Praise for *The Diseasing of America's Children*

"I haven't met a four-year-old who doesn't have a short attention span and act hyper at times. With his commonsense approach, John Rosemond questions a culture that increasingly makes the leap from typical behavior to a diagnosed disease. He empowers parents to question whether children need to be controlled by medication or can be changed by more effective parenting."

—E. D. Hill
Fox News Host and
Author, *I'm Not Your Friend, I'm Your Parent*

"At last, a science-based compendium of rationales for a commonsense approach to child behavior. This excellent and well-referenced work should inform and guide every parent, educator, and health professional. For most children, helping them to mature mentally and emotionally while helping them to develop self-control is the key to producing a happy, healthy, and successful child. Psychotropic medications are often part of the problem, not the solution. John Rosemond and Dr. Ravenel are to be congratulated on a work that I will recommend to everyone."

—Joseph R. Zanga, MD, FAAP, FCP
Joyner Distinguished Chair in Primary Care;
Past President, American Academy of Pediatrics; and
Past President, American College of Pediatricians,
Brody School of Medicine at East Carolina University

"Thoroughly researched and a great read, this book makes perfect sense. It will enlighten, liberate, and empower parents and professionals alike."

—Dr. Kevin Leman
Author, *Have a New Kid by Friday*

"In *The Diseasing of America's Children*, John Rosemond and Dr. Bose Ravenel confront the historical and societal origins of the behavioral 'big three': attention-deficit/hyperactivity disorder (ADHD), oppositional defiant disorder (ODD), and early onset bipolar disorder (EOBD). In part 1, the authors reveal the pseudoscience behind the psychiatric labeling and drugging of America's youth. In part 2, they provide fifteen commonsense solutions for difficulties arising from impaired self-control. Cowritten by two reformed professionals who boldly speak truth to power, this is a triumphant work that calls to mind the words of the late George Orwell: 'In times of universal deceit, telling the truth becomes a revolutionary act.' May this book inspire other acts of a revolutionary nature in the effort to save the brains and souls of the nation's children."

—Grace E. Jackson, MD
Psychiatrist and Author, *Rethinking Psychiatric Drugs*

"Rosemond and Ravenel offer insightful explanations for the exploding diagnosis of ADHD among American children. Their radically simple approach to correcting inattention and problem behavior makes this book a must-read for any parents persuaded to medicate their children."

—Den A. Trumbull, MD
Vice President, American College of Pediatricians,
Gainesville, Florida

"This book will be a bombshell in pediatrics and has dramatically revolutionized my approach to kids who present with the symptoms of ADHD."

—C. Ellis Fisher, MD, FAAP
Pediatrician, Gastonia Children's Clinic,
Gastonia, North Carolina

THE DISEASING OF AMERICA'S CHILDREN

Exposing the ADHD Fiasco and Empowering Parents to Take Back Control

John Rosemond, MS
and Bose Ravenel, MD

THOMAS NELSON
Since 1798

NASHVILLE   DALLAS   MEXICO CITY   RIO DE JANEIRO   BEIJING

The Diseasing of America's Children

© 2008 by John K. Rosemond and S. DuBose Ravenel

Published in Nashville, Tennessee, by Thomas Nelson. Thomas Nelson is a trademark of Thomas Nelson, Inc.

Thomas Nelson, Inc., titles may be purchased in bulk for educational, business, fund-raising, or sales promotional use. For information, please e-mail SpecialMarkets@ThomasNelson.com.

Library of Congress Cataloging-in-Publication Data

Rosemond, John K., 1947-
  The diseasing of America's children : exposing the ADHD fiasco and empowering parents to take back control / John K. Rosemond and Bose Ravenel.
    p. cm.
  Includes bibliographical references and index.
  ISBN 978-0-7852-2886-8 (hardcover)
  1. Attention-deficit hyperactivity disorder--United States. 2. Medical misconceptions. I. Ravenel, Bose.
  II. Title.

RJ506.H9R666 2008
618.92'8589--dc22

                                                                                    2008023298

Printed in the United States of America
08 09 10 11 12 QW 9 8 7 6 5 4 3 2 1

*John Rosemond dedicates this book to his son, Eric,
who got the ball rollin' some thirty years ago.*

*Dr. Ravenel dedicates this book to the parents in his practice who
have trusted that there is a better way to correct learning and behavior
problems than to rely on drugs, and whose feedback has been a source
of continued learning, inspiration, and inestimable reward.*

CONTENTS

CONTENTS

ACKNOWLEDGMENTS

JOHN ROSEMOND THANKS . . .

Steve Laube, the greatest literary agent a guy could ask for, for his support, encouragement, and Christian fellowship.

Pediatrician Dr. Ellis Fisher of Gastonia, North Carolina, for taking the time to review the manuscript and render invaluable suggestions, as well as for his inspiring Christian fellowship.

Dr. Bose, for taking so much time away from his private pediatrics practice to see this book through to completion, for his invaluable research, and for his uncanny ability to detect the absurd in what often passes for science.

Dr. Kevin Leman, for his friendship, support, and wonderful sense of humor.

My wife and best friend of forty years, Willie, with whom all things are possible.

DR. RAVENEL THANKS . . .

Dr. Edward B. Christopherson, psychologist and leading behavioral pediatrics expert, for igniting the spark during a 1991 mini fellowship.

Dr. Howie Glasser, who has further encouraged and inspired me through his Nurtured Heart approach to child behavior problems.

John Rosemond, for helping me discover the joys of being a rebel with a cause.

My understanding wife, Susan, for her support and encouragement, as well as her optimism and forbearance during the research and writing of this book.

TOGETHER, JOHN AND DR. BOSE THANK . . .

Dr. David B. ("Dr. Dave") Stein, for his meticulous clinical research, his pioneering writing on the subject of ADHD, his inspiration, and his continued courage in the battle against psychological correctness.

Debbie Wickwire, Joey Paul, Jennifer Stair, and Jennifer Greenstein at Thomas Nelson for believing in our mission and for challenging us to write the best book possible.

READ THIS FIRST!

WE PULL NO PUNCHES IN THIS BOOK. IN SOME CASES, WE NAME names. However, as much as we are critical of the statements and work of certain people, we truly believe that the individuals in question, named and unnamed, are convinced they are toiling in the best interest of America's children. We are convinced that money is a driving force in the attention-deficit/hyperactivity disorder (ADHD) marketplace; however, it is not unethical to make money, and we are by no means accusing specific individuals of unethical professional conduct. But we do believe that certain individuals in what we call the ADHD Establishment are guilty of behavior that is not consistent with a scientific attitude—specifically, of making definitive statements based on flimsy evidence and even, in some cases, downright bad science.

Science depends on verifiable, objective evidence and experimental results that can be replicated by other scientists. Where ADHD is concerned, neither verifiable, objective evidence nor replicable experimental results exist to support the claims of the ADHD Establishment. We are convinced, therefore, that the science behind ADHD and the other childhood behavior disorders it has birthed (primarily, oppositional defiant disorder and early onset bipolar disorder) is not science at all. At best, it's very bad science, but we do not believe the people behind this bad science are bad people. It's important that the reader know this before beginning this book, because our pull-no-punches attitude could otherwise lead to wrong conclusions.

We've written this book to expose what we feel is a travesty of science that is causing harm to children. We've written this book to empower parents to take back control of their children by recognizing the misinformation they have been given and disentangling themselves from a medical–mental health–pharmaceutical behemoth that is selling diseases that have no objective reality. But more than anything, we've written this book in the hopes it will begin a creative dialogue that will advance the state of child psychology, child psychiatry, and pediatric medicine. We sincerely believe the status quo is not healthy for anyone—children, parents, schools, or mental health and medical professionals. It needs to be challenged, upended, taken apart, and fixed. We hope this book helps to begin that process.

INTRODUCTION

*It is dangerous to be right in matters on which
the established authorities are wrong.*
—Voltaire, 1751

A FAIR NUMBER OF PEOPLE, WITHOUT HAVING EVEN READ IT,
have told us this book is going to make a lot of people very upset. Such is
the inevitable consequence of saying that the emperor has no clothes, of
telling the truth when the truth threatens powerful vested interests. In
this case, the emperor is what we call the ADHD Establishment.

The ADHD Establishment consists primarily of certain pediatricians,
psychiatrists, neurologists, psychologists, parent and patient advocacy
groups like Children and Adults with Attention Deficit Disorder
(CHADD), and the pharmaceutical industry. In recent years, this coalition has collaborated in an effort that has resulted in the manufacture of
diseases that do not exist. In other words, these diseases—attention-deficit/
hyperactivity disorder (ADHD) and its diagnostic offspring, oppositional
defiant disorder (ODD) and early onset bipolar disorder (EOBD)—are
fictions. (Although we are skeptical concerning the recent significant
increase in the estimates of children with pervasive developmental disorder, of which autism and Asperger's syndrome are subsets, we withhold

judgment as to whether PDD is a manufactured disease. At this time, we feel comfortable saying only that the diagnosis is being dispensed some-what recklessly.)

This coalition has managed to convince parents, teachers, journalists, and medical and mental health professionals that the aforementioned fictions have an objective reality. To do so, its members have made and continue to make statements that are not supported with valid scientific evidence. They say things like "We know . . ." when they don't know, and "The evidence is clear . . ." when it is anything but clear, and "There is no longer any doubt . . ." when the only people lacking doubt are themselves and the credulous people who believe them.

This coalition has managed to disease millions of American children with fictitious illnesses and in so doing has made an incredible amount of money. *Never have mental health professionals made so much money from one childhood mental health diagnosis as they have made from ADHD,* and it may well turn out to be the most lucrative psychiatric diagnosis, adult or child, ever. In addition, drug companies have made billions off the sales of drugs prescribed to treat a disease that does not meet scientific criteria for disease.

In March 2008, during a phone conversation with one of my[1] former graduate school professors, he said, "No one really knows how a kid gets ADHD." I replied, "A kid gets ADHD in the office of a physician or a mental health professional."

That is the long and short of it. Cancer, diabetes, and pneumonia are diseases. Their reality can be verified with X-rays, blood tests, and other reliable scientific means. Some members of the ADHD Establishment say ADHD can be seen in brain scans, but that's simply not true. There is no specific brain scan image consistently associated with what the Establishment says is ADHD. Establishment members frequently refer to a "chemical imbalance" in the central nervous system, but this is a fic-tion. It turns out there is no such thing as a neurochemical *balance*; therefore, the idea of a neurochemical *imbalance* has been snatched from thin air (see chapter 3). Medical researchers are looking for a cure for cancer, diabetes, and other physical diseases. The ADHD Establishment says ADHD is a physical disease, but no one in the Establishment is looking for a cure. Actually, the only cure for a disease that does not exist is to discredit the disease-mongering. That is our purpose in this book.

Mind you, once upon a time, both of the authors believed in ADHD and the other childhood behavior disorders it has spawned. Both of us dispensed these diagnoses and either recommended or prescribed medication, believing that in so doing we were being no less helpful than if we had recognized that a child was suffering with tuberculosis and helped him obtain proper treatment. "It takes one to know one," the saying goes, and we absolutely know what we are talking about because we are both reformed, repentant former members in good standing of the ADHD Establishment. There was a time when we participated in pulling the proverbial wool over our own eyes. Once blind, we now see, and what we see is . . . no other word describes it quite so aptly as *appalling*.

We are appalled by the damage we see being done to America's children, families, and schools by professionals who seem to have mislaid their objectivity and are willingly accepting as fact what is not scientifically verifiable. We are appalled at the scope of professional denial involved. When one shows members of the ADHD Establishment hard evidence that the "diseases" in question are fictions, they deny that the evidence has any meaning. Establishment members often ridicule anyone who dares to challenge their self-appointed authority. One way they do this is by simplifying opposing arguments so that they sound absurd, as in "John Rosemond says if you let your child watch television, he's going to develop ADHD." If they do not openly ridicule, they often condescend, which is ridicule of a subtler sort.

True scientists are distinguished from pseudoscientists in that the former say things to this effect: "We may be wrong." True scientists qualify their conclusions as being based on the best evidence available at the time and are quick to admit that evidence not yet discovered may well disprove their theories. Members of the ADHD Establishment rarely, if ever, say such things. They generally insist that they are the final word on the subject and that anyone who disagrees with them is misinformed or just being contrarian. This is not the attitude of scientists. It is the attitude of demagogues and ideologues, and indeed, when members of the Establishment are challenged, they more often than not engage in demagoguery.

For example, certain Establishment members have inferred and even boldly stated that I am harming children by preventing them from obtaining proper treatment. They set up the straw man; then they knock it down. The Establishment's other emotional appeal is to charge people who disagree with them of blaming parents. By claiming that ADHD is a genetic condition, the Establishment adroitly groups ADHD with Down syndrome and Fragile X syndrome. Everyone knows that parents are not to blame for Down or Fragile X. The problem is that whereas scientists know precisely what genetic defects lie behind Down and Fragile X, the supposed genes that cause ADHD have not been discovered. Nonetheless, in the absence of any objective proof of genetic cause, the Establishment says they *know* ADHD is caused by genes. We say otherwise; therefore, we are supposedly *blaming* parents.

In the sciences, one can *know* something based on verifiable evidence, or one can *know* that verifiable evidence does not exist with which to draw hard-and-fast conclusions. The latter condition applies here. As we will demonstrate in later chapters, we *know* that no ADHD genes have been discovered, no ADHD gene transmission theories have been prove· no ADHD biochemical imbalance has been quantified, and no specific ADHD brain condition has been identified.

We are *not* preventing children from obtaining proper treatment. We are trying to help parents to realize that in this context, *proper* is not proper at all. The red flags we are raising are not the problem. The problem is the ADHD diagnosis and the typical mode of treatment. We are *not* blaming parents. As the subtitle of this book states, we are attempting to empower parents to take back control of their children. We are trying to help parents recognize the misinformation they have received about ADHD and disentangle themselves from a professional-corporate alliance that is intent upon protecting its very valuable real estate.

We are alarmed that so many parents in America are allowing members of the Establishment to "manage" their children for them through the use of powerful, potentially hazardous psychotropic drugs. As we will show you, these drugs are unnecessary. We have seen enough children diagnosed with ADHD begin behaving functionally at home and school without medical intervention to know that this is not a medical issue. We further know that parents who accept responsibility (not blame) for their children's problems take the first step toward self-empowerment and disentangling. We know this is in the best interests of the parents and children in question.

In science, the burden of proof falls upon the person or persons who advance a new theory. In this case, the burden of proof falls upon members of the ADHD Establishment. It's up to them to prove that what they are saying is true. We have no obligation to prove that what they are saying is *not* true. Nonetheless, we will prove that what they are saying has not been verified, that they don't *know* what they claim to know. Maybe, someday, the Establishment will provide satisfactory evidence proving what they say about ADHD. We doubt that day will come, but if it does, we will still have nothing to apologize for. We are simply reporting the facts.

Let us know what you think of this book by e-mailing us at diseasingkids@aol.com.

John Rosemond, family psychologist
Dr. Bose Ravenel, pediatrician
Gastonia and High Point, North Carolina
March 2008

PART 1

Exposing the ADHD Fiasco

CHAPTER 1
FIVE SLIPPERY WORDS

It depends on what the meaning of the word "is" is.
—President Bill Clinton

Discussions about attention-deficit/hyperactivity disorder (as well as oppositional defiant disorder and early onset bipolar disorder) can get complicated very quickly. The complications generally involve one or more of five slippery words: *believe, real, work, have,* and *know.*

As I was walking out of an auditorium in Lexington, Kentucky, where I had just spoken to some three hundred people, mostly parents, a woman approached me and said, "So I take it you don't believe in ADHD."

During the presentation, I had done my best to debunk some widely held falsehoods concerning ADHD, including that it is an inherited or gene-based condition. Because the diagnosis had become so ubiquitous, I realized that several parents in the audience would have questions.

"What does *believing* in ADHD require?" I asked her.

She looked at me with a slightly embarrassed smile. "Well, you know . . . that it's *real.*"

I could tell this was going to be a somewhat thorny conversation.

Before I could answer her, we had to come to agreement concerning what the word *real* means with regard to this supposed disorder. Does it mean that ADHD has objective reality, that it is the behavioral result of physical anomalies that can be seen and measured? Some psychologists, physicians, and researchers *believe* that it does and is. They *believe* that ADHD can be seen in brain scans, detected by electroencephalography, that it exists in the form of structural abnormalities in the brain and/or imbalances in the brain's chemistry. The emphasis in the previous two sentences is meant to draw attention to the fact that in the field of ADHD, *belief* is all there is. Science, however, is not about belief. It is about objective, verifiable, replicable evidence, of which there is none where ADHD is concerned.

One of the characteristics of postmodernity—the curious times in which we twenty-first-century Americans live—is that if enough people *think* something is true, it takes on a consensual reality that is as powerful, and sometimes more so, than a fact that can be verified by objective means of detection or measurement. Furthermore, once something has acquired consensual reality, people—and even people who ought to know better, people with scientific credentials—will often deny that facts are facts.

The fact is that none of the claims that ADHD has a biological cause has been verified through scientific experiments that upon replication yield the same results. On that basis, therefore, ADHD is not *real*, not yet at least. Then again, one can ignore all the claims of genes, microscopic brain lesions, and chemical imbalances and limit the notion that ADHD is *real* to its phenomenology—to the undeniable fact that large and ever-increasing numbers of children display the defining behaviors (or "symptoms," as delineated in the most recent revision of the *Diagnostic and Statistical Manual*, the diagnostic guidebook for the mental health professions) to a significant degree. From that perspective, ADHD is very *real* indeed.

But is ADHD a "disorder"? Does its nomenclature accurately reflect that there is something amiss with the children in question, that for whatever reason—biological or otherwise—they can't "think straight," and thus their behavior is often chaotically disorganized? Or is attention-deficit/hyperactivity disorder simply a more scientific-sounding way of referring to what, not so long ago, people simply called a spoiled brat? Is the term just one more example of how political correctness has corrupted language? This point of view has it that the ADHD child's behavior problems are indeed *real* but that there is nothing inherently *wrong* with the child. In many ways, the hurricane of controversy that swirls around the topic of ADHD is in fact an argument concerning whether or not it is *real*, and if so, in what sense of the term.

Since I didn't have enough time to help this woman understand these sorts of distinctions, I simply said, "I think ADHD is very real in the sense of the behavior problems that are being described. I just don't believe that the things many, if not most, diagnosing and treating professionals are saying about ADHD are factual."

"So you don't believe the medicines really work?" she asked.

Ah! The third of our slippery terms—*work*. This mother had likely been persuaded that if administration of a drug like Ritalin results in significant diminishment of symptoms for several hours, we have *prima facie* evidence that ADHD does indeed have biological reality (i.e., the drugs supposedly correct a fictitious biochemical imbalance).

I said, "The answer to that question depends on whether you are defining *work* in the short-term or the long-term sense."

"But why would the medicines work at all if ADHD wasn't real?" she astutely challenged.

"Has one of your children been diagnosed with ADHD?" I asked her, fairly certain of the answer.

"Our five-year-old son," she said. "My husband has been diagnosed with it as well, and we suspect that our second child may also have it, but it's too early to tell for sure. He just turned two."

Now I knew where she was coming from. As the parent of a child diagnosed with ADHD, she was trying to determine whether or not I agreed with what therapists had told her, and if not, why. Her last question—why do the medicines work at all if ADHD isn't real?—reflects the circular logic characteristic of the Establishment's rhetoric. In the final analysis, the Establishment's ability to continue to profit from the "diagnosis" and "treatment" of ADHD is entirely dependent on mixing claim and fact as if they were one and the same, thus arriving at predetermined conclusions. To wit:

Unsubstantiated CLAIM: Attention-deficit/hyperactivity disorder is a genetically transmitted disease.

Unsubstantiated CLAIM: Attention-deficit/hyperactivity disorder takes the form of a chemical imbalance and/or structural and functional abnormalities in certain areas of the brain.

Established FACT: Certain prescription drugs often reduce the defining symptoms of ADHD for a period of three to approximately twelve hours, depending on the drug, its dosage, and its form, at which point symptoms return. In other words, these prescription drugs do indeed seem to "work" for a period of time defined in hours; they do not, however, work in the sense of eventually eliminating symptoms altogether. Penicillin truly *works* by eliminating the disease; the medications in question do not eliminate ADHD. Further, as we discuss in chapter 5, they have the potential of causing more problems than they solve, if they solve any.

Established FACT: The drugs in question affect the central nervous system, which includes the brain, usually resulting in a longer attention span (enhanced ability to shut out distractions and focus on a single task) and, therefore, better impulse control.

Unscientific CONCLUSION: Since the drugs in question act on the central nervous system in ways that alleviate symptoms (albeit temporarily), ADHD must be a "disease" located in the brain.

The problem, as we will examine in greater detail later, is that *anyone's* attention span—adult or child—is likely to improve after taking a therapeutic dose of a stimulant. The Establishment's argument leads to the conclusion that *everyone* has something wrong with their brain and needs stimulants to correct whatever that something is. Preposterous, indeed, but at least one well-known ADHD Establishment professional questions whether there is such a thing as a "normal" brain.[1]

Back to my conversation with the woman in Lexington. After I explained that just because medicines appear to "work" in the short term doesn't prove the existence of a disorder, she responded, "Well, I do agree it's overdiagnosed."

"Agree with whom?" I asked.

She paused, taken slightly aback, and then replied, "Well, you think it's overdiagnosed, right?"

"Again," I said, "that depends on just exactly what it is we're talking about. For example, you think ADHD is a *real* physical disorder in some objective sense. I have yet to see proof of that. Therefore, I think that even one diagnosis is overdiagnosis. But if you define ADHD as simply a set of behaviors that describe significant numbers of children of this generation, behaviors listed in the *Diagnostic and Statistical Manual*, I would have to say that ADHD is grossly underdiagnosed."

"How so?" she asked, obviously perplexed.

"Because a lot more children display that set of behaviors than have been diagnosed with ADHD. I'd estimate that five out of ten of today's kids fit the DSM description to a degree sufficient to justify the diagnosis, especially during their preschool years.

"Now let me ask *you* something," I continued. "Do you think it's possible that nearly half of America's children have something seriously wrong with their brains, some kind of inherited chemical imbalance? And if the something in question is genetic, then why do teachers who taught before 1960 testify that they hardly ever saw kids who fit the description?"

"I really don't know," she admitted.

"I understand," I said, nodding reassuringly. "Those are the sorts of questions I'm trying to get people to think about." And with that, and a courteous smile, I told her it was nice talking with her and went on to the other folks who were waiting to ask questions of me.

Until that conversation in that lobby in Lexington, I'd been struggling with how to begin this book. I realized we now had our beginning. My exchange with that mother reflected, in a nutshell, the problems inherent in any attempt to have a productive, logical conversation with someone who *believes* in ADHD. Quite simply, there is no logic to the positions taken by the ADHD Establishment, not to mention that objectivity is completely lacking. To put it bluntly, many of the professionals who specialize in the diagnosis and treatment of ADHD simply cut ideas from whole cloth. Where they lack objective evidence to support their claims, they invent fiction.

When I ask the parent of an ADHD child how the diagnosing professional explained the origin of the problem, the most common response is that the child inherited it from the father. When I ask, "Inherited what exactly?" the most common answer is "a biochemical imbalance."

Let's take a closer look at what it means to have a so-called biochemical imbalance. The term implies that there exists a measurable state of biochemical balance. The fact is no such state exists. The biochemistry of the brain, of the central nervous system, is in a state of ongoing ebb and flow, wax and wane, flux. One set of neurochemical proportions gives way to another, then another, then another, and so on. Anger is characterized by one set of chemical proportions, happiness by another. But within any episode of anger, at any given moment in the episode, the brain's chemistry may be different than it will be one second later or was one second before. Furthermore, the biochemistry of anger or any other emotion varies from person to person. What then does it mean that a person has a "chemical imbalance"? Relative to what?

And thus we come to the fifth of our slippery terms—*know*.

A child psychiatrist, irritated that I wasn't blithely accepting his point of view, once insisted, "We absolutely *know* that ADHD is an inherited disease, that it has to do with problems in the brain, and that it can only be effectively treated with medical interventions!"

Know? In reality, this irritated psychiatrist and his colleagues in the ADHD Establishment *know* nothing of the sort. They *believe* ADHD is inherited, that it involves problems located in the structure and chemistry of the brain—premises that support the conclusion that the treatment of ADHD (and therefore the larger share of the resulting income stream) belongs to medical doctors. For more than thirty years, researchers supported by grants, taxpayer dollars, and apparently inexhaustible pharmaceutical company funds have been trying to find objective evidence to support these beliefs, and for more than thirty years and counting, they have come up empty-handed. Meanwhile, scientists have solved far more complex medical problems. This is of no significance, however, to many of these researchers (some of whom have claimed to have found "proof" that ADHD is a disease when subsequent analysis of their research reveals they have found nothing of the sort). They believe, and they are scientists; therefore, they *know*.

The bottom line: the ADHD Establishment cannot recruit believers to their position with facts, because there are no facts that support their position. As you will soon see, the cold, hard facts support another position entirely. So the ADHD Establishment recruits believers by appealing to people's emotions—specifically and primarily, the emotions of parents of children who have been diagnosed with ADHD. It goes without saying that people are emotional concerning their children.

In this book, our premise is simple and straightforward: ADHD, as defined by the ADHD Establishment, is a fiction. To support this fiction, the ADHD Establishment spins a web of elaborate theories unsupported by verifiable data or even common sense. We will see that the same set of propositions also applies to the diagnoses of the other two most popularly diagnosed childhood behavior disorders: oppositional defiant disorder (ODD) and early onset bipolar disorder (EOBD).

Our ultimate purpose is equally straightforward: to separate fact and fiction so that parents become able to take back control of their children.

So, on with the show!

CHAPTER 2
REDEFINING CHILDHOOD

Nothing is too absurd for some philosopher to have said it.
—Blaise Pascal

AN INTERNET SATIRE TITLED "THE ETIOLOGY AND TREATMENT of Childhood" develops a humorous and clever line of thought by positing that by its very nature, childhood is a disorder identifiable by such symptoms as dwarfism, knowledge deficits, emotional immaturity, and legume anorexia.[1] The author's intent is to mock the smug seriousness of psychologists and psychiatrists, but as we will show, a number of contemporary influences are bringing about a radical reshaping of the definition of childhood—and therefore how adults perceive and respond to children— such that this satire is beginning to appear more prophetic than funny.

Behaviors that have long been recognized as either typical of early childhood, matters of individual or gender difference, or the upshot of unfinished discipline or a lack thereof have been and are being redefined by the American mental health establishment as constituting one or more "disorders." Unruly, defiant children become the carriers of oppositional defiant disorder (ODD) and are treated with powerful drugs or combinations thereof. "Terrible" two-year-olds who become nearly apoplectic if they are denied their self-centered demands are diagnosed as having early onset bipolar disorder (EOBD)—and again, treated with more drugs. Children who are shy and avoid certain peer-group social situations are diagnosed with social anxiety disorder, Asperger's syndrome, or pervasive developmental disorder (PDD)—the frequent result being still more drugs. Active, distractible boys who have difficulty sitting still are labeled with attention-deficit/hyperactivity disorder (ADHD), for which more drugs have been developed than for the preceding three diagnoses combined. Increasingly, children so snared in the mental health machine receive more than one diagnosis under the pretext that these disorders often occur in pairs or clusters.

From 1952 to 1994, the number of mental disorders listed in the *Diagnostic and Statistical Manual* (DSM) increased from 112 to 374, of which diagnoses of childhood emotional and behavior problems figured significantly. Not surprisingly, this increase in diagnostic nomenclature parallels a corresponding increase in the number of children found to have these so-called mental illnesses as well as the number and kinds of drugs used to treat them. These drugs are produced and aggressively marketed by pharmaceutical companies that influence (through selective funding) and in many cases even host much of the research that leads to these drug treatment practices. In some cases it is difficult to tell which came first, the diagnosis or the drug used to treat it.

The most prevalent childhood behavior disorder diagnosis is attention-deficit/hyperactivity disorder. Behaviors symptomatic of ADHD include inattentiveness, impulsivity, hyperactivity, forgetfulness, and a disorganized approach to tasks. The usual end result is below-par grades in school as well as exasperation on the part of the child's parents and teachers. During the last twenty-five years, estimates of the prevalence of ADHD have gone from one in thirty-three children to as high as one in ten. When one factors in estimates for the prevalence of ODD and EOBD—both of which are alleged to often coexist with ADHD—the figure goes up to approximately one in six children afflicted by one behavior disorder or another (and many teachers contend that the figure is significantly higher). That means that in any given first-grade classroom of twenty-five children, four are likely to have serious mental illnesses characterized by erratic moods and/or behavior.

No one who attended school in the 1950s or 1960s remembers sitting in a classroom with anywhere near that many troublesome classmates, even during a time when class size was far greater than it is today. Almost every baby boomer can recall an occasional kid who got into more than his share of trouble, but *occasional* is the operative qualifier. How in the world have we gone, in just two generations, from an occasional child who was occasionally disruptive to one in six kids with near-constant discipline issues? Answering that question requires some historical perspective.

A SHORT HISTORY OF CHILDHOOD BEHAVIOR DISORDERS

The story of childhood behavior disorders began in 1902 when British pediatrician George Still described children with a variety of behavioral disturbances—descriptions that prefigure what we today call ADHD, ODD, and EOBD. In Still's view, the behavior problems in question reflected moral deficiencies rooted in heredity or caused by physical disease.

Following the global pandemic of encephalitis that occurred between 1917 and 1926, severe behavioral disturbances were seen in many child survivors, including hyperkinesis (a persistently high level of generally purposeless motor activity). Following this observation, prominent medical theorists proposed that any significant degree of overactivity or impulsivity was the result of underlying brain damage, even if objective evidence of such damage was lacking. This assumption gave rise to the term "minimal brain damage," which encompassed not only hyperactive children but also those with learning disabilities. The term was later changed to "minimal brain dysfunction," but with the publication of

DSM-II in 1968, enough doubt had been cast on the brain damage/dysfunction hypothesis that the latter term was also discarded, and "hyperkinetic reaction of childhood" (HRC) was officially adopted.

The symptoms of HRC prefigured those now given for ADHD in the latest edition of the DSM (DSM-IV, published in 1994, with text revisions in 2000): hyperactivity, impulsivity, inattention, distractibility, and so on. Around this same time, researchers began noticing that forms of amphetamine, a powerful central nervous system stimulant, produced a paradoxical effect in many of these same children. Instead of exacerbating their hyperactivity and impulsivity, which might be expected, amphetamines in low doses produced noticeable *temporary* improvements in self-control and attention span, along with significantly lower activity levels. Because amphetamines act on the central nervous system, researchers assumed that these behavioral improvements confirmed the presence of a malfunction in the brain. Thus began the circular reasoning that is reflected today in much of what is said by members of the ADHD Establishment.

Attention-deficit disorder replaced hyperkinetic reaction of childhood in the DSM-III (1980). Since then, each successive update of the DSM (1987, 1994, 2000) has seen the defining criteria for ADD—changed to ADHD with the publication of DSM-III-R in 1987—shift back and forth, as if lines in the sand were being periodically erased and redrawn. Professional consensus has been achieved only as a result of significant compromise among those considered to be experts in the field and has been driven largely by professional politics, not increased diagnostic discrimination, much less objective evidence of a valid disease state. Because objective definitional criteria for ADHD are lacking, the diagnosis is a judgment call. In fact, this same defect characterizes the diagnostic criteria for *all* of the psychiatric disorders enumerated in the DSM. It will surprise many readers to learn that not one of these supposed "mental illnesses" is supported by compelling evidence of an underlying biological disease state.

In the current version of the DSM, the American Psychiatric Association has the following to say about the very notion of mental disorders:

> It must be admitted that no definition adequately specifies precise boundaries for the concept of 'mental disorder'. The concept of mental disorder, *like many other concepts in medicine and science,* lacks a consistent operational definition that covers all situations. . . . In DSM-IV there is no assumption that each category of mental disorder is a completely discrete entity with absolute boundaries dividing it from other mental disorders or *from no mental disorder.*[2] (Reprinted with permission from the *Diagnostic and Statistical Manual of Mental Disorders,* Fourth Edition, Text Revision [Copyright 2000]. American Psychiatric Association)

The APA wants the reader to believe that diagnostic categories that lack empirically defined boundaries are the norm in medicine and science. This is simply not true. Without exception, the reality of a physical disease can be verified objectively and its boundaries can be precisely defined. A trained clinician will not mistake strep throat for cancer of the larynx, for example. Likewise, every single proposition in the hard sciences of physics, chemistry, and biology rests on physical evidence. There is no confusion between hydrogen peroxide (H_2O_2) and water (H_2O), or a gas and a solid. Of all the legitimate medical and scientific professions, only psychology and psychiatry claim to know the existence of things that have not been, and in many cases cannot be, verified objectively. In saying "we're no different from anybody else," the APA is determinedly trying to conceal the fact that mental illnesses do not qualify as illnesses at all for exactly this reason: they *cannot* be objectively defined so that their boundaries clearly distinguish one from another. There is great confusion between one mental disorder and another and even, in many cases, even mental illness and a state of good mental health. In short, the APA is in denial concerning the fact that psychiatry and psychology do not qualify as hard sciences, not by a long shot. In fact, because they deal predominantly in matters of faith (challengers of which, as the authors can attest, risk being branded as professional heretics), they more closely resemble religion than science.

With regard to ADHD, the current DSM lists eighteen defining behaviors, none of which is pathological *per se* (Figure 2.1).

DSM-IV-TR CRITERIA FOR ADHD

A. Six or more of the following symptoms of inattention have been present for at least 6 months to a point that is disruptive and inappropriate for developmental level:

INATTENTION
1. Often does not give close attention to details or makes careless mistakes in schoolwork, work, or other activities.
2. Often has trouble keeping attention on tasks or play activities.
3. Often does not seem to listen when spoken to directly.
4. Often does not follow instructions and fails to finish schoolwork, chores, or duties in the workplace (not due to oppositional behavior or failure to understand instructions).
5. Often has trouble organizing activities.
6. Often avoids, dislikes, or doesn't want to do things that take a lot of mental effort for a long period of time (such as schoolwork or homework).
7. Often loses things needed for tasks and activities (e.g., toys, school assignments, pencils, books, or tools).
8. Is often easily distracted.
9. Is often forgetful in daily activities.

B. Six or more of the following symptoms of hyperactivity-impulsivity have been present for at least 6 months to an extent that is disruptive and inappropriate for developmental level:

HYPERACTIVITY
1. Often fidgets with hands or feet or squirms in seat.
2. Often gets up from seat when remaining in seat is expected.
3. Often runs about or climbs when and where it is not appropriate (adolescents or adults may feel very restless).
4. Often has trouble playing or enjoying leisure activities quietly.
5. Is often "on the go" or often acts as if "driven by a motor."
6. Often talks excessively.

IMPULSIVITY
1. Often blurts out answers before questions have been finished.
2. Often has trouble waiting one's turn.
3. Often interrupts or intrudes on others (e.g., butts into conversations or games).

Figure 2.1 (*Reprinted with permission from the* Diagnostic and Statistical Manual of Mental Disorders, *Fourth Edition, Text Revision [Copyright 2000]. American Psychiatric Association.*)[3]

Not one of the symptoms is described with any precision. The word "often" is used in every single criterion. A more precise quantifier is never used, which is to say that the criteria are not quantified at all. This is hardly scientific. What's more, the number of behaviors required in either category, six of nine, is completely arbitrary. Why six? Why not five? Why not seven? And if that weren't enough, the APA has provided a category called "attention-deficit/hyperactivity disorder, not otherwise specified" for diagnosing the condition when ADHD behaviors are *thought* or *seem* to be present but fall short of DSM-IV criteria. In other words, the fact that a child's behavior doesn't match the DSM definition for ADHD doesn't mean he doesn't have some form of ADHD. If a child suspected of having it doesn't qualify, he can still qualify. What's next? "Attention-deficit/hyperactivity disorder, not otherwise specified, sorta-kinda"? This sort of impreciseness and obfuscation can and, we assert, *does* have but one purpose: the "diseasing" of as many children as possible. The equivalent of this in the legal profession is known as fishing for clients.

What the APA can't see, other professional bodies can. The American Academy of Pediatrics in its practice guidelines for pediatricians, states: "DSM-IV criteria remain a consensus without clear empirical [research] data supporting the number of items required for the diagnosis. . . . Furthermore, the behavioral characteristics specified in DSM-IV, despite efforts to standardize them, remain subjective."[4] (Reproduced with permission from *Pediatrics*, Vol. 105, pages 1158–1170, Copyright © 2000 by the AAP.) In 1998, the National Institutes of Health convened a special conference of the world's leading authorities on ADHD. These expert participants in a later text summarizing the state of the science found "no evidence of a natural threshold between ADHD and 'normal' behavior. . . . Thus, there is little evidence at this time to suggest that there is a natural boundary for the diagnostic category of ADHD."[5] Whereas the experts have agreed among themselves that ADHD is an arbitrary construction, they will not admit the same to the public.

The further problem is that a good number of professionals simply ignore DSM criteria when diagnosing ADHD. In a 1996 survey of five hundred pediatricians and psychologists, it was determined that only 9 percent relied on DSM criteria in making the diagnosis.[6] Researchers from Duke University found that in a rural Appalachian population of 375 children ages nine to thirteen who had been diagnosed with ADHD,

214 (57 percent) did not fulfill DSM criteria and 62 of these, or 29 percent, *had no ADHD symptoms at all.*[7]

Findings of this sort are not surprising to us. On numerous occasions, we have seen children diagnosed with ADHD who presented few if any symptoms. It has seemed to us, in fact, that some therapists use the diagnosis as a matter of convenience: to wit, insurance companies will not pay a therapist for working with a child who is annoying, immature, or unmotivated, but they will pay if the annoying, immature, unmotivated child is found by a certified professional to "have" ADHD. During my private practice years (1980–90), I became familiar with a number of children who had been evaluated by a certain private-practice team that included psychologists, educational specialists, and occupational therapists. The reports this team generated differed only in that the names of the children and test data were changed, strongly suggesting that the expensive "evaluation" was a mere formality, that a child referred to this group was assumed beforehand to have ADHD. Parent and professional reports indicate that "ADHD factories" of this sort are not uncommon nationwide. Likewise, Dr. Ravenel has read a number of evaluation reports in which therapists have admitted they are recommending the administration of medication in the absence of qualifying ADHD symptoms.

We are reminded of a 1972 study in which a number of high-functioning, very normal individuals presented themselves to several psychiatric institutions complaining of severe symptoms characteristic of schizophrenia. They were all evaluated, diagnosed with schizophrenia, and admitted to the institutions' closed wards. Amazingly, even though these faux patients displayed no symptoms beyond evaluation, none were ever recognized by a psychiatrist as a fake.[8] The long and short of things seems to be that if one presents himself or is presented to a mental health professional, said professional is likely to assume that the person in question has a disorder of one sort or another and the ensuing evaluation is almost certain to confirm the assumption. (For someone to even *think* he or she has a mental problem, in the absence of dysfunctional behavior, can be construed as symptomatic of a disorder.) As this pertains to children, ADHD, ODD, and EOBD are the diagnoses *du jour*. Who knows what the future may bring?

In the eighteenth and nineteenth centuries, physicians thought people with mental disorders were biologically defective, that they behaved abnormally because of inherited criminal personalities, smaller-than-average brains, deformed crania, and so on. It was generally agreed that because these defects were inherent to a person's biology, mental illnesses could not be cured. Thus, the almost certain "treatment" for anyone who behaved out of the ordinary was incarceration in a mental institution, usually for life.

For the mental health professions, the twentieth century was an age of enlightenment during which it became recognized that persistent emotional discomfort and maladaptive behaviors were most likely due to historical and situational variables and not immutable biological states. This meant that the disturbed or distressed individual, if properly motivated and directed, could change. The last twenty-five or so years has seen a regression in mental health practice, away from an emphasis on identifying and addressing the reasons behind maladaptive behavior and toward the retroassumption that mental disorders represent pathological brain states that are permanent and therefore require ongoing medical treatments. In this regard, ADHD and its diagnostic cousins have provided therapists with a means of ensnaring children and their parents in a treatment process that is expensive and—because these same therapists claim these disorders cannot be cured but only controlled—theoretically never-ending.

The diagnosis of growing numbers of children with ADHD is abetted by attempts to "dumb down" the diagnostic criteria to children as young as two.[9] The fact that each of the eighteen symptoms listed in the DSM describes typical toddler behavior—high activity level, short attention span, distractibility, disorganized behavior, difficulty waiting one's turn, and so on—is increasingly irrelevant to today's diagnosticians. This trend toward "medicalizing" normal childhood behavior is decried in an editorial by Peter Conrad, PhD, department of sociology at Brandeis University: "One can only wonder, with the increased diagnosis of ADHD and affective disorders in children, how many of these cases may reflect fundamentally developmental or situational rather than clinical issues. From a social perspective, defining more and more children's behaviors as medical problems diverts our attention from the possible social and psychological origins of these difficulties."[10]

Lest one think that the diagnosis of ADHD in toddlers represents the ultimate diagnostic "stretch," the notion of ADHD in *infants* has actually invaded the medical literature. Patricia O. Quinn, a Washington, D.C. developmental pediatrician, has written several books on ADHD, including one titled *Attention Deficit Disorder: Diagnosis and Treatment from Infancy to Adulthood*.[11] Quinn is by no means the only person in the field claiming that fussiness and a high activity level during infancy may be early indicators of ADHD.

MORE GRIST FOR THE MILL

Oppositional defiant disorder (ODD) first appeared in the 1987 revision of the DSM (DSM III-R). Controversy concerning this diagnosis was immediate, centering primarily on the fact that although clinical studies had been conducted prior to legitimizing the diagnosis, the results of those studies were not reported in the DSM and do not seem to be available for examination elsewhere. The question becomes, what is the American Psychiatric Association trying to conceal?[12]

Before we answer that question, however, let's take a look at the criteria for this alleged disorder from the current version of the DSM (Figure 2.2). To qualify for the diagnosis, four of the eight behaviors listed must

---

DSM-IV-TR CRITERIA FOR ODD

1. Often loses temper.
2. Often argues with adults.
3. Often actively defies adults or refuses to comply with adults' requests or rules.
4. Often deliberately annoys people.
5. Often blames others for his or her mistakes or misbehavior.
6. Is often touchy or easily annoyed by others.
7. Is often angry and resentful.
8. Is often spiteful and vindictive.

Figure 2.2 (*Reprinted with permission from the* Diagnostic and Statistical Manual of Mental Disorders, *Fourth Edition, Text Revision [Copyright 2000]. American Psychiatric Association.)* [13]

---

be present for at least six months and cause "significant impairment in social, academic, or occupational functioning."

As was the case with DSM criteria for ADHD, "often" is used without exception, but there is no established standard by which "often" can be specifically defined. In fact, indeterminate language characterizes the description. Taking the fourth criterion, how does one determine that a four-year-old is "deliberately" annoying people? Is it not possible that the people in question are simply easily annoyed, especially by children; that they are afflicted with knee-jerk annoyance of children disorder (KJACD), characterized by little tolerance for the normal high-energy antics of the very young? The answers to these two questions, respectively, are "there is no way of making such a determination" and "yes." Similar questions can be asked of the other seven diagnostic criteria, the answers to which would be similarly revealing. Oppositional defiant disorder, therefore, exists only in the eye of the beholder.

Research psychologist Paula Caplan has come to a similar conclusion. In the course of trying to determine the effect of gender bias on the diagnostic process, Caplan investigated whether existing research even so much as confirmed the existence of certain categories of mental disorder found in the DSM. She investigated three diagnostic categories—autistic disorder, oppositional defiant disorder, and obsessive-compulsive disorder—and found that none of the research contained objective data to define the boundary between normal and disordered. She concluded, *"Those prescriptions cannot be said to have been derived from any scientific work whatsoever."*[14]

Dr. Caplan, a former consultant to the American Psychiatric Association for the DSM revision process, is a specialist in teaching and writing about research methods and was chosen by the American Psychological Association as an "eminent woman psychologist." For someone of her stature to be criticizing the foundations of psychiatric/psychological diagnosis means the process is seriously flawed.

So now we know what the APA is trying to hide: there is no empirical support for the ODD diagnosis. It is an invention. As Caplan points out, no scientific work has been done that would establish the reality of something called oppositional defiant disorder. Furthermore, as is the case with ADHD, children usually receive this spurious label strictly on the basis of reports concerning their behavior obtained from parents and teachers. Giving a child a diagnosis without firsthand verification of symptoms is sloppy, to say the least. No conscientious medical doctor would ever diagnose a child with, say, bronchitis without examining the child. The lack of any empirical cutoffs with respect to diagnostic criteria along with the absence of research that would support the validity of the diagnosis, coupled with sloppy (and perhaps unethical) diagnostic procedures means children are being labeled as "having" ODD simply because their behavior is annoying, threatening, and frustrating to the significant adults in their lives. That may say more about those adults than it does those children. But there is a further, even more vexing problem.

Nearly every medical website we searched suggested that ODD is inherited and/or caused by defects in the child's biology. Some references suggested that ODD might be the result of *temperamental* factors, but again, the term implies the presence of some innate quality. Anyone who's had significant experience with children of various ages would agree that most toddlers—so-called terrible twos—fit the description. It is normal for children between eighteen and thirty-six months, approximately, to have little tolerance for frustration, to refuse to accept responsibility for misdeeds, and to be annoying (and relentlessly so). Characteristically, toddlers are also easily annoyed, vindictive, and defiant. That's six of the eight defining criteria, so we need go no further. In other words, ODD is not a defect that some children have and some do not; rather, almost all children exhibit the defining behaviors during toddlerhood. How, then, can one explain that whereas nearly all two-year-olds have an innate defect, inherited or otherwise, the defect seems to go away in most of them before their fourth birthdays? The answer is that no logical explanation exists.

Quite obviously, oppositional defiant disorder is nothing more than a contrivance, a pseudodiagnosis cut from the whole cloth of the emperor's fabled clothes. Nonetheless, otherwise intelligent people are convinced that it is a reality and feel that the only issue is its underlying cause. This indicates that education, intelligence, and proper credentials do not necessarily make for intellectual rigor, because intellectually rigorous people would say that to debate the cause of something that has not been proven to even *exist* is to put the cart a good distance in front of the horse. Intellectually rigorous people would say that the very existence of the horse must be ascertained before any attention is given to locating the cart. Most alarming, this lack of intellectual meticulousness characterizes the writings of some of the most influential people in the field. Take Dr. Demitri Papolos of the Albert Einstein College of Medicine, who with his wife, Janice, is the author of the best-selling *The Bipolar Child.*

In addition to a well-read book, the Papoloses have a newsletter that goes out to thousands of parents and professionals, and they have appeared on numerous talk shows to educate the public concerning the nature and extent of early onset bipolar disorder (also called pediatric bipolar disorder). In their book, they attribute temper tantrums and other vexing behaviors *during toddlerhood* to the presence of EOBD. The Papoloses acknowledge the absence of any hard scientific evidence that would validate their theory, yet they maintain that EOBD is a real, verifiable entity. They claim that in some bipolar children, the onset of symptoms occurs during infancy with tantrums, irritability, and general restlessness and further argue that up to 33 percent of children diagnosed with ADHD actually have EOBD.[15]

Early onset bipolar disorder is not yet included in the *Diagnostic and Statistical Manual*—meaning, it is not recognized by the APA as a valid diagnosis—but that doesn't bother the Papoloses. They suggest that professionals can apply an existing DSM diagnosis, "bipolar disorder not otherwise specified," to children who do not meet the DSM-IV criteria for bipolar disorder.[16] Getting around the fact that EOBD is not yet a recognized diagnosis in this fashion means that diagnosing professionals can now obtain reimbursement from insurance companies, HMOs, and Medicaid for treating children who supposedly have a problem that, as is the case with ADHD and ODD, doesn't really exist.

The Papoloses provide a list of EOBD symptoms, including the following that they identify as "very common" (our comments are italicized and enclosed in parentheses):

- Separation anxiety (*Agitation over impending separation from parents has long been recognized as normal in children eight to thirty months of age and is often associated with parents who have difficulty separating from their children. In other words, it is usually impossible to determine whose anxieties came first, the parent's or the child's.*)
- Rages and explosive temper tantrums (*Full-blown emotional meltdowns over even small frustrations are not unusual during the second and third years of life.*)
- Oppositional defiant behavior (*This is nothing more than a typical feature of the "terrible twos."*)
- Distractibility (*Needless to say, young children are easily distracted.*)
- Hyperactivity (*Parents of toddlers have forever described their children as "getting into everything" and "running them ragged."*)
- Risk-taking behaviors (*Such as climbing on the counter to get at the cookie jar? Or running away from parents in a shopping center? The fact is, young children often do not know that what they're doing involves significant risk.*)
- Difficulty getting up in the morning (*The idea that difficulty getting moving in the morning may be a sign of a biological defect moves the authors to speechlessness.*)[17]

Obviously, most of the Papaloses' symptoms are typical of toddlers, which is consistent with their claim that EOBD can be detected as early as infancy. They even suggest that it might be possible to detect it *in utero*. In *The Bipolar Child*, the Papaloses report that a good number of the mothers they interviewed remembered their babies were highly active in the womb—hard kicking, lots of rolling and tumbling—and suggest the possibility of a connection between such prenatal activity and later bipolar disorder.[18]

Lest one scoff at the notion that the above list of supposed symptoms represents childhood bipolar disorder and the proposal that highly active fetuses may have EOBD, it is sobering to look at the Papoloses' recommendations for treatment, including their recommendation concerning the parent-child relationship, specifically that parents not appear to their children to be attempting to dominate or control them.[19] It is difficult to see how the Papoloses are recommending anything other than giving in to the child, accommodating his demands and outbursts, which common sense would say is going to make the behavior problems that much worse. This seemingly counterproductive approach is consistent, however, with their overall hypothesis: EOBD is the result of an immutable biological defect. If so, then authoritative discipline (of the sort the authors often recommend and have often found to be successful in such cases) is moot.

Furthermore, and paradoxically, authoritative discipline may make the problem worse. That leaves psychotropic (specifically, mood-stabilizing) drugs, which the Papoloses say "should be considered as a first line of treatment" and early on, before the supposed disease "warps the psychological development of a child and destroys the life of a family."[20]

Someone searching the Internet for information on bipolar children is likely to land on the website of the Juvenile Bipolar Research Foundation, which describes itself as a "charitable organization dedicated to the support of research for the study of early-onset bipolar disorder."[21] The director of research for this charitable organization is none other than Demitri Papolos, MD. Anyone who registers with the website can download, for free, the sixty-five-item "Child Bipolar Questionnaire," developed by Papolos, which JBRF will score for free. We are to believe that many behaviors once regarded as simply childish (complaints of boredom, fidgetiness, goofiness) and immature or merely signs of unfinished discipline (argumentativeness, blaming others for mistakes, interrupting conversations) are now markers of pediatric bipolar disorder. As we've seen with DSM criteria for ADHD and ODD, Papolos's diagnostic instrument is replete with imprecise language, as in "has difficulty arising in the AM" and "has difficulty making transitions."[22] As one researcher comments, "most normal children would score at least modestly."[23]

In *The Bipolar Child*, the Papoloses propose that significant numbers of children diagnosed with ADHD actually have EOBD. Or they have both, in which case the Papoloses explain how to differentiate between the two. In the case of tantrums, for example, they contend that ADHD-associated temper tantrums are triggered by sensory and emotional overstimulation while those associated with EOBD are triggered by limit setting, as in parents saying no.[24] It should be needless by now to point out that the Papoloses' contentions in this regard rest on no solid science.

Where EOBD is concerned, the Papoloses revisit what we have already seen concerning ADHD and ODD:

- Arbitrary, ill-defined, and unscientific diagnostic criteria
- Unproven theories about causation
- Treatment recommendations that presume "chemical imbalances" and other unverified brain pathologies

Unfortunately, the Papoloses' writings are having a profound influence on professional thinking and practice. Reviews of their book often gush with acclamations like "groundbreaking,"[25] and "classic and life-saving."[26] Their writings have contributed significantly to the diagnosing of more and more young children with bipolar disorder, a supposed mental illness that was once regarded as not likely to occur prior to late adolescence.

According to *Archives of General Psychiatry*, from 1994 to 2003 the percent of psychiatric diagnoses represented by EOBD increased fifteen-fold. In 2007, authoritative estimates of the prevalence of EOBD were as high as 6 percent.[27] As we've seen happen with ADHD, it is all but certain that as the diagnosis becomes more and more of a proven money-maker for the professional community, incidence estimates will increase.

The authors of that same *AGP* paper emphasize the need for "researchers and clinicians to reach a consensus concerning diagnostic criteria and assessment methods."[28] In effect, they are admitting that although the diagnosis is proliferating like the proverbial hotcakes, no professional consensus exists concerning how or by what standards the diagnosis should be made. Furthermore, by calling for consensus, they also tacitly admit that EOBD is lacking scientific corroboration. Whenever a consensus of opinion is invoked as the basis for diagnostic guidelines, science is lacking. When the scientific validity of a diagnosis has been established, opinion becomes moot.

WHERE ARE WE HEADED?

Most people think that mental health professionals are in the business of selling treatment, but treatment is actually their secondary product. The primary product, the product a therapist must sell to the designated buyer before he can begin dispensing therapy, is a diagnosis, the buyer of which is an insurance company or health maintenance organization, known as a third-party payer (TPP). Furthermore, the diagnosis must be listed in the DSM. In effect, the therapist "sells" the TPP on the notion that the patient has an APA-approved mental disorder. If the TPP "buys" the diagnosis, it will pay for therapy, within specified limits. As recently as the 1970s, it was rare for TPPs to pay for mental health services, so most people paid for their own. In those days, mental health professionals sold therapy. In many cases, people received therapy without even receiving a diagnosis. Those days are gone, thanks to lawyers.

A company that makes its money by selling soap products is going to be highly motivated to develop more and more soap products. Likewise, a profession that generates income by selling diagnoses is going to be motivated to come up with more and more diagnoses to sell. The number of diagnoses listed in the DSM has more than tripled in the last fifty years. The APA would claim that improvements in psychiatric science have enabled them to discover more than 250 new mental disorders during that time. But there is very little of what could properly be called science involved here. The discovery of a new diagnosis is often just smoke and mirrors. Besides the accolades that accrue to those who discover new "syndromes" and "disorders," there's the money to be made, and a lot it is, especially when children are involved. An adult may choose to simply cope with his own emotional problems but is far less likely to do so when the problems involve his child.

The mental health community saw how readily parents bought that children who weren't doing well in school had ADHD, so next came ODD and parents of unruly, disobedient children bought that. Now we have EOBD, and parents of children who are provoked to rage at the sound of "no" for an answer are buying that. And the beat goes on. First, the APA invents a new diagnosis, thus creating a new client base; second, it uses non-science and other nonsense to "medicalize" the supposed disorder; third, it expands the boundaries of the diagnosis so as to capture more and more clients in the new diagnostic "net."

This is exactly what's happened with all of the diagnoses we've discussed thus far, and it's happening as we write with childhood depression and autism. With respect to the latter, it's significant to note that whereas autism was recently estimated to affect one in one thousand American children, it is now estimated by such authoritative sources as the Center for Autism and Related Disorders and the American Academy of Pediatrics to affect one in 150 children.[29,30] That's a 667 percent increase! This has not happened because some new pathogen or toxin has entered the uterine or neonatal environment; it's happened because where there was once only autism disorder, there is now such a mind-boggling array of "autism spectrum disorders," including Asperger's syndrome, childhood disintegrative disorder, and—here we go again—pervasive developmental disorder *not otherwise specified,* that any child whose behavior falls even slightly outside the norm is in danger of being "diagnosed" with autism or one of its variants by some "expert." (We will, for the moment, concede that there is a legitimate, relatively rare condition known as autism, notwithstanding that, as noted by Paula Caplan, its diagnostic parameters are not objectively described.)

A number of parents have reported to me that clinicians have diagnosed their three- and four-year-old children with Asperger's syndrome largely on the basis of preschool teacher reports that they are shy, prefer to play alone rather than in groups, or don't make eye contact when adults are talking to them. The fact is that most kids who are shy and retiring at age four eventually grow out of their social awkwardness. Likewise, pervasive developmental disorder (PDD) is being applied to children who don't talk or seem very interested in talking by age two (this describes three of my seven grandchildren, all of whom were talking fine by age three), appear fixated on one or two toys to the exclusion of everything else (this describes two of my grandchildren, both of whom developed broader play interests as time went on), and react negatively to changes in routine (not unusual for young children; in fact, many adults, including my very psychologically healthy wife, don't like changes in routine). Needless to say, there is no proof that those behaviors are pathological; nevertheless, PDD is identified as a "neurological disorder."[31] Childhood behaviors people once thought were simply unremarkable person-to-person variations in personality and temperament have become or are becoming indications of brain disease. This begins to look suspiciously like disease-mongering. In that vein, one researcher suggests that this trend represents a new version of "Munchausen's syndrome, where some significant other wants the individual to be ill and these significant others derive some gain from these proxy illnesses."[32]

David Reitman, PhD, associate professor of psychology and editor of *The Behavior Therapist*, has written a tongue-in-cheek "Modest Proposal for a New Diagnostic Classification: Intrinsic Motivation Deficit Disorder

(IMDD)." He states, "Mental health professionals previously frustrated in their attempts to identify enough cases of ADHD or ODD to keep their practices afloat will welcome this common and easily diagnosed condition as a focus of clinical attention."[33] Although satirical, and quite humorous at that, it would not be surprising to see the APA include some variant on IMDD in the next edition of the DSM. As a matter of fact, in his best-selling *The Myth of Laziness*, pediatrician Mel Levine argues that children who appear lazy are most likely suffering from "output failure" caused by neurodevelopmental weaknesses.[34]

Writing in *Pediatric News*, a newsletter distributed free of charge nationwide to pediatricians, Dr. David W. Willis, behavioral-developmental pediatrics director at the Northwest Early Childhood Institute in Portland, Oregon, proposes that the incidence of childhood mental health disorders is growing so dramatically as to outstrip the current supply of mental health practitioners. He cites research purporting to show that 20 percent of children ages nine to seventeen are affected by one mental disorder or another and observes that "these disorders may manifest as difficult behaviors at younger ages." He then issues a call to pediatricians, encouraging them to identify these children as preschoolers and either begin treatment or make appropriate referrals, noting that pharmaceuticals will soon be developed to use as "preventive therapy for children with genetic susceptibility to mental health problems."[35] The long and short of Willis's proposal: it may soon be deemed appropriate to administer drugs to children who may not yet be exhibiting problem behaviors but are thought to have a "genetic susceptibility" (a fictitious concept the authors will deal with in chapter 3) to mental illness. Thus, even children with no observable problems may well, and soon, become grist for the mental health mill.

The U.S. government is even getting in on the act. The New Freedom Commission on Mental Health—an Orwellian moniker if ever there was one—established in 2002 by President Bush, calls for mandatory mental health screening of American school-age children. That's right, *mandatory*, as in parents will no longer be able to choose whether or not their kids are examined by mental health professionals. But that's not where this will end, because you can bet that the parents of a child found, upon examination, to have a "disorder" will be compelled to present said child for "treatment" under threat of being charged with child neglect. If this is "new freedom," then the moon is a big wheel of Swiss cheese.

As with all matters concerning a child's health care, the decision to have a child undergo psychological evaluation is and should forever be a prerogative reserved exclusively to the child's parents—the extremely rare exception, in the case of parental incompetence, for example, acknowledged. The New Freedom Commission is an outrageous attempt to infringe upon parental rights, and if the commission's recommendations are followed, things promise to only get worse. Should its recommendations ever pass Congress, millions of American kids will end up being diagnosed with various "disorders" and "mental illnesses," thus giving a huge pump to the economies of the psychological, psychiatric, and pharmaceutical industries. Public schools will have to expand programming to children identified as having these so-called special needs. This will require money, and lots of it. Ultimately, entitlements under the Americans with Disabilities Act will blossom, further burdening the American economy.

Thankfully, there is someone in President Bush's own party who recognized the threat posed by this "new freedom." Congressman and 2008 presidential candidate Ron Paul, MD (R-Texas) introduced a bill, the Parental Consent Act of 2007, that forbids federal funds from being used for mental health screening of children without the express, written, voluntary, and informed consent of their parents. Paul has previously written that "only tremendous public opposition will suffice to overcome the lobbying and bureaucratic power behind the president's New Freedom Commission."[36] The lobbies to which he somewhat obliquely refers are primarily those representing the interests of the mental health and phar-maceutical industries.

In this context, the phrase "no child left behind" begins to take on a meaning different from that originally intended. Although the No Child Left Behind legislation was designed to ensure that no child would grow up without a proper education, it appears that we are rapidly approaching a time when no child will grow up without a psychiatric diagnosis and a prescription.

CHAPTER 3
BIOLOGY IN WONDERLAND

"Who makes a decision . . . as to whether a child has hyperkinesis,
or is just a bored, bright, creative, pain-in-the-neck kid?"
—psychiatrist Cornelius Gallagher, chairman of the APA
committee on the *Diagnostic and Statistical Manual*[1]

"We have hunted for big, simple neuro-pathological explanations
for psychiatric disorders and have not found them."
—genetics researcher Dr. Kenneth Kendler[2]

DURING THE PAST FIVE YEARS, IN MY FREQUENT TRAVELS AS A
public speaker, I have been gathering information by means of an informal
poll. When a parent (more often than not, a mother) tells me that her child
has been diagnosed with ADHD, ODD, and/or EOBD, I ask, "And what
did the diagnosing physician or therapist tell you caused your child's problems?" The actual words vary of course, but the fundamental answer does
not: an inherited biological problem, usually a biochemical imbalance.

- "He told me my child was born with an imbalance in his
  brain. He determined that that sort of thing runs in my
  family."
- "She said my child's brain is wired differently from most kids'
  brains, and that he probably inherited this from his father."

- "We were told that his problems were genetic, and that he can't help behaving the way he does."

When I ask if the therapist performed or ordered any physical examination or genetic testing, the parent looks puzzled and then answers that no, the therapist did not.

To which I respond, "That's amazing, don't you think, that the therapist was able to tell that your child has a biological problem without performing or ordering any medical tests, and he was further able to discern that your child inherited the problem without ordering genetic testing?"

More than one parent has asked, "Are you saying he just made that stuff up?"

It may be a tad unfair to accuse therapists of making these things up, but it is perfectly accurate to say they are snatching them from the thinnest of air. No valid medical procedures are used to arrive at these bogus conclusions. It further surprises many parents to learn that although physicians and therapists make claims of this sort as if they are established, incontrovertible, and not open to discussion, they are nothing more than theories— theories, furthermore, that are not supported by good scientific evidence. There is no compelling proof to the effect that the behaviors constituting ADHD (as well as ODD and EOBD), or specific behavior(s) of any sort for that matter, are or can be inherited. Equally conjectural are the notions that ADHD is caused by an "imbalance" in the proportions of chemicals that mediate brain activity and/or abnormalities in certain brain structures. Taken together, these theories constitute the *disease model* of childhood behavior disorders—*disease* because it holds that childhood behavior disorders are caused by faulty biology. Its counterpoint is the *developmental model*, which holds that childhood behavior disorders develop as a consequence of detrimental life circumstances, including such things as overexposure to television and video games, a diet deficient in nutritional value and/or high in manufactured chemicals, and a lack of proper discipline.

The disease model would easily win a popularity contest among not only the lay public (because laypersons understandably tend to believe unequivocal statements made by people with capital letters after their names), but diagnosing and treating professionals as well (because they attend postgraduate courses that teach this model). Nevertheless, as the reader will eventually discover, the preponderance of objective evidence clearly favors the developmental model. In fact, when one examines the known facts, the disease model begins to look not just wrong, but absurd. Because the position they have staked out is not scientifically tenable, proponents of the disease model must of necessity defend it with statements and information that are scientifically unsupportable, misleading, and even illogical.

Dr. Ravenel once sat in on an online exchange between a free-thinking psychologist and a psychiatrist during which the latter compared "mental illness" (a category that includes childhood behavior disorders) to Alzheimer's disease. The psychologist astutely pointed out that the problem with this argument is that Alzheimer's biological basis has been established beyond doubt, while that is not the case regarding *any* psychiatric disorder listed in the DSM-IV (including depression and schizophrenia). Statements concerning the biological basis of Alzheimer's, therefore, tell us nothing about the supposed biological basis of, say, attention-deficit/hyperactivity disorder. The psychiatrist responded that the psychologist was ignoring *conclusive* findings about brain structure and related cognitive and behavioral problems but conveniently omitted any citation of such "conclusive" evidence. He was wise to do so, because there is none.

IS ADHD IN THE GENES?

An Internet search of the phrase "ADHD genes" brings up numerous references to articles and public statements by various researchers and treating professionals in which the claim is advanced that ADHD is primarily, if not entirely, a matter of inheritance.

- Writing in the prestigious *American Journal of Human Genetics* (2002), researchers from the University of California and Oxford claim "there is strong evidence for a genetic etiology of the disorder" and then immediately admit that the actual effect of the genes they have identified seems "very small." They further claim to have discovered that the same gene(s) may be implicated in both autism and ADHD. The authors write as if it is beyond question that genes cause both conditions, when proof of genetic causation has yet to be established for either (nor has any other biological basis).[3] In response, Dr. Fred Baughman Jr., an eminent physician and outspoken critic of the ADHD Establishment, points out that it is "inherently deceitful" to assert a biological cause for a supposed disorder that has not been validated as a disease. He boldly and correctly asserts that "this article should never have been published in a respected scientific journal."[4]

- The website of the British Broadcasting Company contains a transcript of a program broadcast on August 23, 2007. Apparently basing her information on an interview with a child and adolescent psychiatrist, the program's moderator states unequivocally that "ADHD is a genetically determined condition that affects the parts of the brain which control impulses, concentration, and attention."[5] Such statements cannot be supported with compelling evidence.

- On a page titled "The Cause of ADD/ADHD Is Genetic" contained on the website of the ADD Medical Treatment Center of Santa Clara Valley (San Jose, California), founder/director Monroe Gross, MD, asserts, "The scientific community now generally accepts that ADD/ADHD is a genetic disorder."[6] The truth of the matter is that the methods and reasoning used to arrive at the conclusion that ADHD is caused by genes cannot be accurately termed "scientific."

- A 2003 article in *Science* magazine—"New Attention to ADHD Genes"—summarizes comments from various researchers to the effect that "ADHD is a one-two punch of susceptibility genes and environmental risks." The researchers admit, however, that they do not know either the specific genes or environmental factors involved.[7]

An individual often identified as a leading authority on ADHD is psychologist Russell A. Barkley, currently a research professor in the department of psychiatry at the SUNY Upstate Medical University in Syracuse, New York. In 2003, Barkley was quoted in an online article as saying he hopes that ongoing research soon puts "the nail in the coffin that ADHD is a myth."[8] Since this article first appeared on the web, one could conclude from Barkley's writings that he appears to have gone beyond hope to all but absolute certainty. In his online professional continuing education curriculum, "Attention-Deficit/Hyperactivity Disorder: Nature, Course, Outcomes, and Comorbidity," revised on November 1, 2007, Barkley says, "Evidence for a genetic basis to this disorder is now overwhelming and comes from four sources: family studies of the aggregation of the disorder among biological relatives, adoption studies, twin studies, and, most recently, molecular genetic studies identifying individual candidate genes."[9] On his own website, Barkley says:

While precise causes have not yet been identified, there is little question that heredity/genetics makes the largest contribution. . . . The heritability of ADHD averages approximately 80 percent, meaning that genetic factors account for 80 percent of the differences among individuals in this set of behavioral traits. For comparison, consider that this figure rivals that for the role of genetics in human height. Several genes associated with the disorder have been identified and undoubtedly more will be so given that ADHD represents a set of complex behavioral traits and so a single gene is unlikely to account for the disorder.[10]

To say that such ill-defined behaviors as "often has trouble keeping attention on tasks or play activities," "often fidgets with hands or feet," and "often talks excessively" are "heritable" simply means that when these descriptions apply, however loosely, to one child in a nuclear family, they are often found to apply to other members of the family as well. So? The fact that laid-back parents are more likely than anxious parents to have laid-back children does not mean that a tendency toward being laid-back is inherited. The fact that parents who vote Republican tend to raise children who, as adults, vote Republican does not mean that something called "Republicanism" is inherited. The fact that children of Catholic parents are likely as adults to attend Catholic churches does not mean that "Catholic behavior" is passed from parent to child.

Barkley's argument also begs the essential question: what, exactly, is being inherited? Efforts on the part of sociobiologists to prove that specific behavior can be inherited have failed miserably. As we will later see, one of the most eminent geneticists in the world categorically denies that predispositions toward certain behaviors can be passed from parent to child through genetic mechanisms. Furthermore, it is misleading to assert cause for a supposed disorder that has yet to be objectively defined. Under the circumstances, the term *heritable* is meaningless and claims of genetic transmission of ADHD from parent to child are fiction.

The truth is that the role of genes in the development of ADHD has been strenuously investigated over the past thirty or so years. Millions of dollars have been poured into this research, but research, no matter how well funded, does not necessarily truth or fact make. In this case, millions upon millions of dollars cannot do away with the fact that no positive, verifiable link between any gene or genes and ADHD has ever been found. Yet numerous professionals who specialize in the diagnosis and treatment of ADHD persist in making claims to the effect that it is inherited. Supposedly the mystery genes in question cause structural anomalies, "wiring" issues, and/or chemical imbalances in the brain which, in turn, cause the behaviors associated with ADHD (as well as ODD and EOBD). We will revisit these unsubstantiated claims shortly.

The genetic hypothesis, especially when it is presented as fact, is the crux of ADHD mythology. Interestingly, it is not only as unsubstantiated today as it was thirty years ago, but it also contradicts genetic fact and flies in the face of plain-old, down-to-earth common sense.

WHERE DID THE GENES COME FROM?

The following are statements of fact: From generation to generation, genes work in a reliably predictable fashion. In popular parlance, they are "passed on" so that within any population group, a trait that is present to a significant degree in one generation inevitably shows up in the next, and the next, and the next . . . and to approximately the same extent. For example, let's say that of all children born in the United States in 2008 who are at least third-generation Americans, 25 percent came into the world with brown eyes. On that basis, we would absolutely know that a representative sample of American birth records from 1945 to 1955 (the grandparent generation) would show that very close to 25 percent of children born during that time sported brown eyes. New genes that suddenly emerge in a population group are called "mutations," and even assuming that a mutation is favored (which no example of has ever been discovered), it would take a long time—far more than a few generations—for any mutation to become significantly widespread.

The question then becomes: if genes cause ADHD, ODD, and EOBD, where is the evidence that significant numbers of American children born from 1945 to 1955 (who therefore attended grades one through five from 1950 to 1965, approximately) exhibited the symptoms associated with these supposed "disorders"? After all, no informed person would deny that these diagnoses are widespread among today's kids.

There is no such evidence. Clearly, the symptom pictures in question were quite rare until the 1970s. During the peak years of the baby boom, America was suffering a teacher and classroom shortage that resulted in an embarrassment of what today would be considered horribly overcrowded classrooms. An elementary school classroom of forty to fifty students taught by one teacher was not at all unusual. My first-grade classroom (in Charleston, South Carolina, 1953–54) held fifty students, taught by one teacher. My second-grade classroom—my mother remarried and my stepfather took us to the suburbs of Chicago—consisted of thirty-seven children, again taught by one teacher.

In third grade, I sat with nearly forty children taught by Mrs. Hoy. Whereas first and second grades are a bit fuzzy, I remember third grade fairly well. Mrs. Hoy did not have to deal with many discipline problems. She occasionally sent a child outside to sit in the hall, but *occasionally* is the operative word, and the exile was more often than not due to not having come to school with completed homework. (I remember sitting in academic purgatory once or twice myself.) She undoubtedly reprimanded a child or two on any given day, but I most clearly remember an orderly yet stimulating learning environment. When Mrs. Hoy taught, we listened. When she gave an instruction, we followed it. I would certainly remember if four or five children (approximately 10 percent, the absolute minimum estimate of the proportion of today's school-age children who supposedly have one or more childhood behavior disorders) presented major behavior problems. But let's face it, my experience might be unique, and my memory might be failing me. To check out that unthinkable possibility, I've asked other people of my generation who attest to having attended overcrowded (by today's standards) classrooms, "Do you recall your teachers spending significant amounts of time on disciplinary matters?" No, they answer. We fifty- and sixty-something boomers all remember the occasional child whose desk abutted the teacher's, the occasional child (usually a boy) who got into more than his fair share of trouble, but no peer to whom I've spoken (I estimate I've spoken directly about this to several hundred, all over the U.S.) remembers children who were hopelessly incorrigible, much less out of control.

No fellow boomer I've talked to remembers a child who threw classroom tantrums, not even in kindergarten or first grade. No one remembers a child who talked back insultingly to a teacher, much less reared back to hit her when she upset him. These sorts of incidents happen with regularity in today's elementary classrooms. For example, I have not spoken to a kindergarten teacher in the past seven years who has not been hit by one of her students in the preceding twelve months. Are all of our memories failing equally rapidly?

I doubt it. In my capacity as a speaker on parenting and family issues, I give some two hundred presentations yearly, all across the U.S. (and every now and then abroad). In the course of my travels, I encounter and converse with more than my fair share of men and women who taught in America's schools during those halcyon days. They consistently confirm that classroom discipline was not a major issue in the 1950s. The not-so-remarkable thing—to a person my age, that is, who was taught by these people—is that these testimonies are virtually interchangeable. In one voice, they attest to calm, orderly classrooms. Not classrooms that were problem free—that would stretch the imagination—but classrooms in which discipline was a relatively easy matter. The statistics not only bear this out, but belie the idea that children learn better in smaller classes. (Historical data is clear on this: effective learning is not a matter of small class size but of good behavior; furthermore, it seems that schools cannot reduce class size fast enough to keep up with the deterioration in classroom behavior and achievement.) In the early 1950s, when the average elementary classroom in America held thirty-plus children taught by one teacher, achievement at every grade level was considerably higher than is the case today. I'm reasonably certain, by the way, that the National Education Association does not want the American public to know that.

PAY ATTENTION TO YOUR TEACHERS

(*As you read the following testimonies from several retired teachers—with details changed to protect the privacy of those individuals—keep in mind what we said earlier: the proportional representation of a certain trait or characteristic within a specific population group tends to remain approximately the same over the span of several generations—more than several, actually, but we'll leave it at that.*)

In 1999, during the morning break of the in-service training I was providing to administrators, teachers, and counselors from a number of schools in Florida, I was introduced to a petite elderly woman—I'll call her Miss Agnes. Much to my surprise, she was in her seventies and still teaching. Granted, she was substitute teaching, but she was subbing nearly every day in one of the Catholic schools in the area.

"I'll teach as long as they'll let me, John," she said, smiling, and proceeded to tell me a story so fascinating and revealing that I have related it to numerous audiences since.

Miss Agnes began teaching shortly after the end of World War II. In 1950, the school at which she taught was expecting an influx of seventy first-graders—five- and six-year-olds—who'd been divided equally between two teachers, she being one of them. The baby boom was in full roar, America was suffering a corresponding shortage of teachers, and classrooms everywhere were overcrowded. The day before the start of school, the other first-grade teacher called the school's principal and abruptly resigned, explaining that her husband had just received notice of his transfer. The principal walked down the hall to where Miss Agnes was setting up her classroom, told her what had happened, and informed her she would have to teach *all seventy children* until another teacher could be found. Seventy desks were promptly moved into the largest classroom in the building, lined up into seven rows of ten desks each, and Miss Agnes undertook what would today be considered an absurdly impossible assignment. In that light, keep in mind that she had been teaching but a few years.

Some pertinent information, to help the reader put a proper context to this fascinating story:

- Outside of Sunday school, most of these seventy kids had never been to a preschool program of any sort, including kindergarten. First grade was their first large-group experience.
- With few exceptions, the children in question, even those who had attended kindergarten, came to first grade lacking academic skills. (In 1950, kindergarten was still a creative, as opposed to an academic, environment.) Most of Miss Agnes's students did not know "number facts" or the ABCs, much less how to read. In those days, parents believed children went to school to learn such things; therefore, most parents believed that academics did not need to be taught—nay, *should not* be taught—before children went to school. My own situation was typical. I entered first grade in 1953. I could sing the ABC song, but I could not correctly identify more than the first three letters of the alphabet, and then only in upper case. I could count to ten, but that was it as far as "number facts" were concerned.
- This being before what I call the "age of parenting neurosis," mothers did not agonize over the issue of late birthdays. If a child's birthday was September 30, and the cutoff for school entrance was October 1, the child went to school. For one thing, he had passed the only existing readiness test, which

consisted of but one question: was his mother ready for him to go to school? Where most 1950s moms were concerned, *eager* was more like it.

- The school in question was a Catholic school—private, in a sense, but not elitist. Some of the parents of those seventy children were working-class folks who had not finished high school, and some were college-educated professionals. Those seventy kids came from all walks of life. In other words, demographics do not account for Miss Agnes's tale.

The following are Miss Agnes's words: "After six weeks, when the principal realized I was having no problems at all, he decided to save money and leave me with them all year long. And John, I really had no problems. Oh you know, an occasional outburst of mischief from one child or another, but no constant outpouring of problems from any one child or from the group. They sat, paid attention, and did their work; and I was able, therefore, to do what I had been trained to do: teach."

Seventy children and no significant discipline problems? Amazing! Though the most amazing aspect of her testimony was yet to come, in order to fully appreciate its significance, one must realize that schools, public and parochial, in the 1950s set the bar of achievement at a certain level and there it stayed. If a student did not clear the bar, he did not go to the next grade according to schedule. In the now politically incorrect vernacular of the day, he *flunked*. Catholic schools tended to enforce this policy more strictly than public schools, but only by a bit. Catholic schools did not lower the bar for any student for any reason, and they certainly did not promote to protect a child's self-esteem. My first-grade teacher was Sister Mary. Believe me when I say that if you came to Sister Mary's class with high self-esteem, she promptly set about to lower it. In this regard at least, Sister Mary was like most adults back then: she did not tolerate displays of high self-esteem in children. Such self-centered posturing was known as "acting too big for your britches" or "being up on your high horse." But I get ahead of myself—more on what I call "the great self-esteem farce" later.

The rest of Miss Agnes's testimony: "Oh, and John," she said, "every child learned to read and write well enough to go to the second grade."

Super amazing to the third power! Well, not actually. Something *amazing* is, by definition, extraordinary. The fact is, Miss Agnes's story is not, by a long shot, extraordinary. As I said earlier, since my encounter with Miss Agnes, I've told her tale to numerous audiences around the U.S. On many of these occasions, while I'm standing at my book table afterward, an older person approaches and tells me a similar story from his or her own teaching career. I've heard at least one hundred such stories since Miss Agnes told me hers, and every time, the retired teacher in question ends the testimony with words to this effect: "And John, I had no significant problems. Excepting the occasional act of mischief and some quite understandable daydreaming, my students sat, listened, and did their work while I taught."

In Connecticut, a retired teacher said, "Praise the Lord that I had no discipline problems [out of the sixty first-graders she taught in 1956, her first year teaching!], because the professors in my teacher education program in college had not taught us anything about classroom behavior management or whatever they call it today."

That's right! There were so few behavior problems in America's schools in the 1950s, not to mention that most of the existing problems were by today's standards minuscule (chewing gum in class, speaking out without raising your hand, talking while in line, and the like), that college professors who prepared America's teachers felt it unnecessary to instruct on how to motivate or discipline students. The fact that parents backed teachers 100 percent where discipline problems were concerned also served to keep children in line.

Several years ago, at a workshop in Georgia, an older woman told me she taught a second-grade class of sixty-five children in the 1950s. Her teaching day began at 8:15 a.m. and ended at 3:15 p.m. Her testimony: "The children were sweet, well-behaved, and very curious. I didn't have to discipline much at all."

In North Carolina, I met a man who in 1962 taught sixty sixth-graders in a self-contained class, by himself. He reported to me that not one of these sixty children presented any significant problem. Discipline was not an issue in his class, he said.

Several years ago, I spoke to a retired Catholic sister who testified that in the late 1950s, in a blue-collar area of Pennsylvania, she was one of two first-grade teachers teaching a combined total of one hundred and eighty-nine students. She taught ninety-four, and the other teacher taught ninety-five! She told me that she had a picture of herself with her class, but I didn't need to see it to believe her story.

She said, "Those children came to my class already disciplined, John. I didn't have to do their parents' job. I just had to do mine."

Mind-boggling! I'll venture to say that one could not scour the U.S. today and handpick seventy first-graders (much less ninety-five!) who could be taught, by one teacher, as successfully as were Miss Agnes's students, no matter how skilled the teacher might be. I'll even go so far as to say one could not find half that number—thirty-five—who could be taught so successfully. Keep in mind that a first-grade class of thirty-five was commonplace in the 1950s. I'm asserting, therefore, that what thousands of teachers were able to do just fifty years ago can no longer be done, *not because good teachers no longer exist,* but because today's teachers are dealing with a host of problems that teachers in Miss Agnes's day did not have to deal with to any significant degree. Without exception, the retirees with whom I've spoken bemoan the problems they began seeing in the early 1970s, problems that had previously been few and far between. By the late 1970s, the problems in question were forcing teachers to do less and less teaching and more and more disciplining. By the late 1980s, these problems were ubiquitous. Furthermore, their ubiquity was starting to drive good people out of teaching. In slightly more than one generation, the previously few and far between was everywhere.

Consider this contrasting story. One Saturday morning in 2003, I was speaking at a church in Alabama. I was standing in the lobby of the church's large sanctuary, "meeting and greeting" as we say in the South, when a woman with a somewhat strained expression approached me and said, "John, I hope you have some encouraging words for me today." When I inquired as to why she needed encouragement, she told me that she had taught first grade for twenty years and had hoped to teach for another twenty, but she was considering taking early retirement before the school year was even over. She taught at an exclusive independent school. I was familiar with the school and knew that, as with most elite academies, its enrollment standards were high and strictly enforced. She had nineteen children in her first-grade class and was assisted by a full-time "paraprofessional" (the elite independent school equivalent of a teacher's aide). I'll stop right here and mention, just in case you haven't done the math, that the teacher-student ratio in this class was one to ten (being liberal with the fraction). Compare this with Miss Agnes's first-grade class in 1950, where the teacher-student ratio was one to seventy.

"John," this teacher said, with great regret in her voice, "out of nineteen students, six came to me already *completely out of control*, and nothing I've done has improved the situation one iota. Discipline problems have been getting worse year by year, but I never anticipated anything like this. Like I said, I need some encouragement."

Six out of nineteen students is approximately one in three, and keep in mind that the school in question has "high" enrollment standards. If we extrapolate that to Miss Agnes's class, she would have been dealing with twenty-three out-of-control children! This contrast may be a bit extreme, but let me assure you that it is not unusual for an elementary teacher today to have five children who are major behavior problems out of a class of twenty-five. That Alabama teacher's story is but one of many such stories of classroom grief I've heard from teachers all over the U.S., and the stories are getting worse every year.

How can one square the obvious significant decline in child self-control from the 1950s to the present with the notion that ADHD, ODD, and EOBD are caused by genes? The answer, of course, is that there's no way to square the facts with the theory. Quite simply, genes are not the culprit.

MYTH BEGETS MYTH

We are not, by any means, saying that in the good old days, children with major behavior problems did not exist. That would discredit us completely. We're saying that the number of kids who exhibited major behavior problems in 1950s and 1960s classrooms was negligble. Retired teachers like Miss Agnes simply do not remember more than the occasional child who displayed the behaviors that establish the diagnoses under discussion. We doubt that so many professional memories could be so uniformly faulty.

But the ADHD Establishment has an answer to this. A number of mental health professionals who specialize in diagnosing and treating ADHD, ODD, and so on have told me that people who taught in the 1950s don't remember kids with the sorts of problems in question because those kids "fell between the cracks." "What cracks?" I ask, to which they reply that kids with ADHD, et cetera, just didn't go to school. They were kept at home.

That's certainly a unique explanation. There is no record of significant numbers of kids not going to school in the 1950s. I mean, we're not talking about kids with severe mental disabilities and might have been institutionalized. We're talking about inattentive, impulsive, and disobedient kids with average and above-average IQs. Indeed, many 1950s schools could not accommodate kids with serious intellectual and/or physical disabilities. Some, perhaps most, of *those* children were kept at home or were living in institutions, but kids with behavior problems didn't stay home. In fact, they *couldn't* have stayed home. By the 1950s, every state had put mandatory attendance laws in place, and nearly every school district employed at least one truant officer or someone on staff who acted as one. If you were out of school for more than a day, and the school had not heard from your parents (who were supposed to call if you were going to be absent), the truant officer was likely to show up at your house, unannounced, just to make sure you weren't playing hooky.

I attended elementary school from 1953 to 1961. All the kids in my neighborhood went to school, and there were so many families with kids moving into my neighborhood that the school was constantly building new wings. That's a lot of kids, and I knew not one school-age child who was not attending school. I knew kids in school who weren't very bright. I knew kids who came from very odd families, the sort we today call dysfunctional. I knew kids who had bad social skills. I knew kids who came from poor families. But I knew not one school-age child who did not attend school, and if there had been such a child in my neighborhood, the word would have gotten around quickly.

I've asked numerous other people my age, people who attended elementary school in the 1950s, "When you were growing up, were you aware of any child of school age in your neighborhood who was not attending school for reasons other than a serious physical or intellectual disability?" The answer has never varied: "Nope."

When confronted with this rather compelling anecdotal data, the professionals in question sometimes come back with, "Well, you know, kids with ADHD, ODD, and so on were probably expelled early on."

Excuse me? During my eight elementary years, I remember one kid getting expelled for something outrageous he did on a school-sponsored eighth-grade trip. (As I said, kids who were impulsive, disruptive, and so on did exist in the 1950s; they were just few and far between.) Again, I ask people my age, "Do you remember significant numbers of children being expelled from the elementary school you attended?" and again they draw blanks. No, "they were expelled" doesn't fly either.

The professional denials know no limits. I've even had two therapists tell me that kids with the sorts of problems under discussion behaved themselves in 1950s classrooms because they were *afraid* of the kinds of discipline that parents and teachers were likely to mete out back in those days. A gene-based brain disease that can be controlled with fear! This is patently ludicrous, but it is a living example of the illogical things members of the ADHD Establishment sometimes say to cover up the fact that they cannot scientifically defend the notion that genes cause disruptive behavior.

A favorite ploy of advocacy groups that represent children and adults with psychiatric diagnoses is to put forth a list of famous people throughout history who've supposedly had the disorder in question. Concerning ADHD, the following people often appear in such lists: Alexander Graham Bell (1862–1939), Hans Christian Andersen (1805–1875), Thomas Edison (1847–1931), Ludwig van Beethoven (1770–1827), Leonardo da Vinci (1452–1519), Galileo (1564–1642), Nostradamus (1503–1566), and—are you ready?—Socrates (469–399 BC).[11] (An official of a support group for parents of ADHD children once told me that Tom Sawyer obviously had ADHD. I didn't have the heart to tell her that Sawyer was a fictional character.)

We can appreciate that people diagnosed with ADHD would be encouraged to know they are in fellowship with the likes of Socrates, but how, pray tell, was it determined that he or any of these other historical figures had ADHD? It is impossible to make a definitive posthumous psychiatric diagnosis from biographical or autobiographical information. One can extrapolate certain conclusions from bio/autobiographical descriptions, but such conclusions are always speculative. Concerning

Edison, for example, we can say with surety that he was creative, entre-preneurial, highly intelligent, and that even as a child he marched to the beat of his own drum. But to say he had ADHD is a stretch. Myth begets myth, and nonsense begets even more nonsense.

A person affiliated with Children and Adults with Attention Deficit Disorder (also known as the National Resource Center on AD/HD) once told me that "ADHD children have always been with us." To make such an assertion is meaningless because it can be neither proven nor disproven. The statement is a sly way of avoiding the central question: is ADHD caused by biology or is it a response to certain environmental/developmental circumstances? In any case, we still have no evidence that teachers in the 1950s or before dealt to any significant degree with class-room behavior problems.

WORD JUGGLING

A growing number of ADHD "experts" seem to be mincing their words when it comes to the claim that ADHD is a matter of genetics. Take physicians Edward M. Hallowell and John J. Ratey, authors of the best sellers *Driven to Distraction* and *Delivered from Distraction*. In the latter, they offer this somewhat bewildering pronouncement about ADHD and genes:

> Although ADHD is highly heritable, no one actually inherits ADHD. Environment plays a crucial role in the development—or nondevelop-ment—of ADHD. All a person can inherit is a proclivity for developing the symptoms of ADHD—a greater susceptibility to ADHD than other people have. Life experiences determine how the genes a person inherits gain—or do not gain—expression. For example, if a toddler watches too much television, that increases the likelihood that the genes predisposing to ADHD will be expressed and the child will develop ADHD. However,

if that same toddler does not watch television, he may never develop ADHD, even though he inherited the genes that predispose him to it.[12]

Hallowell and Ratey cannot support any one of the above statements with objective proof. In at least one case—the statement that life experiences determine how genes express themselves—the claim is not correct as stated. Life experiences do not determine the color of one's eyes or hair, the length of one's index finger, the size of one's jaw, and the list goes on.

Hallowell and Ratey are not geneticists, but Richard C. Lewontin is—an evolutionary geneticist, to be exact. Lewontin was the Alexander Agassiz Professor of Zoology and Biology at Harvard University, a highly prestigious position. His books include *Not in Our Genes* (coauthored with neurobiologist Steven Rose and psychologist Leon J. Kamin). Lewontin, a certified superstar in the field of genetics, maintains that the notion of genetic *predispositions*—Hallowell and Ratey use the terms "proclivity" and "susceptibility" to mean the same thing—cannot be verified. [13] It would appear, therefore, that Hallowell and Ratey are cutting ideas out of whole cloth. Furthermore, they are trying to have it both ways by claiming that genes are behind ADHD, but the genes in question are "asleep" until certain aspects of the environment cause them to "wake up" and begin causing trouble. Concerning the idea that certain aspects of the environment turn on certain genes, Lewontin says that while this model seems to depend upon environmental triggers, it is "completely genetically determined, independent of the environment."[14]

In other words, Hallowell and Ratey's assertion that certain environmental circumstances activate genes that are otherwise inactive is a dexterous means of making it seem as if they aren't really saying that genes cause ADHD, when that is precisely what they are saying. Then again, an equally strong argument could be made to the effect that Hallowell and Ratey are *unwittingly* admitting that ADHD is a predictable response to certain environmental circumstances. After all, if Lewontin is right and genetic predispositions do not exist, then we are left with the environment alone as the cause of ADHD. For the moment, however, we are going to set that aside and return to an in-depth analysis of several of Hallowell and Ratey's contentions.

1. *The ADHD gene is inactive until it is turned on by some aspect of the environment.* As one example of how a feature of the environment might turn on the ADHD gene, Hallowell and Ratey say that a toddler who carries said gene actually develops ADHD because he watches "too much" television. They are careful not to quantify how much television watching is necessary to activate the sleeping gene because they don't know, and they are banking that their readers won't challenge them on this point. One might ask if "too much" refers to cumulative hours, or average hours watched per week, or whether "too much" television is the same for a two-year-old carrier of the ADHD gene as it is for a fourteen-year-old carrier. One might ask why watching "too much" television activates the ADHD gene and not, say, spending "too much" time looking out the window of a moving vehicle? Or, is there an upper age at which, if the ADHD gene has not yet been turned on, it *cannot* be turned on; it becomes permanently disabled? Hallowell and Ratey don't explain the complex mechanics behind this mysterious genetic black box because they can't. They simply assert that something works in a certain way, and that is supposed to be that.

2. *The environment can turn on the ADHD gene but cannot turn it off.* If aspects of a "carrier's" environment can turn on the sleeping ADHD gene, activating its "proclivity," then it is reasonable and logical to assume that eliminating those same aspects of the environment will turn the gene off. But Hallowell and Ratey say that ADHD cannot be cured by simply manipulating the environment. Apparently, once the ADHD gene is turned on, it goes "rogue" (our term) and from that point can only be controlled (but never put back to sleep again) with proper management, often including medication. This is the crux of the mythology propagated

by the ADHD Establishment: ADHD, being the result of genes, cannot be cured but only controlled, and that because the disorder is fundamentally one of faulty biology, medical means are generally necessary to establish said control. (To their credit, Hallowell and Ratey say that medication is often helpful, but not always, and that to be effective it should be part of a more comprehensive treatment/management plan.)

3. *It may be possible to determine that a person has ADHD using a measure of brain-wave activity.* Hallowell and Ratey claim that a procedure called qEEG, or quantitative electroencephalogram, is 90 percent accurate in identifying the brain-wave pattern that characterizes ADHD (they use the term ADD). Supposedly, people with ADHD show a pattern of "underarousal"—meaning a predominance of slow waves over faster waves—in certain areas of the brain's outer layer, or cortex.[15] Hallowell and Ratey do not explain the link between this cortical condition and problems with inattention and/or impulsivity. To us, it appears as if they sought a scientific method of supposedly verifying a nonscientific diagnosis, and they found one. Furthermore, their 90 percent reliability claim has not been verified by other researchers. A 2003 review of literature failed to find a clear relationship between qEEG measures and a diagnosis of ADHD, noting that anomalies found cross over diagnostic categories, meaning qEEG is not a reliable diagnostic indicator.[16] (The fact that brain-wave signatures crossed diagnostic categories is predictable given that, as Caplan has found, no clear boundaries separate one psychiatric diagnosis from another.) Cigna HealthCare will cover qEEG for certain applications (e.g., epilepsy), but not for ADHD because it is considered "experimental, investigational, or unproven" in that context.[17]

4. *American life can cause something called pseudo-ADD.* The remote control, a generally fast pace of life, television sound bites, fads, and other aspects of a culture devoted to instant gratification and expediency induce an ADHD-like state that is endemic to America, say Hallowell and Ratey. Many Americans have pseudo-ADD, they say, but although the

symptoms are alike, this is not to be mistaken for true ADHD. The symptoms of true ADHD are persistent; the symptoms of pseudo-ADHD are less intense and intermittent.[18] But wait! The diagnosis is always based on either reports from third parties (in the case of a child, parents and teachers) or self-reports (in the case of an adult). And each of the DSM criteria, to apply, must occur "often." Where is the line to be drawn between often and intermittent? In effect, Hallowell and Ratey are unwittingly admitting that the science of ADHD is not science at all. It is mystification, confusion piled on top of confusion, red herring thrown after red herring. If people can develop symptoms of ADHD by being exposed to the techno-frenzied pace of American culture, then some people's symptoms are going to be more prominent than others, are going to occur more "often" than others. Those folks are going to qualify for the diagnosis. In short, Hallowell and Ratey effectively admit that the environment is the culprit here. They definitely make a better case for environment than biology.

The contention that ADHD is gene-based is contention, period. Several ADHD researchers, including Dr. Stephen Faraone, director of medical genetics research at SUNY Upstate Medical University in Syracuse, New York, insist that firm support for a genetic element in the etiology of ADHD is provided by evidence from both studies of identical twins reared apart and studies of adopted children. (An online biography identifies Faraone as "the top-ranked psychologist in the world.")[19] But according to genetics researcher Jay Joseph, author of *The Gene Illusion*, this contention is based on faulty interpretation of data. Joseph points out the flaws in these researchers' interpretations, including methodological flaws in the studies themselves and the confounding influence of environmental factors.[20]

In his ongoing effort to prove that ADHD is coded in the genome, Russell Barkley often refers to the findings of Australian twin studies in which identical twins (identical genomes) were more likely than fraternal twins (as genetically different as non-twin siblings) to "share" ADHD. Presumably, the difference is due to the greater genetic similarity of identical twins, but that assumes that the environment influences twins, whether identical or fraternal, equally. That assumption turns out to be false. In *Not in Our Genes*, Richard Lewontin and his coauthors point out that parents, teachers, relatives, and friends tend to treat fraternal twins with much greater appreciation for their differences than is the case with identicals. Compared with fraternals, identical twins are far more likely to dress similarly (if not alike), play together, study together, and share the same friends.[21] Therefore, the finding that identicals are more likely than fraternals to share ADHD characteristics is most accurately explained in terms of environmental differences. In the final analysis, and no matter how one looks at it, the argument that ADHD is gene-based falls flat.

IS ADHD IN THE BRAIN?

Having eliminated the possibility that childhood behavior disorders are gene-based, the question still remains: is it plausible that a noninherited biological basis for ADHD does in fact exist? Dr. C. Keith Conners, a pioneer in the diagnosis of ADHD, thinks so. In a brochure published by the manufacturer of a stimulant often used to "treat" ADHD, Conners is quoted as saying, "It is now widely understood and accepted that ADHD is a real medical condition with a neuro-biologic [i.e., brain and central nervous system] basis."[22] Conners developed his widely used scales for rating the presence and magnitude of ADHD behaviors in the 1970s, and he is considered an expert on ADHD matters. Despite his credentials, his contention that ADHD is a "real" brain-based disease is not supported by real evidence. His colleagues say so, and rather definitively.

In 1998, an overwhelming majority of experts attending the National Institutes of Health Consensus Conference, after days of reviewing all of the available evidence, agreed there is no compelling evidence to the effect that ADHD is caused by or significantly and reliably associated with physical or biochemical "irregularities" (e.g., deficiencies in the left temporal lobe, biochemical imbalances) in the brain. They furthermore agreed that no objective test or set of criteria exists with which to accurately diagnose ADHD.[23] A 2002 textbook, *Attention Deficit Hyperactivity Disorder—State of the Science*, contributed to by a number of recognized authorities in the field and proclaimed by its editors to be "an up-to-date, state of the art review of what is known concerning the disorder by the world's leading authorities on each of the topic areas," reported that the 1998 Consensus Conference findings remained unchanged.[24] No verifiable empirical data has come along since that would justify revising that position. Interestingly enough, Conners was one of the contributors to that textbook. In it, he says, " . . . no single cause of ADHD has yet been identified, and its exact etiology and pathophysiology remain obscure." He adds, " . . . ADHD symptomatology has a central nervous system basis (as do all normal and abnormal behaviors, thoughts and emotions). By way of caution, such brain-behavior correlations do not constitute proof that ADHD reflects a disordered physiological or anatomic state."[25]

Obviously, Conners's statement in the pharmaceutical brochure mentioned above is contradicted by what he wrote in *Attention Deficit Hyperactivity Disorder—State of the Science*. (In a letter responding to Dr. Ravenel's query regarding this discrepancy, the pharmaceutical company product manager writes: "Dr. Conners has reviewed and approved the normalization brochure you are referring to, where statements . . . were directly taken from an interview with him."[26] The company's representative did not address the discrepancy, although that had been the thrust of Dr. Ravenel's inquiry.) The brochure is given to physicians by representatives who are trying to convince those physicians to prescribe stimulants for children displaying ADHD symptoms. *State of the Science* is a compilation of writings from various researchers in the ADHD field. It was written for practitioners, not the general public. Why would Conners say one thing in one context and something completely different in another? Could it be that what Conners and other ADHD experts are willing to admit to one another—that there is no hard evidence of brain disease in ADHD—they are not as willing to admit to consumers?

William B. Carey, pediatrician and coeditor of a leading pediatric textbook (*Developmental-Behavioral Pediatrics*, 1999), writes: "The assumption that ADHD symptoms arise from cerebral malfunction has not been supported even after extensive investigations" and "No consistent structural, functional, or chemical neurological marker is found in children with the ADHD diagnosis as currently formulated."[27] Carey is but one of many investigators who have arrived at this conclusion. However, since he wrote those words, a number of researchers claim to have found changes in the structure and function of the brain by using various methods of brain scan. Does this research represent a "breakthrough" in understanding ADHD?

BRAIN SCAN BABBLE

In recent years, considerable attention has been paid to brain-imaging studies and their alleged implications for psychiatric diagnoses, including ADHD. The imaging techniques include single photon emission computerized tomography (SPECT), positron emission tomography (PET), magnetic resonance spectroscopy (MRS), and functional magnetic resonance imaging (fMRI). Functional neuroimaging results in a "picture" of the brain from which metabolic or biochemical information can be extrapolated, thereby pinpointing areas of the brain that might be dysfunctional.

Announcements to the effect that neuroimaging studies have discovered changes in the brain associated with ADHD are usually greeted with great fanfare in the popular media. On November 13, 2007, for example, a riot of media reports hailed a study purporting to show that crucial parts of the brains of children with ADHD develop more slowly than brains of normal children. Researchers compared the brain images of 223 children diagnosed with ADHD with the same number not so diagnosed, reporting that brain regions that suppress inappropriate actions and thoughts, focus attention, control movement, and are essential to memory develop more slowly in ADHD kids, the lag being as much as three years.[28]

A careful reading of the entire news release, however, illustrates the virtual absence of any true significance to the purported findings of the study—dramatic comments to the contrary notwithstanding. A leader of the study, Dr. Phillip Shaw, of the National Institute of Mental Health, is quoted as saying that the delay in brain development "could only be detected when a very large number of children with the disorder were included."[29]

In other words, researchers could not distinguish the brains of ADHD children from those of the normal children on an individual basis, so they added up minuscule differences between individuals in a sufficiently large total number that the sum total score for ADHD brains was higher than the total for the normal group. By summing statistically insignificant differences, these researchers were able to present a composite picture of what they claim to be the typical ADHD brain—voila!—sure enough, the ADHD brain looks very different from a supposedly normal brain.[30]

The further, and more significant, problem with this research is that 80 percent of the ADHD kids in the study had been taking stimulant medications since being diagnosed. Given that the diagnosis of ADHD is highly suspect, that the diagnostic procedures and parameters are unscientific to begin with, what the study actually compared was a group of children of which most had been taking stimulant medications with a group of children who had not. Even if we allow for the moment that neuroimaging did in fact detect significant brain differences between the two groups of children, those differences should rightly be attributed to

61

medication. Following this line of thought, it is reasonable to posit that if an external agent such as a stimulant drug props up a certain child's brain function (in this case, the functions of attention span and impulse control), the part of the child's brain associated with that function would eventually show delays in development. As analogy, if an individual with a broken leg uses a crutch to take pressure off the leg well beyond the point at which the leg bone has healed, the muscles of the assisted leg will eventually atrophy. Indeed, as this analogy would predict, the lead author in the study reported that the greatest delays in brain maturation were found in precisely those areas most involved in attention and motor control.[31]

In a particularly incisive article for *Chronicles* magazine, Fred Baughman calls attention to the fact that all of the ADHD brain-imaging research to date is similarly flawed.

From 1986 to 1998, nine MRI (Magnetic Resonance Imaging) brain scans were performed on psychostimulant-treated groups diagnosed with ADHD. The professional bigwigs concluded that since *all* showed brain atrophy, the culprit must be ADHD. The possibility that the "treatment" itself was causing the atrophy was dismissed.[32]

At the 1998 National Institutes of Health (NIH) Consensus Conference on ADHD, Baughman publicly confronted one of the researchers in question, asking " . . . why didn't you mention that virtually all of the ADHD subjects . . . have been on chronic stimulant therapy, and that this is the likely cause of their brain atrophy?" He received this reply: "I understand that this is a critical issue and in fact I am planning a study to investigate that. I haven't done it yet."[33] To our knowledge, said researcher has yet to investigate that pertinent question.

Even Hallowell and Ratey point out this same problem with respect to a 1986 brain-imaging study in which brain shrinkage was detected in 58 percent of young adults diagnosed with ADHD. Baughman quotes them as saying, " . . . since all of the patients had been treated with psy-chostimulants, cortical atrophy may be a long-term adverse effect of this treatment."[34]

In 2002, researchers reported finding significantly smaller-than-nor-mal brain volumes in children diagnosed with ADHD but *not* given medication.[35] These findings were embraced by the ADHD Establishment and reported by numerous media outlets. Overlooked, however, was the fact that the normal children in the control group were more than two years older on average, taller, and heavier than the ADHD kids in the experimental group. It is well known that the larger the child, the larger the brain. That the researchers, physicians all, ignored the far more logical interpretation of their findings says they approached the question "Are the brains of ADHD children smaller than normal?" with no objectivity. Instead, they seem to have constructed a study that would confirm what they already believed to be true.

A leading figure in the brain-imaging field is psychiatrist Daniel Amen, the recipient of a Distinguished Fellow Award from the American Psychiatric Association and a clinical professor of psychiatry and human behavior at the University of California, Irvine. Amen claims that a brain-imaging method called SPECT (single photon emission computerized tomography) is an invaluable technology for understanding psychiatric disorders such as depression and ADHD. Perhaps in part because he has been an eminently successful entrepreneur (a two-scan evaluation at one of Amen's four clinics [two in California, one in Washington State, and one in Virginia, cumulatively doing four hundred to five hundred scans per month] costs several thousand dollars), Amen has become a highly controversial figure in psychiatric circles—a visionary or a shrewd self-promoter, depending on whom one asks. His fundamental thesis is that aberrant behavior derives from abnormalities in the brain, abnormalities that other forms of brain imaging don't detect as well as SPECT, if they detect them at all. Amen is a good salesman, for sure—by all accounts, he's engaging, funny, and persuasive—but more than one investigator has said that what he's doing is not supported by scientific evidence.

George Bush, psychiatry professor at Harvard Medical School, has said that Amen has never, to his knowledge, "published any data, or provided one shred of evidence that an independent investigator would be able to reproduce."[36] The fact that Amen has not published his findings in peer-reviewed journals has moved people like Helen Mayberg, professor of psychiatry and neurology and brain-imaging researcher at Emory University, to ask "Where's his data?" In January 2005, the American Psychiatric Association's nine-member Council on Children, Adolescents, and Their Families issued an independent position paper opposing the use of SPECT for diagnosis of psychiatric conditions in child and adolescent psychiatry.[37]

WHAT ABOUT CHEMICAL IMBALANCES?

The term *chemical imbalance* has taken on a popular validity that it doesn't deserve. Whereas nearly every parent of a child diagnosed with ADHD, ODD, or EOBD reports the diagnosing professional explaining the supposed disorder in terms of a chemical imbalance in the brain, there really is no such thing. To speak of imbalance requires knowing what constitutes a state of balance, and such a state is impossible to determine, if there even is such a thing. The brain is in a constant state of activity, even when the individual is asleep. Brain chemistry is in an equally constant state of flux; therefore, measures of an individual's brain chemistry (assuming, for the sake of argument, that is even possible) at two different moments sixty seconds apart would result in two different sets of data. The argument, however, is moot because whereas brain-imaging techniques can measure electrical activity, blood flow to various brain areas, or brain anatomy, there is no known way of measuring brain chemistry.

In an article critiquing the claims made by pharmaceutical companies to the effect that drugs known as selective serotonin reuptake inhibitors, or SSRI antidepressants, correct chemical imbalances in the brain, investigators Jeffrey Lacasse and Jonathan Leo assert that no peer-reviewed article has ever been published that would "directly support claims of serotonin deficiency in any mental disorder, while there are many articles that support counterevidence."[38] Even Wayne Goodman, chair of the FDA psychopharmacology Advisory Committee, later admitted that Lacasse and Leo were correct, saying that the notion of chemical imbalance is nothing more than a "useful metaphor," but not something he could bring himself to actually say to a patient.[39]

We propose that the only thing "useful" about a notion that has no scientific validity is its value as a marketing device. Obviously, the notion that certain drugs correct brain-based chemical imbalances is a contrivance designed to appeal to the credulous consumer of psychiatric services and pharmaceutical products. It's not a metaphor; it's a falsehood. Parents of children diagnosed with ADHD do not report that the diagnosticians say "to use a metaphor, it's *as if* your child has a chemical imbalance in his brain." They unfailingly report that these diagnosticians tell them their children *have* chemical imbalances in their brains, period. We've talked to hundreds of parents who have related this explanation to us. We seriously doubt that so many parents could have all misunderstood what diagnosticians were saying. As an explanation that explains nothing, the chemical imbalance canard is yet another example of the misleading statements often made by professionals who specialize in diagnosing and treating childhood behavior disorders.

THE BENEFIT OF DOUBT?

Let's say, for purposes of discussion, that someone eventually finds a "consistent structural, functional, or chemical neurological marker" common to children diagnosed with ADHD. Wouldn't that prove that

ADHD is a brain-based disease? No, it would not, because such evidence would still beg the question: does the brain irregularity cause ADHD behaviors, or does something about a child's developmental environment or even *the ADHD behaviors themselves* cause the brain irregularity? Does the chicken come before the egg or vice versa?

Solid research has shown, and beyond any reasonable doubt, that abnormalities in the brain can be caused by features inherent to a child's environment (e.g., a chaotic, conflict-ridden family life; significant time spent watching television and/or playing video games; a lack of disciplinary structure; poor nutrition). There is even good evidence to the effect that such brain differences can also be brought about by a child's own behavior! How a child is taught to read significantly influences brain development, for better or worse.

The good news in this regard is that the brain possesses the remarkable ability to "repair" itself once environmental and/or behavioral problems are corrected. The implication is that a child's brain that has been "corrupted" by television watching, poor nutrition, bad reading instruction, or lack of proper discipline can be set right again by eliminating electronic media, instituting proper nutrition, correct teaching methods, and/or establishing effective disciplinary guidelines and procedures. In short, the more we know about the brain and brain development, the more it looks as if what we are calling ADHD (and by extension, the other childhood behavior disorders as well)—even if it is found to be associated with brain differences—can very possibly be corrected without medical interventions.

CHAPTER 4
THE POLITICS OF DIAGNOSIS

"No, no!" said the Queen. "Sentence first—verdict afterwards."
"Stuff and nonsense!" said Alice loudly. "The idea
of having the sentence first!"
—*Alice's Adventures in Wonderland*, by Lewis Carroll[1]

WHEN ASKED TO PROVIDE HARD SCIENTIFIC EVIDENCE OF THEIR contentions to the effect that ADHD is a gene-based disease of the brain, ADHD Establishment spokespersons are fond of saying things like "there is great agreement" and other references to professional consensus, as if consensus constituted irrefutable proof. But the mere fact that a large group of scientists agree on something does not mean the debate is over. In the final analysis, appeals to professional consensus are nothing more than attempts to intimidate into silence those who would disagree with some "scientifically correct" position.

In an article available on his website, author and physician Michael Crichton takes on the issue of consensus science: "Consensus is the business of politics. In science consensus is irrelevant.... Consensus is invoked only in situations where the science is not solid enough."[2]

Indeed, the "science" behind the claims of the ADHD Establishment is not science at all. It is consensus, period.

In the February 2008 issue of Delta Airlines' *Sky* magazine, author Gary Taubes (*Good Calories, Bad Calories: Challenging the Conventional Wisdom on Diet, Weight Control, and Disease*) is interviewed concerning his challenge to traditional nutritional dogma. At one point, commenting on how bad nutritional science came to dominate professional thinking and drive professional advice, Taubes refers to

> ... medical doctors and nutritionists poorly trained in what it takes to do good science. These people believed they knew what the answers were before they did the rigorous experiments needed to find out. Worse, they believed they had an obligation to tell the public and spread the word before they did the research. And once they did the studies, and they didn't get the results they expected, they ignored them.[3]

If one substitutes "neurologists, psychiatrists, and psychologists" for "medical doctors and nutritionists," what Taubes says is equally true concerning the "science" behind childhood behavior disorders. In a word, it's sham. But it's a sham that has duped lots of intelligent people, including most American educators, most of the physicians who treat America's kids, most of America's mental health practitioners, most people in the mainstream media, and last but not least, most of America's parents.

The three most common ways children become diagnosed with ADHD are

1. Teachers raise "red flags" concerning classroom behavior and/ or academic performance and may even suggest ADHD as a possible diagnosis and recommend testing.
2. Parents complain to pediatricians or family physicians of ongoing behavior problems that seem impervious to discipline.
3. Parents independently seek private psychological or

psychiatric services because of concerns regarding behavior or school performance.

IDENTIFIED AT SCHOOL

Many children diagnosed with ADHD are first "identified" by their teachers, usually before the fourth grade. A teacher will notice that a child is off task a great deal, often seems "out of it" or "off in his own little world," doesn't complete work, and makes lots of careless errors. The child may also be a behavior problem: disruptive, argumentative, impulsive, and bossy with peers. The teacher may or may not ask the school social worker, school psychologist, or some other member of the school-based evaluation team to observe the child in class and confirm her impressions. In either case, she will share her concerns with the child's parents, leading up to the subtly advanced suggestion that the child may have ADHD and should probably be tested. (Most states prohibit teachers from making declarative statements of a diagnostic sort, and most states also prohibit school psychologists from making what is considered a medical diagnosis, so teachers and other school personnel are usually very circumspect when it comes to this issue. A teacher may say, "Your child is having problems in my class and I think it might be a good idea for you to consider having him tested," but she is probably not going to say, "Your child has ADHD.")

By this time, the teacher has probably attended at least one in-service on ADHD given by a local professional who specializes in its diagnosis and treatment. Not knowing any better, she has likely swallowed ADHD Establishment propaganda hook, line, and sinker. She is completely convinced that by bringing the possibility to the attention of the child's parents, and suggesting that they have their child tested, she is doing the child a great service. Because of the peculiarities of special education law (Individuals with Disabilities Education Act), today's teachers also have to tiptoe around any children who present anything more than occasional, garden-variety discipline problems.

Classroom discipline problems are a major issue in America's schools, and if teachers are to be believed, the magnitude of the problem is increasing every year. It goes without saying that discipline takes away from instructional time. As standardized achievement test results have become more and more crucial to a school's rating and even funding, teachers have come under increasing performance pressure from their administrators. This greatly increases the likelihood, and understandably so, that teachers will look for the most expedient way of dealing with problem children—including children who present no outstanding discipline problems but are generally inattentive and off task—one that involves the least amount of time and effort on their part and provides a "solution" as quickly as possible. Medication provides exactly that.

The problem is compounded by the fact that today's teachers, by and large, obtain little disciplinary cooperation from parents. Not infrequently, teachers who discipline children come under fire from parents. Furthermore, when parents complain to administration about a teacher's discipline, there is significant likelihood that administration will side with the parents in order to keep the peace. Both of these all-too-common circumstances increase the incentive teachers have for referring discipline problems outside the system.

Finally, public school administrators have sensitized teachers to the fact that parents can and sometimes do sue retroactively. Supreme Court Associate Justice Anthony M. Kennedy, dissenting on a 1999 Court ruling, wrote that current special education law severely limits the ability of schools to "take disciplinary action against students with behavior-disorders, even if the disability was not diagnosed prior to the incident triggering discipline."[4] In other words, if a school disciplines a child who is *later* diagnosed with ADHD, ODD, and/or EOBD, and a psychologist or psychiatrist says the offense was related to the diagnosis, the child's parents can sue the school for disciplining a "disabled" child. If that sounds crazy, the authors concur.

DIAGNOSIS BY PHYSICIAN

Parents of a child identified at school may opt to talk to their child's pediatrician (PD) or family physician (FP) about the issues raised by the teacher. In that case, the PD/FP may not even talk to the child's teacher. He may simply listen to the parents' story and ask a few questions about the child's behavior at home. If he's especially "thorough," he will call the teacher and obtain a firsthand verbal report from her. He may even ask her to fill out the teacher portion of Conners' Rating Scale, in which case he will have the parents fill out the parent portion. Keep in mind that the teacher is probably hoping the child will be put on medication, which means that her responses to either questions asked by the physician or the Conners' items cannot be considered objective. If the parents are having discipline problems with the child, there is also incentive for them to skew their responses in a diagnostic direction.

Also increasing the likelihood of diagnosis is the fact that most PDs and FPs have received scant training in child behavior. When it comes to disciplinary issues, therefore, their approaches often reflect personal biases, on-the-job experience, or what they've been told in seminars they've attended, including seminars on ADHD, ODD, and EOBD. Almost without exception, the latter are sponsored by pharmaceutical companies and feature speakers who promote the medical model. Pediatricians and family physicians usually walk away from these seminars convinced that ADHD, et cetera, are real diseases and that the most effective treatment approach includes medication. Compounding the problem is that most PDs/FPs see six to ten patients an hour. They rarely have the time to sit down and provide quality counseling to parents concerning behavioral matters, and it's rare for a pediatric behavioral specialist to be on staff in a pediatric office. Under the circumstances, writing a prescription provides a physician with a means of being as "helpful" as possible in the shortest amount of time. For all these reasons, the likelihood is significant that the PD/FP will make the ADHD diagnosis and put the child on medication.

Some physicians, however, prefer to refer diagnostic responsibility to psychologists, usually because they feel a psychologist's evaluation will be more thorough and his/her treatment plan more comprehensive. Since few pediatric or family practices have psychologists on staff, these referrals are usually made to psychologists working in independent private practices.

DIAGNOSIS BY PSYCHOLOGIST

Parents wind up in the office of a psychologist (or child psychiatrist, but we will use the term *psychologist* generically to include both professional categories) because they've been referred by their child's school or pediatrician or they've heard through the grapevine that the psychologist in question knows what he's doing when it comes to ADHD. If the school has not already tested the child, the psychologist will almost surely do so. It's important to understand that the school did not test the child to determine whether or not he had ADHD. In most states, schools are not authorized to render the diagnosis. The school tested to see if the child qualified for special education services. The testing done by a psychologist in private practice is a different matter. Clinical psychologists are allowed by law to make the ADHD diagnosis.

Having been in private practice for more than a decade, I can say with confidence that the psychologist knows what diagnosis he's most likely to render after fifteen minutes of talking to the parents, maybe even after nothing more than talking with the mother over the phone when the first appointment was being made. Nonetheless, after a parent interview, he will probably schedule the child for a battery of tests that measure IQ, academic achievement, and developmental integrity. He'll also ask the parents and teacher to complete behavior checklists. Needless to say, the tests are not medical in nature. In many cases, absent clear indication that the child's problems may be due to or complicated by developmental deficits, the need for testing is questionable. Keep in mind that of the eighteen DSM criteria for ADHD, not one is test-based. Without exception, they refer to behavioral characteristics that can be verified by interviewing the parents and having the child's teacher fill out a questionnaire. When done under the pretense that they are diagnostic, the administration of this expensive battery of tests (usually costing in the range of $1000 to $2500) serves the purpose of creating the illusion that the therapist is doing something scientific in order to determine the exact nature of the problem.

If pressed on the issue, psychologists will say they don't give the tests to make the diagnosis, but only to obtain information that might be helpful in developing a treatment plan. That is not, however, what many if not most parents hear. They hear, "I need to give your child tests in order to make a valid diagnosis." We have spoken to hundreds of parents about this issue. Not one parent has ever told either of us that the psychologist who tested their child explained that tests are not necessary to make a diagnosis but are being given only to render a broader picture of the child's strengths and weaknesses so as to facilitate a more effective treatment plan.

Incidentally, I once shared the above information with a parent audience in a large southeastern city. Several weeks later, I received an e-mail from a mother who told me that she subsequently demanded her money back from the psychologist who had misrepresented the purpose behind the $1500 battery of tests he had administered to her child, whom he diagnosed with ADHD. He promptly wrote the refund check, knowing that if he didn't, he might ultimately answer to his licensing board.

Assuming a diagnosis of ADHD ensues, the therapist's explanation will likely be consistent with the disease model. He will tell the parents that the disorder is gene-based, involving chemical imbalances, inadequate development in the left frontal lobe, and so on. Interestingly enough, although girls receive approximately 25 percent of ADHD diagnoses,[5] and some sources claim the actual incidence among females is much higher,[6] fathers (i.e., males) are almost always identified as the carriers of the gene. To make this determination, the therapist will ask questions like "As a child, did you sometimes have problems paying attention in class?" and "Is your desk often in a state of disorganization?" The father's answers, skewed by the fact that he is being subtly encouraged to answer in the affirmative, will "confirm" that he passed the fictitious ADHD gene to his child. As have both of the authors, a disproportionate number of adult males will flunk an adult-ADHD test.

(In all fairness, there are psychologists out there who are very conservative when it comes to making the diagnosis, who will not seize the opportunity to secure income from every parent who walks through their doors. In our experienced estimation, these constitute a minority. An even smaller number of psychologists have come to the realization that ADHD itself is a fabrication and will not dispense the diagnosis.)

The genetic explanation absolves both parents and child of any and all responsibility for the problem. The therapist may even tell the parents that nothing they could have done would have changed the trajectory of the child's life. This explanation, however unscientific, instantly alters the parent-child dynamic. The child, up to this point a source of great frustration (and consequently, guilt), becomes a victim. He cannot help the way he behaves. The genetic explanation effects almost instantaneous changes in how the parents view the child and respond, therefore, to his misbehavior. Frustration is replaced with compassion. Exasperation is replaced with patience. The parents become less abrupt, more proactive; less prone to threats, more relaxed and understanding. Ironically, even though it is a contrivance, the genetic explanation brings about functional modifications in parent behavior and the parent-child relationship. The child, in turn, is very likely to begin behaving more functionally as well, with or without medication. But that almost surely comes next. It is the rare psychologist who does not recommend medication as a primary feature of an ADHD treatment plan.

The disease model enables the psychologist to sell the parents on the notion that drugs are necessary. At this point, the therapist—if he is not himself able to prescribe drugs—brings other elements of the ADHD Establishment into the picture. He refers the child to a pediatrician or child psychiatrist who confirms the diagnosis and prescribes one or more of the pharmaceuticals currently used to treat ADHD.

In many cases, the psychologist will also convince the parents that ADHD children suffer secondary psychological problems stemming from repeated experiences with criticism, punishment, and failure, adding up to depressed self-esteem, if not depression itself. If so, and if he recommends as such, the parents will begin paying for individual therapy sessions that are probably a waste of the parents' time and money. There is no compelling evidence that children, on average, benefit from either play therapy or what is called "talk therapy."

In short, the disease model serves the interests of the parents, the therapist, the prescribing physician, and the manufacturer(s) of the drug(s) prescribed. The only person the disease model does not benefit is the child.

Before closing this short chapter, we should emphasize that many therapists are not aware they are acting as accomplices to a diagnostic fiasco. The typical therapist, even one who specializes in the diagnosis and treatment of ADHD, is sincere. He is convinced that what he's doing is right and proper and in the best interest of his patients. Everything he's read in professional publications and every seminar he's attended on ADHD substantiates the disease model for the simple reason that articles contradicting the disease model are not likely to be approved for publication by the professional review boards, and no seminar contradicting the disease model is likely to be approved for continuing education credit by certifying professional committees. So, as we've already said ("Read This First"), diagnosing professionals are not necessarily wittingly opportunistic. Many of them have simply been taken in by Establishment mythology.

CHAPTER 5

THE POLITICS AND PERILS OF PHARMACEUTICALS

*And it seems to me . . . that there will be within
the next generation or so a pharmaceutical method
of making people love their servitude.*
—Aldous Huxley, *Brave New World Revisited, 1958*

THE UNITED STATES IS CURRENTLY THE WORLD LEADER IN PHARmaceutical research and marketing. In recent years, pharmaceutical companies have developed a host of new drugs that have made significant inroads into treating and curing a number of life-threatening physical diseases. They have also spent amazing amounts of money developing drugs to treat psychiatric disorders, including ADHD. The difference, however, is that while the biological reality of physical diseases such as cancer or diabetes can be verified, no biological abnormality has been reliably associated with any psychiatric disorder. As already discussed, the claims made by psychiatrists and psychologists to the effect that certain psychiatric disorders are gene-transmitted and involve chemical imbalances are nothing but claims. The drugs used to treat these disorders, therefore, are as theoretical as the disorders themselves. Scientists know how penicillin works, but no one can really explain why psychotropic drugs work, when they work.

The further problem is that whereas the effectiveness of drugs used to treat physical diseases can be measured, judging the effectiveness of psychotropics rests on subjective testimony from the patient or someone close to the patient (in the case of a child, usually either a parent or a teacher). This brings into play what is known as the Hawthorne effect: *when someone is singled out for special treatment, his or her task performance will tend to improve.* So when an individual takes or is given a psychotropic and either he or someone else reports improvement along some dimension, the question begs as to whether the improvement was due to the chemical properties of the drug or simply because the individual is being given special attention. The Hawthorne effect probably explains why in any study comparing responses to psychotropics versus responses to placebo pills, a certain number of people will respond quite positively to the placebos. Some even report improvements that exceed those reported by patients who are taking the real drug. They believe they are getting help; therefore, they feel better. It's even possible for placebos to fool third parties. A teacher who believes a child is taking a medication to improve attention span may report a significant improvement even though the child is only taking a placebo—and this may occur even when the child is unaware of taking anything at all.

For these reasons, the research done to support psychotropic drug use doesn't rest on the solid scientific foundations that characterize research done on drugs used to treat verifiable physical ailments. It's shakier and inspires considerably less confidence. In the final analysis, therefore, acceptance by physicians and patients of a psychotropic drug's efficacy depends largely on effective marketing, and pharmaceutical companies have developed marketing to an art form. It's virtually axiomatic to say that when marketing drives acceptance of a product, the actual ability of the product to live up to its press is questionable.

As regards the medications used to treat ADHD, a significant and growing body of evidence strongly suggests that science has been compromised to the almighty dollar. As is all too often the case with the selling of a political candidate, the marketing of ADHD medications is replete with exaggerated claims, minimal disclosures, and deceptive advertising. Pharmaceutical companies have capitalized on the myths that permeate the subject of ADHD to manufacture and encourage even more myths about their products. It's time American parents knew, as Paul Harvey says, "the rest of the story."

PHARMACEUTICAL MARKETING

The development and manufacture of pharmaceuticals is a highly profitable enterprise. Unlike most manufacturing sectors, for example, pharmaceutical company profits tend to remain constant even during economic downturns. In 2001, during a recession, the ten American drug companies listed in the Fortune 500 ranked far above all other industries in average net return as a percentage of both sales (18.5 percent) and assets (16.3 percent). At the same time, the median net return for all other Fortune 500 industries was only 3.3 percent of sales. In 2002, as the downturn continued, pharmaceutical profits dropped only slightly.[1]

In view of this impressive profit record, it should come as no surprise that pharmaceutical companies exercise significant influence in the political arena. According to Dr. Marcia Angell, former editor of the prestigious *New England Journal of Medicine* and author of *The Truth About the Drug Companies: How They Deceive Us and What to Do About It*, the pharmaceutical industry has one of the largest lobbies in Washington. The industry's trade association, PhRMA, spent more than $450 million on lobbying from 1997 through 2002. That's more than $70 million per year! Company lobbyists in 2002 included 26 former members of Congress and another 342 individuals formerly on Congressional staffs or with other government connections. From January 2005 through June 2006, drug companies and their trade groups employed more than one thousand lobbyists and spent $155 million on lobbying, primarily to protect drug patents and preventing the importation of low-priced Canadian drugs.[2]

When pharmaceutical companies strive to influence political decisions, they are only taking advantage of the First Amendment, but the fact that they also make strong efforts to influence how researchers conduct experiments and report results is another matter entirely. Consider, for example, the mutually beneficial relationship that now exists between pharmaceutical companies and researchers at the National Institutes of Health (NIH), a publicly funded institution entrusted with a key role in promoting and hosting scientific research on drugs. Senior NIH scientists can, and not infrequently do, supplement their incomes by accepting consulting fees and stock options from drug companies that deal with the Institute. Such financial connections were prohibited in the past, but in 1995 the director of NIH lifted the restrictions, and from then on there have been no limits to the amount of money its researchers could accept from outside work. According to a *Los Angeles Times* investigative report, this has been a financial windfall for NIH scientists.[3] It's reasonable to propose that such compensations can have a profound compromising effect on a researcher's objectivity.

The pharmaceutical industry has extended its influence into academia as well. According to a report published in the *New England Journal of Medicine*, pharmaceutical companies have provided individual faculty members, departments, and even entire universities with powerful financial and nonfinancial incentives to participate directly in the development of drugs, devices, and diagnostic tests. The most common vehicle used to assure such commitment is equity or stock options assigned to the investigator and the institution where the work is performed.[4]

CLINICAL TRIALS ON TRIAL

For the Food and Drug Administration to license a new drug, it must be given to individuals who have the disease at issue in carefully controlled tests known as clinical trials. Approval of a new drug requires only that two clinical trials be demonstrated to show that the drug is superior to a placebo.

What the general public does not know is that pharmaceutical companies are not required to publish the results of trials failing to show benefit, but only to file them with the FDA. For example, if only two of a dozen studies conducted on a particular drug found favorable results, the findings of the other ten are filed with the FDA, but their findings will probably never be revealed to the public or even to physicians who are subsequently encouraged to begin prescribing the drug. This is known as the "file drawer" phenomenon.[5]

This practice came to light in 2002 when investigators took a thorough look at *all* the clinical trials conducted to test the effectiveness of SSRI antidepressants on depressed children and adolescents, including those that had been filed but not published. When all the results were combined, the placebo pills (usually sugar pills) were found to be 80 percent as effective as antidepressants. There was only a two-point difference between SSRI and placebo on a sixty-two point scale commonly used to rate depression. The most unsettling finding, however, was that SSRIs as much as *quadrupled* the risk of suicide in children and teens.[6,7,8] As a result of these and subsequent studies, formal warnings have been issued in both the United Kingdom and the United States by the respective oversight agencies. It is important to realize that these warnings stem not from *new* research findings, but from information *already known* to drug companies.

Then there's what's known as "wash out" and "placebo lead-in." In a typical psychiatric drug trial, any medications participants may be taking prior to the study are abruptly stopped in order for them to "wash out" and theoretically not affect the outcome. Participants are then given a placebo in place of the drug under study for a seven- to ten-day "lead-in" period.[9] Any symptoms they experience during that time are assumed to represent the underlying disorder for which the trial drug is being proposed. It's quite possible, however, that these symptoms are often negative responses to sudden withdrawal from powerful psychotropic medications, and that any positive outcome reported in response to the experimental drug may be more accurately explained as relief from that withdrawal.

In a related maneuver, any subjects who responded positively to the placebo during "lead-in" are eliminated from the study. Remaining participants are then divided into two groups—one group that takes the drug under study and one that takes the placebo. But the comparison is obviously unfair because the study's outcome is already weighted heavily in favor of the new drug.

INVESTIGATORS UNDER INVESTIGATION

Drug trials are done in private practitioners' offices as well as in leading medical schools and research hospitals. Pharmaceutical companies often make direct payments to physicians and institutions for every patient entered into a trial. Such payments may amount to hundreds of dollars per patient. Research physicians are also frequently extended the opportunity to receive additional payment for presenting company-produced information to other physicians at meetings, seminars, and conferences.

Reading through a list of medical journal articles favorable to ADHD drugs, one repeatedly comes across the same authors and coauthors. It stretches the imagination to think that this finite group of individuals could produce such an overwhelming amount of research-based literature while engaged in active medical careers. As it turns out, after a trial is completed, the researcher(s) may only be asked to sign a study report prepared by a company-hired professional who also analyzed the study results. In some cases, when issues have arisen concerning the effectiveness or safety of a particular psychotropic, nominal authors have complained that they were not allowed to make changes in the article or even to see all the data.

Gene Haislip, a former official of the U.S. Drug Enforcement Agency who directed the DEA's office of Diversion Control, has been engaged for a number of years in efforts to raise public awareness about the over-prescribing of stimulants to young children. He has said, "I have doubts that the truth is driving this issue. It seems that market forces and money are behind it." He goes on to express his suspicion that the objectivity of a small group of ADHD researchers whose work is funded by pharmaceutical companies has been compromised. He further suspects that ADHD patient advocacy groups that receive drug company financial support have become "fronts" to facilitate the process of getting children on stimulants (more on that imminently).[10]

Even more telling is the firsthand experience of Dr. William Pelham, as reported by *AlterNet*, an Internet magazine. Pelham has been a leading ADHD researcher for some thirty years and is author of more than 250 research papers on ADHD, many with the support of industry grants. He is also a former member of the scientific advisory board of McNeil Pharmaceuticals, marketers of Concerta®, a popular ADHD stimulant. In 2002, he received a lifetime achievement award by the world's largest and most influential ADHD patient advocacy group, Children and Adults with Attention Deficit/Hyperactivity Disorder (CHADD).

Between 1997 and 1999, Dr. Pelham conducted one of three studies McNeil used to support the claim that hardly any children taking Concerta experience problems with appetite, growth, or sleep. In two of the three studies, including Pelham's, children were not accepted as subjects unless they were already taking and responding well to another form of methylphenidate. In other words, the studies were front-loaded with already successful patients, thus significantly reducing any possibility they would report side effects. In the *AlterNet* article, Pelham calls this "really misleading."[11]

The children enrolled in Pelham's study were treated with a combination of methylphenidate and behavioral methods. Pelham describes how, when his paper was in prepublication at the journal *Pediatrics*, pressure was exerted by ranking pharmaceutical company personnel to alter some of what he had reported, including his recommendation that medication be used in combination with behavior therapy. *Pediatrics* is read primarily by pediatricians; therefore, the pressure put on Pelham to alter his research paper amounted to an attempt to withhold valuable information from the primary dispensers of stimulant medications. As such, it also had the intended effect of ensuring that greater numbers of ADHD kids would be treated with stimulants alone rather than provided the benefit of behavior therapy. In most cases, that would have the effect of increasing the length of treatment, thus increasing the amount of money a pharmaceutical company made off any given child.

After Pelham's insistence on including some reference to the behavioral component of his intervention, the company performed another research analysis and produced another paper, to which they attempted to obtain his endorsement. Despite his objections, the article was sent to a prestigious child psychiatric journal. The company sent the revised paper to Pelham, seeking his endorsement, but he would not sign off on what he saw as a "whitewash" in favor of drugs. The article was then published in the journal without his being told, but including his name as an author.[12]

MISLEADING ADVERTISING

In a brochure published by Shire, U.S. (manufacturer of Adderall®) and targeted to physicians, ADHD is said to be associated with a "physical problem in the brain" along with "a chemical imbalance . . . in the brain," and that medications like Adderall "are thought to correct the chemical imbalance in the brain."[13] Facts can be annoying things. It is a fact that no studies to date have confirmed beyond reasonable doubt that impulsivity and short attention span—the two primary symptoms of ADHD—result from physical problems or chemical imbalances in the brain. As discussed in chapter 3, the very notion of a "chemical imbalance" is a fiction. Under the circumstances, for Shire to claim that ADHD medications correct an imbalance in brain chemistry is unscientific.

Furthermore, it has been established beyond question that these stimulant medications have the same effect on normal individuals as they do on individuals exhibiting ADHD symptoms: *temporarily* improved attention span, concentration, and self-control.[14] One must therefore conclude that nearly *everyone* is afflicted with chemical imbalances and other unspecified problems in their brains!

ADULT ADHD

The biogenetic theory of ADHD makes it relatively easy to convince the parents of a child so diagnosed that one or both of them contributed genetically to the child's "disease." As a consequence of this as well as the general marketing of ADHD as a "lifespan disorder," the treatment of adult ADHD has become big business. Needless to say, it is a business built on fictions and propaganda.

A respected medical information website, WebMD, once included an ADHD Assessment Questionnaire sponsored by Eli Lilly, manufacturer of Strattera®. Representative of the general nature of the questions is "When you have a task that requires a lot of thought, do you often avoid or delay getting started?" It's safe to say most adults would answer "Yes." Scores are divided into categories ranging from "Very Severe ADHD Behaviors" to "Mild ADHD Behaviors." It is significant to note that no "Absent ADHD Behaviors" category exists. The impression is subtly advanced, therefore, that everyone has some degree of ADHD and would do well to have the possibility checked out, which one could easily do by clicking a link that will connect the respondent to a list of physicians in his or her locality who specialize in treating ADHD.[15] One can reasonably presume that even with the disclaimer to the effect that only a physician "can make a definite diagnosis," most of the physicians listed will agree with its results. To give credit where credit is due, the person who devised this clever scheme is a marketing genius.

A diagnosis of adult ADHD has obvious appeal to people who do not possess a functional work ethic (which is not to say this applies to all adults who have accepted the diagnosis). To avoid losing their jobs because of bad work habits, such a person can study a list of adult ADHD symptoms, complain of forgetfulness, disorganization, and distractibility to psychiatrists or even their personal physicians, and be all but guaranteed a diagnosis. Remember that adult ADHD is diagnosed on the basis of self-report. Because ADHD is covered by the Americans with Disabilities Act (albeit with caveats), their employers may now have to make "accommodations" for these individuals, including giving them more time to finish tasks, not assigning them more than one task at a time, and the like. (In *Answers to Distraction*, for example, Drs. Edward Hallowell and John Ratey advise an ADHD adult male who says he's been fired from every job he's ever had to take advantage of ADA by "asking for the accommodations that you probably have not been asking for."[16]) In the final analysis, an employer may end up paying a full wage to a perfectly normal adult who has been diagnosed with ADHD for doing half the work the wage is worth. Needless to say, the proliferation of this fictitious disorder in the workplace threatens to seriously damage the American economy.

Along these same lines, I once heard the story of a woman in her midtwenties who was attempting to get into medical school. After failing the timed entrance exam twice, her parents had her evaluated by a psychiatrist who diagnosed her with ADHD. The woman's wealthy father showed a letter from the psychiatrist to the dean of the medical school and basically threatened a lawsuit if his daughter was not given an indefinite amount of time to take the entrance exam. The dean relented, and the young woman passed the exam on her next untimed try. Assuming she graduated (courtesy of even more accommodations, one assumes), she is not required to tell any of her patients that she is disorganized, distractible, and prone to memory lapses. Amazingly enough, this story was told to me by the young woman's father, who beamed with pride throughout the telling, obviously convinced he had only seen to it that justice was done.

In the next section, America's foremost ADHD advocacy group claims that ADHD has "severe" consequences. The only severe consequences the authors have been able to discover are those to the American work ethic, workplace, and economy.

IS CHADD REALLY LOOKING OUT FOR YOU AND YOUR CHILD?

The largest and most influential patient advocacy organization in the ADHD Establishment is Children and Adults with Attention Deficit/ Hyperactivity Disorder (CHADD), a twenty-thousand-plus member organization based in Landover, Maryland. CHADD claims to provide "accurate, evidence-based information about ADHD"[17] to parents and the public. Is that so?

In the section of its website where treatment options are summarized, CHADD recommends "multimodal treatment" including "medication, when necessary." It goes on to say that "for many children with AD/HD, medication *may be* an integral part of treatment."[18] That's appropriately cautious. However, on the website of the National Resource Center on AD/HD (which is identified as "A Program of CHADD" and which is seamlessly linked to CHADD's main website), CHADD is considerably less equivocal. Here, it again recommends multimodal treatment, including behavior management and medication, but is careful to say that it does not regard these as "either-or options," but rather modalities that should be used in concert.[19] Elsewhere on the National Resource Center website, it says that "Treating AD/HD in children *requires* medical, educational, behavioral, and psychological interventions."[20] The only medical intervention subsequently mentioned is medication. Then, in a blatant case of research cherry-picking, CHADD cites only two studies, both of which seem to support the position that medication is necessary to optimal treatment outcome.[21] Ignored are studies in which behavioral treatment alone produced results as good as or better than a multimodal approach, including a 2007 study in which preschool children ages three to five with or at high risk for ADHD showed significant improvement in behavior simply as a result of parent education.[22] Also not mentioned by CHADD is research conducted by Dr. William Pelham, as well as data obtained from the most ambitious study to date of ADHD treatment outcomes, showing that the efficacy of medication declines over time.[23] It's significant to note that according to figures from the 2006–2007 Annual Report posted on the CHADD website, pharmaceutical companies by the end of that fiscal year (June 30, 2007) had contributed $1,169,000, or about 26 percent of the budget.[24]

After receiving the CHADD Hall of Fame Award in 2002, Dr. William Pelham was interviewed for *Attention*, the organization's monthly magazine. In the interview, Pelham said that methylphenidates (stimulants) have serious limitations, especially when used in the absence of other treatment modalities. He told his interviewer that nonmedical therapies should be the treatment of first choice for ADHD and that medication should only be employed as an adjunct, when absolutely necessary. When the interview was published, large chunks had been cut, including Pelham's comments concerning the limitations of stimulant medications. In a foreword to the unedited version of the article he provided *AlterNet*, Pelham writes that some of the strongest advocates of stimulant treatment "including CHADD—have major and undisclosed conflicts of interest with the pharmaceutical companies that deal with ADHD products."[25]

Although it claims to provide scientifically accurate information about ADHD, the information on its website includes unproven contentions such as ADHD is a neurobiological disorder as well as a "lifespan disorder" (i.e., never goes away). CHADD is dismissive of any evidence to the effect that ADHD's defining behaviors might be caused by inadequate discipline, overexposure to electronic media, or poor nutrition, calling these "popularly held," which implies they have no scientific credibility. Rebuffing the claim that ADHD is an invention, and not a scientifically valid disorder, CHADD as much as admits that it relies not on data that is objective, verifiable, and replicable, but rather on consensus science. On its National Resource Center on AD/HD website, CHADD reprints an article from *Attention* stating, ". . . there is general consensus that AD/HD is a valid disorder with *severe*, lifelong consequences."[26]

Even using the term "severe" when describing the consequences of a disorder that has not been proven to exist is absurd, overdramatic, designed to appeal to emotion. The consequences of third-degree burns are severe. Even if ADHD is someday proven to have objective reality, its worst-case individual consequences are far from severe.

CHADD cannot lay credible claim to objectivity. Where ADHD is concerned, it promotes the medical model and denies evidence of psychosocial cause or even influence. It appears that pharmaceutical companies who have donated significantly to CHADD are getting their money's worth.

STIMULANTS: HYPE VERSUS REALITY

The value assigned to stimulant medications depends on whether one is considering short-term or long-term effects. There is no doubt but that in the short term, stimulants promote attention span and concentration. Depending on the form of the drug and its dosage level, that positive effect will last from three to twelve hours. The real issue, however, is whether they are beneficial in the long term, or as beneficial as other, nonmedical interventions. A helpful analogy might be to a person who experiences headaches on a daily basis. Aspirin would solve the problem in the short run but would not address the underlying problem causing daily headaches. Furthermore, long-term aspirin use can seriously damage the gastrointestinal system. Likewise, evidence is mounting to the effect that long-term stimulant use is not just risky, but may also be counterproductive.

MTA STUDY

The Multimodal Treatment Study of Children with Attention Deficit/ Hyperactivity Disorder (MTA) is regarded by many in the ADHD Establishment as the "crown jewel" of ADHD research and is often referred to by professionals who are attempting to justify stimulant use as a first choice. MTA published findings in 1999, 2004, and 2007, involving 576 children. Cosponsored by the National Institute of Mental Health and the Department of Education, researchers compared the outcomes of intensive stimulant treatment alone, medication combined with a reward-based behavioral approach, behavior management alone, and typical community treatment that included the use of stimulants in 67 percent of the children. The authors of the study include some of the "stars" of the ADHD Establishment, including Drs. William Pelham, James Swanson, Peter Jensen, and Keith Conners.

It turns out that MTA does not live up to its press. Its design flaws—including that observers who rated outcomes knew in advance which children were in which groups—all but completely invalidate the results. But moving that consideration to the side for the moment, it is significant to note that although the study is often cited as proof of the efficacy of stimulants, a majority of the children's parents and teachers rated the outcome of behavior management over that of medication. Furthermore, after the study began, stimulant-treated children engaged in nearly four times more delinquent behaviors than did children in the nonmedication groups, with more days of prescribed medication being associated with more serious delinquency.[27] One of the authors of the MTA study was Dr. William Pelham. In a 2007 British Broadcasting Company interview, Pelham said he thought that MTA's authors "exaggerated" the benefits of medication. After much consideration, he concluded, "There's no indication that medication is better than nothing in the long run."[28] A startling admission, to say the least.

OTHER ADHD RESEARCH

Researchers reviewed all the studies on stimulant treatment of ADHD in 2001, and from the highest quality studies among the 2,402 identified concluded that "*broad generalizations about the usefulness of* [methylphenidate] *should probably be avoided, particularly due to the lack of long term trial evidence.*"[29] They also pointed out that poorly designed trials are more likely to exaggerate positive treatment effects than are better designed ones.

In 2007, the Oregon Evidence-Based Practice Center (OEPC), a collaboration among several organizations including the Kaiser Permanente Center for Health Research, updated their 2005 report on the efficacy of drug treatment for ADHD. After analyzing thousands of research papers found through the most sophisticated and respected database search engines available, including the FDA website, the report's authors concluded that medication treatment does not appear to result in significant improvements in academic performance, behavior, or social achievement.[30]

In 2008, the *Los Angeles Times* reported on a UCLA study of 188 Finnish teens with "probable or definite ADHD." Researchers observed that outcomes among American teens, most of whom are treated with ADHD drugs, are similar to the outcomes found among Finnish teens, most of whom are *not* treated with these drugs, leading the *Times* writer to conclude: "Does medication make a difference in the long run for kids suffering from the disorder? New research suggests that it doesn't."[31]

THE MYTH OF THE "PARADOXICAL EFFECT"

One popular notion has it that the stimulants frequently prescribed to treat ADHD behaviors "cause people with ADHD to slow down, but cause non-ADHD people to speed up." Hundreds of parents of children diagnosed with ADHD have told the authors that their children's therapists told them this. Countless numbers of teachers have told me that they've heard this from mental health professionals during in-service sessions or consultations. It simply isn't true.

Yes, when the drugs in question are given to hyperactive children, their activity levels usually subside considerably. That is not due to some unique effect these drugs have on the fictitious "ADHD brain." Stimulant medications enhance a person's attention span and ability to concentrate on a task at hand. Disregarding the very occasional occurrence of idiosyncratic side effects, they have the same effect on everyone. The simple explanation is that as a person's attention span lengthens, his activity level will come down. Said differently, as a person's ability to focus on a single task improves, the person will be more able to sit still.

In the case of a hyperactive child, the difference in pre-medication and post-medication activities levels is going to be more than simply obvious; it's going to be striking. If, however, the same medication is given to a person who is not hyperactive, who is generally able to sit still, focus on and complete tasks, the pre- and post-medication difference is going to be negligible, if even observable. Nonetheless, that person will probably report that he or she felt more absorbed in the task, better able to screen distractions, and the like. The stimulant had the same effect on both the hyperactive child and the nonhyperactive individual. (Knowing this, parents of children with no ADHD symptoms have been known to solicit pediatricians and family practitioners to render an ADHD diagnosis and prescribe stimulants for the seeming purpose of giving their children an academic "edge" in the classroom, or, if a good number of a child's classmates are already taking stimulants, to assure the child will not be disadvantaged.)

Notice that the nonhyperactive individual did not "speed up" in response to the medication. The fact that the street name for stimulant drugs is "speed" does not mean they cause people to begin running at "fast-forward." When a person's attention span is improved by one of these meds, he or she will probably complete tasks more quickly than usual, but their physical movements will not appear rushed. A person taking a "street dose" of one of these drugs may become anxious, jittery, and restless, but street doses are considerably greater than therapeutic doses.

If all of this is well-known, and it is, why do so many people who claim expertise in ADHD perpetuate this myth? Because the myth of the so-called paradoxical effect reinforces the greater myth that the nervous system of a person with ADHD is very different from that of a non-ADHD person. If their nervous systems are not the same, then their reactions to central nervous system stimulants will not be the same.

ARE ADHD STIMULANTS SAFE?

ADHD: A Complete and Authoritative Guide, published by the American Academy of Pediatrics (AAP), states that the side effects of stimulant drugs are *generally* mild, mentioning such benign things as stomachaches, decreased appetite, headaches, difficulty falling asleep, jitteriness, a "rebound" effect (after the drug wears off, an above-baseline increase in ADHD behavior), and tics.[32] "Generally" is the operative term, obviously, because AAP neglected to mention a number of other verified side effects including psychotic episodes, elevated blood pressure, increased pulse rate, growth impairment, and depression. The publication also fails to mention that older children taking prescribed stimulants sometimes share their medications and even sell them to other children who take them recreationally or to enhance their own classroom performance. An increase in vulnerability to "street drugs," including cocaine, as well as increases in smoking have also been noted in some studies. Omission of any mention of these known or potential side effects in an AAP publication presented as a "complete and authoritative guide" for physicians speaks to the degree to which even professional medical organizations have been taken in by pharmaceutical company propaganda.

What follows is a discussion of known or potential side effects and other drawbacks of ADHD stimulants.

COGNITIVE CONSTRICTION

The term *cognitive constriction* refers to shrinking down the breadth of one's thinking processes. It is intuitive and predictable that if one takes a drug that is known to narrow one's focus, enabling the individual to ignore what otherwise would distract, awareness of things other than the immediate object of attention would be restricted. In other words, what we call "creative thinking" would be diminished. It is interesting to consider what might have happened if Albert Einstein had lived when "distractibility" and "daydreaming" were viewed as symptoms of a supposed brain disease, and if he were treated with stimulants during his formative and productive years. This is not a far-fetched conjecture, since his name has been mentioned by members of the Establishment as an example of famous historical figures who probably had ADHD.

Although the AAP Guide mentions cognitive constriction, it is said to be "rare." A report published prior to the Guide, however, suggests it may occur more than rarely. In one study, nearly half of the subjects taking methylphenidate for ADHD demonstrated some degree of narrowing in their thought processes and problem-solving abilities.[33] Psychiatrist Peter Breggin has described how both overfocusing and obsessive-compulsive behaviors have been associated with stimulant treatment in children, pointing out that teachers and parents may sometimes interpret these as *improvements* rather than as negative side effects of their treatment.[34]

DRUG SHARING AND DRUG ABUSE

A 2006 study by the Substance Abuse and Mental Health Services Administration and sponsored by Eli Lilly (manufacturer of Strattera, a nonstimulant ADHD medication), included the estimate that twenty-one million people twelve years of age and older have used stimulants for nonmedical reasons. Of these, nearly three million have abused ADHD stimulants *exclusively* and thirty-nine thousand have developed stimulant dependence as a result. Furthermore, the study's authors state that these figures are probably conservative.[35]

Although the ADHD Establishment will admit that there is conflicting evidence on the question of whether taking stimulants for ADHD increases or decreases the risk for abusing other drugs, its members often reference a 1999 study purporting to show that ADHD children who were treated with medication were less likely than nonmedicated ADHD children to later abuse drugs.[36] The study, done by a prominent member of the Establishment with admitted ties to the pharmaceutical industry, has two significant limitations that render its conclusions doubtful: First, there were only nineteen children in the untreated group, a sample size generally regarded as inadequate. Second, the percentage of untreated children who developed drug problems was far greater than the rate in the general population, raising questions concerning the manner in which the researcher selected his subjects.

Other, better-designed studies paint a different picture. A study initiated in 1974 that followed 492 ADHD children for twenty years found that stimulant-treated children were much more prone to cocaine and nicotine dependence than nonmedicated children. Cocaine use was found among 27.4 percent of subjects with one year or more of stimulant treatment compared to only 15 percent with no exposure to stimulants.[37]

Researchers reported their findings from following 147 hyperactive children for thirteen years into early adulthood. Although apparent associations between stimulant treatment and later use of cocaine were largely accounted for by controlling for independent risk factors such as coexisting conduct disorder, there still remained an increased risk for cocaine use following stimulant treatment in high school. The authors posed the possibility that stimulant treatment in high school might produce a "sensitizing effect" toward risk of using cocaine.[38]

INITIATION, ADAPTATION, AND ADDICTION

Drs. Steven Hyman, director of the National Institute of Mental Health (NIMH), and Eric Nestler have described how stimulant drugs increase the level of the neurotransmitter dopamine. As intake of a stimulant remains constant over time, it serves to *initiate* long-term changes in brain function that occur as the brain adapts to the presence of the alien chemical. Hyman and Nestler postulate that this adaptation is responsible for the addictive potential of stimulants.[39] In other words, changes in brain cell function induced by a stimulant produces adaptations in the brain that, in turn, lead to long-term alterations in brain function which then ensure that the individual will experience significant unpleasant symptoms if the drug is stopped.

Grace Jackson explains the same idea in terms of what she calls "allostasis"—the opposite of "homeostasis." The latter refers to the manner in which living organisms maintain stability through constancy, in essence seeking equilibrium. Allostasis refers to adaptations made by individuals in response to internal and external stresses. She speculates that several common phenomena observed in children on stimulant drugs can be explained by this process:

- The initial beneficial effect of the stimulant wears off, leading the parent to report that the drug has "stopped working." The child's physician generally responds either by increasing the dose or changing to a different stimulant.
- The child experiences what is known as "rebound" as the

effects of the drug wear off. In other words, the child becomes more than typically active, distractible, easily frustrated, and so on. These symptoms are often interpreted by the clinician as a recurrence of symptoms of the underlying disorder, but Jackson speculates that they actually represent a withdrawal response; the child's brain has adapted to the drug and now requires it to maintain homeostasis.[40]

In a related study, researchers performed brain scans of an ADHD patient following three months of methylphenidate treatment and then scanned again one month after stopping the drug. Changes in certain brain structures raised the possibility that prolonged stimulant use may lead to changes in the brain that will make it increasingly difficult for the individual to function well without the drug.[41]

The addictive potential of these drugs to parents who give them to their children has, to our knowledge, never been discussed, so we will.

PARENTS BECOMING "ADDICTED" TO GIVING A CHILD MEDICATION

It is all but certain that stimulant medication provides nothing but a short-term solution to ADHD behaviors. For many parents, however, even a three- to twelve-hour solution to disruptive behavior justifies continuing to give their children medication. Most parents of ADHD kids say they are using behavioral methods in conjunction with medication, but the authors are generally skeptical of these reports. After all, one cannot discipline behavior that's been effectively suppressed by medication—behavior, in other words, that isn't there. It's more logical to assume that many parents eventually become *addicted*, in the psychological sense, to giving their children medication. As soon as they discover that a dose of stimulant brings significant relief (to them) within thirty minutes, they come to rely more and more on the medication. In the process, their children become more and more undisciplined, which causes their parents to request ever-increasing doses, and 'round and 'round they go.

DEPRESSION

ADHD has long been associated with depression. It is widely reported that depression is present, or at least likely to develop, in as many as one-third of all ADHD children, referred to as comorbid depression—meaning that depression develops in these children as a second, coexisting diagnosis. Russell Barkley finds this comorbidity for depression in ADHD to range from 15 to 75 percent, including 45 percent of adolescents.[42]

The question remains, however, as to whether or not stimulant treatment raises the risk of depression. A rapid increase in the diagnosis of EOBD has brought this even further into relevance. It has been suggested by proponents of diagnosing EOBD, even in the acknowledged absence of criteria for childhood diagnosis, that many cases of what appears to be ADHD are actually EOBD and that the development of depression following an earlier diagnosis of ADHD and treatment with stimulants is explained by the natural history of bipolar disorder. Both the "comorbid" depression associated with ADHD and the EOBD allegedly accounting for many cases of childhood depression fail to take into account the real possibility that depression in these children is caused by their medication treatment for ADHD. For example, psychiatrist Grace Jackson says that a common side effect of stimulants, the well-known "rebound" effect as the most recent dose is wearing off, can easily be interpreted as bipolar.[43]

Martin Seligman argues that children may be more likely to develop depression when parents protect them from frustration and adversity and less likely when parents foster optimism by allowing their children to learn, over time, to overcome obstacles.[44] Many parents of ADHD children believe them to be incapable of dealing functionally with challenging situations, especially academic and social. It's reasonable to suggest that parents who opt for medication may be more protective than parents who, in the face of similar problems with their kids, opt for nonmedical strategies. Seligman's thesis suggests that medicated children may be more prone to depression because their parents tend to be more protective. Along the same lines, psychologist Albert Bandura theorizes that psychological health is significantly dependent on maintaining a sense of personal control, which Bandura terms "self-efficacy."[45] Prolonged dependence upon drugs to inhibit impulsive or inattentive behaviors may undermine that very sense of personal control and competence, causing the individual to be more vulnerable to depression.

PSYCHOTIC EPISODES

Psychotic episodes attributable to stimulant drugs are widely believed to be uncommon, but a 1999 Canadian study suggests otherwise. Of ninety-eight children treated for ADHD with methylphenidate, six developed psychotic symptoms during their treatment. It's important to note that none of these kids had been diagnosed with any other psychiatric disorder before treatment began; furthermore, psychotic symptoms resolved for all six children after stimulants were discontinued.[46]

The package insert for Adderall XR®, an amphetamine-class ADHD medication, states that psychotic symptoms "*can be caused by stimulants at usual doses*" in children and adolescents.[47] One is moved to wonder why, if the manufacturer of a leading ADHD stimulant warns of psychotic reactions, the AAP fails to mention the possibility in their *Authoritative Guide*.

An FDA ruling in February 2007 directed ADHD drug manufacturers to inform patients about certain possible psychiatric and cardiovascular risks of stimulant medications. The release of this alert included reference to an approximate one in one thousand risk of "hearing voices, becoming suspicious for no reason, or becoming manic, even in patients who did not have previous psychiatric problems."[48] The Canadian study referenced above suggests that a risk factor of one in one thousand may be an underestimate.

STATE-DEPENDENT LEARNING

Psychologists have long known that an individual who has learned certain material while under the influence of a drug will not have optimal recall unless he is again under the influence of the same drug. This is known as state-dependent learning and has obvious ramifications for the stimulant-medicated child. It suggests, for example, that a child who learns his multiplication tables while under the influence of an ADHD stimulant will have less than optimal recall if he is not under stimulants. More significantly, a teenager who takes and passes driver's education while under the influence of methylphenidate may not drive as well on days when he is not medicated.

INCREASED BLOOD PRESSURE, HEART RATE, AND CARDIAC RISK

Although long-term effects on blood pressure or heart rate have not been proven, research has shown that there are significant short-term increases caused by stimulants. One study in adults given a common ADHD stimulant showed a 16.9 percent increase in systolic blood pressure and a 12.3 percent increase in the diastolic reading ninety minutes after a dose.[49] Other research has documented significantly increased systolic and diastolic blood pressure among stimulant-treated children after three years of follow-up.[50]

In February 2006 the Drug Safety and Risk Management Advisory Committee of the Food and Drug Administration voted by a narrow margin of eight to seven to recommend a controversial "black box" warning concerning the risks ADHD stimulants pose to cardiovascular health. A prominent cardiologist subsequently pointed out that among twenty-five cases of sudden death in individuals who had been taking ADHD stimulants (as determined by the FDA's Adverse Event Reporting

System), nineteen of those deaths involved children eighteen and younger. In this regard, it's worth mentioning that only an estimated 10 percent of serious adverse events are reported to the FDA surveillance system.[51] Although the proposed black box warning was not adopted by the FDA, the agency did issue a requirement for changes in the labeling of stimulants to include a warning about cardiovascular risks for children with known *or* unrecognized cardiac abnormalities.

Two U.S. Department of Health and Human Services agencies announced in September 2007 that a comprehensive study is to be launched to evaluate the potential for increased risk of heart attack, stroke, or other cardiovascular problems from the use of ADHD drugs. The two agencies are the Agency for Healthcare Research and Quality (AHRQ) and the U.S. Food and Drug Administration (FDA). This decision reflects the fact that the medications used to treat ADHD can increase heart rate and blood pressure, and the potential adverse effects of long-term use are unknown.[52]

In summary, one would have to conclude that the risk of potential cardiovascular complications from prolonged treatment with stimulants, especially if continued for many years, is significant—both from a theoretical and from a practical point of view.

IMPAIRED GROWTH

Even though it is an established fact that stimulants suppress appetite, many stimulant proponents maintain that stimulants do not affect children's growth or that any such effect is insignificant. An ever-increasing body of evidence shows, however, that growth impairment is a distinct possibility. For example,

- Australian researchers found that stimulants were associated with progressive declines in height and weight in 86 percent of treated children.[53]

- Researchers at Yale University compared growth rates of stimulant-treated children in two large pediatric practices with their untreated siblings. At three-year follow-up, significant reductions in height were seen among 76 percent of boys and 90 percent of girls.[54]
- The MTA study previously discussed showed that consistent use of stimulants stunts the growth of children at a rate of approximately one inch every two years. That same study also questioned the theory, oft-repeated by drug companies and therapists alike, that children make up the growth deficit over time.[55,56]

Grace Jackson references studies that have found an association between stimulants and deficiencies in growth hormone and raises the possibility that these effects upon growth hormone could, in turn, have a disruptive effect upon the brain.[57]

In the spirit of being fair and balanced, it must be said that most children taking the drugs in question, under proper medical supervision, will not experience any of the possible reactions noted above or any bad side effects at all. Nonetheless, after a careful and thorough review of the evidence, we have come to the conclusion that ADHD stimulants pose a certain degree—we believe it is significant—of potential physical, emotional, behavioral, and social risks to children. By virtue of the fact these drugs are highly controlled, they do not qualify as "safe" by any stretch of the term. If they were safe, obtaining them would not require a prescription. Furthermore, we have come to the conclusion that the problems they are used to treat are better treated using the methods we describe in chapters 8 and 9.

PART 2

Making Sense

CHAPTER 6
A SIMPLE EXPLANATION

All things being equal, the simplest explanation is the best.
—A paraphrase of Occam's razor

The supreme goal of all theory is to make the irreducible
basic elements as simple and as few as possible.
—Albert Einstein

IF THE SYMPTOMS DESCRIBING ATTENTION-DEFICIT/HYPER-activity disorder, oppositional defiant disorder, and early onset bipolar disorder (and those disorders yet to come) cannot be adequately explained in terms of genes, biochemical imbalances, or structural anomalies in the brain, what then does explain them? In this chapter, we will turn our attention to an explanation that not only makes sense but is supported by good science.

Before we tackle that issue, however, a pertinent question begs: do the authors believe that these disorders are overdiagnosed? No we do not, not if we define them in strict accord with DSM-IV criteria (or, in the case of EOBD, the criteria proposed by psychiatrist Demitri Papolos). We are convinced that if a research team were able through some Orwellian act of Congress (see our comments on the New Freedom Commission in chapter 2) to assess every child in America between the ages of five and twelve, and said team adhered strictly to DSM (and

Papolos's) guidelines, they would find that close to half of all elementary-age children in America qualify for at least one of these diagnoses.

Along these lines, I have asked a good number of elementary school teachers to estimate the number of kids in their classes who are frequently inattentive, restless, easily distracted, disruptive, and have difficulty concentrating and finishing work on time (i.e., children who fit the DSM criteria for ADHD). The general answer, converted to a percentage, has never been less than 20 percent and has been as much as 75 percent. That's considerably higher than the 6 to 10 percent figure usually put forth by the ADHD Establishment and does not even include those children who fit the criteria for ODD and/or EOBD. Teachers who have taught for twenty years or more consistently report that some of the worst-behaved children they encountered in their first five years of teaching would be considered relatively well-behaved today. They also report that many of the best-behaved children in their classes today would have been considered ill-behaved in the classes they taught twenty years ago. That the DSM criteria—objectively and dispassionately applied—describe so many of today's kids is alarming, if not chilling. The way things seem to be shaping up, the not-so-distant prospect of most of America's children being on one drug or another—administered for the supposedly altruistic purpose of helping them *function* more effectively—is hardly preposterous.

What could possibly account for the obvious fact that a disproportionate number of America's kids exhibit glaring deficiencies in attention and self-control as represented by the diagnoses under discussion? The answer is found in the diagnostic criteria themselves, of which the following is a collective summary:

- Short attention span
- Impulsive (lacking in self-control)
- Frequent periods of high, unfocused activity
- Difficulty staying focused on a task until completion

- Easily distracted
- Unwilling to engage in tasks requiring sustained effort
- Easily frustrated (loses temper easily)
- Vehemently denies responsibility for wrongdoing
- Impatient, demands instant gratification, difficulty waiting his or her turn
- Oppositional and/or defiant toward adult authority, often belligerently so
- Highly attention-seeking, intrusive (lack of respect for boundaries)
- Unpredictable mood swings
- Frequent rages and explosive tantrums when thwarted, denied, or frustrated

As does *every single one* of the supposed symptoms of ADHD, ODD, and EOBD, the above behaviors are characteristic of toddlerhood, which is why that developmental stage has long been known as the "terrible twos." In other words, we are not talking about behavioral conditions that *some* children have and other children do not have; rather, these are behavioral conditions—or, more accurately, *one* behavioral condition that manifests in various ways—typical of *all* toddlers. "Terrible twos" is actually somewhat of a misnomer because the characteristic behaviors usually appear sometime during the second year of life when the child realizes he is a separate, autonomous individual and begins to assert his resolve to not simply master the environment (including the people therein), but to dominate and control it. As parents of this age child will attest, this sea change does not happen gradually, but it has a sudden and startling onset. The following account is far from unusual:

One night, two doting parents put to bed an eighteen-month-old boy who has been to that point in time the epitome of "adorable." Upon entering his room the next morning, they are met by a child who acts as if he is possessed by demons. He fights them as they change his diapers. He throws wild tantrums when they don't immediately accede to his demands, which become increasingly unreasonable. He seems like a whirling dervish during the day, moving from one thing to another without any seeming purpose other than to touch, disrupt, and destroy. No mood lasts for long. One minute he's be cheerful, the next he's peevish and petulant. When they tell him not to do something—don't climb on the coffee table—he throws them a defiant look and proceeds to climb on the coffee table. When they tell him to do something, however mundane, he screams "No!" at the top of lungs that seem unusually powerful for a twenty-five-pound body. When his parents take him into public places, he disturbs the general peace with shrieks and screams that cause other shoppers to consider calling the local child abuse authority. When put to bed, he rages until they pick him back up and continues to disrupt their lives until midnight, when he finally falls asleep only to awaken them, screaming hysterically, at five o'clock in the morning. And so it goes. In short, this once cuddly, adorable child becomes, overnight, an unholy terror—chaos personified.

As is the little boy in the above not-so-hypothetical story, the typical toddler is defiant, persistent, and demanding (i.e., ODD); petulant, prone to unpredictable mood swings, and given to sudden, violent outbursts if he doesn't get his way (i.e., EOBD); unfocused, highly active—but often without seeming purpose—easily distracted, and impulsive (i.e., ADHD). These characteristics not only comprise ADHD and its diagnostic offspring, but also reflect the inherent amorality of the pre-socialized child, a child who obviously believes that what he wants, he deserves to have, by any means necessary, and that no one has a right to stand in his way—a belief system that mirrors the mind-set of sociopaths and criminals. And yes, we are most definitely saying that the toddler is a criminal in the making. One does not have to teach a toddler antisocial behavior. Violence directed toward others, lying, stealing, selfishness, defiance of legitimate authority—they all come naturally to this age child. As I have said in previous books, "curing" toddlerhood—exorcising antisocial behavior and setting the child on a prosocial course—by the third birthday is the foremost challenge of parenthood.

Given that *all* toddlers to one degree or another present the behaviors that define the "big three" childhood behavior disorders, the notion that they represent an abnormal biological condition falls flat on its face. These supposed disorders obviously represent a *normal* developmental condition. Furthermore, this normal developmental condition—the so-called terrible twos—exists today as it existed one thousand years ago, and it will typify toddlers one thousand years from now (assuming we're still around).

Now we're getting somewhere! A *developmental* theory of ADHD, et cetera, provides us with an explanation that makes far more sense and certainly conforms more to the evidence than does a genetic/neurological one. It also explains the ease with which teachers during the peak years of the baby boom were able to manage successfully, by themselves, early elementary classrooms comprised of thirty-five or more children.

Prior to the psychological parenting revolution that occurred in America in the 1960s and early '70s, parents "cured" the antisocial nature of toddlerhood by the time their children were three years old. (Exceptions to this general rule existed, of course, but they were rare.) Today's parents, by and large, are failing to do so. In the former case, children came to school adequately socialized and reasonably well behaved. They paid attention to adults and did what adults told them to do. It did not really matter, therefore, how many of these respectful, obedient (albeit still mischievous) children were crammed into one classroom. They were *teachable*.

By contrast, many of today's children come to school still possessing, and significantly so, toddler characteristics: inattention, impulsivity, inability to focus on a task and see it through to completion (distractibility), and various noncompliant habits. Thus an elementary teacher today spends a disproportionate amount of classroom time dealing with disciplinary matters. It is still theoretically possible for a competent teacher to teach, by herself, forty or more well-behaved elementary age children. The problem would be finding, in a given school district, that many kids who are as well behaved as were their counterparts in the 1950s, before American parents began listening to psychologists and other mental health professionals spin child-rearing fables.

DIFFERENT APPROACHES = DIFFERENT OUTCOMES

Psychologist Russell Barkley, psychiatrist Edward (Ned) Hallowell, CHADD, and other spokespersons for the ADHD Establishment steadfastly maintain in their writings that ADHD is not a consequence of poor parenting. However, that judgment depends on one's definition of *good* parenting. It is undeniably true that many parents who are "good" by today's standards—parents who work very hard to always do the right thing by their kids—have children who qualify for the ADHD diagnosis. But "good" parenting today looks considerably different from what was considered good parenting in the 1950s and before. From the perspective of now-elderly folks who raised their children during the post-WW II baby boom (1946–1964, inclusive), the behavior of today's parents often appears foolish and counterproductive. The parents in question aren't necessarily bad parents. They're simply parents who are operating within a post-1960s set of child-rearing mores—a set of parenting dos and don'ts that are 180 degrees removed from old-fashioned, traditional parenting standards.

Until the late 1960s, a stable set of biblically based parenting standards prevailed in America. (The standards in question were so thoroughly embedded in the fabric of American culture that even people of no faith raised children accordingly.) These parenting values had been carried to these shores by the first settlers and handed down, unaltered, from generation to generation. A long out-of-print text illustrates how this traditional child-rearing paradigm was even embraced among professionals until the new way of thinking infiltrated psychology. In *Training Children in Self-Discipline and Self-Control,* two prominent psychologists of the time proclaimed, as the title of their book reflected, that self-discipline and self-control should be parents' primary objectives. They also argued that parents should simply correct misbehavior and not search for reasons why it occurred. Lastly, and amazingly, they asserted that lay help was likely to be more helpful than professional help. We agree on all three counts.[1]

As a general disdain for "old" ways of doing things began to develop during the tumultuous, deconstructive 1960s, American parents began dismissing the advice of their elders and embracing advice dispensed by psychologists and other mental health professionals. The authors contend that with no more than a handful of exceptions, these supposed experts have been dispensing, for the most part, bad advice. This bad advice has resulted in an epidemic of dysfunctional (albeit well-intentioned) parenting, and just as dysfunctional parenting had consequences back then, it has consequences now. The difference being, however, that whereas dysfunctional parenting was sporadic back then, it is endemic today. The symptoms of this culture-wide dysfunction are stress, anxiety, frustration, guilt, and more and greater problems with children than our great-grandparents could have imagined. How did we end up in such a mess?

In the 1960s, a cultural paradigm shift occurred. America entered the '60s informed by tradition and respectful of traditional authority. It exited the '60s informed by the new electronic media, disdainful of tradition, and cynical toward traditional forms of authority, including parental authority. During that raucous decade, America became a postmodern, progressive society, a society that embraced "out with the old, and in with the new!"

The rise of clinical psychology coincided with this paradigm shift, and psychologists and other mental health professionals began using the bully pulpit given them by the media to demonize traditional marriage (supposedly bad for women), the traditional family (supposedly inherently pathological), and traditional child rearing (supposedly bad for children). As a consequence of this disingenuous, cut-from-whole-cloth propaganda, America embraced a nouveau "parenting" ethic that bore absolutely no resemblance to the one that had preceded it. Up until that time, it had been axiomatic that parents reared their children much the same way they themselves had been reared. Baby boomers put an end to that. They were the last generation of American children to be raised the old way, and they were the first generation of American parents to raise their children the new way—the way according to psychobabble.

Traditional child rearing emphasized proper training of a child's character, the linchpin of which is respect for others. The new paradigm—in previous writings, I call it postmodern psychological parenting—emphasizes the development of high self-esteem. It never fails to surprise people to learn that a significant body of recent research has revealed that an elevated sense of self-esteem is highly associated with antisocial behavior; which is to say, people with high self-esteem have generally little respect for others. Because high self-esteem is now as American as apple pie, the idea that it is not a prosocial attribute tends to perplex.

Upon hearing the bitter truth about high self-esteem, today's parents will often exclaim, "But I want my child to possess self-confidence!" First, it is a mistake to think that if one does not have *high* self-esteem, then one has *low* self-esteem. The actual opposite of high self-esteem, however, is not depression, but a character that embodies the traditional, biblical values of humility and modesty. Second, there is no evidence whatsoever that people who are humble and modest and therefore highly mindful of others lack the belief that they are capable of overcoming life's challenges, and there is good evidence that *people who pursue high self-esteem through achievement are especially vulnerable to depression.* Martin Seligman, PhD, professor of psychology at the University of Pennsylvania, proposes that the quest for high self-esteem has actually depressed the mental health of America's kids.[2] Mind you, people with high self-esteem feel they are capable of dealing with life's challenges, the problem being that they often aren't willing to put forth the effort to do so. In other words, high self-esteem is often associated with low motivation. People with high self-esteem also tend to overestimate their abilities. In that light, which of the following is likely to be the safer driver: a sixteen-year-old with high self-esteem or a sixteen-year-old who is humble and modest?

Respecting others eventually leads to self-respect, which is by no means synonymous with self-esteem. Self-respect develops as a person does things for other people. It is the knowledge that one is capable of making a valuable contribution for the good of others. It is not dependent upon income, status, or the like. Self-esteem develops in response to praise, contrived success experiences (e.g., a child who produces a medio-cre theme receives an A because the teacher wants to reward him for his effort), and accomplishments that are motivated primarily by a desire to enhance the self, whether in other people's eyes or one's own. Self-respect-ing people build culture; self-esteeming people, because they are intent upon *self*-gratification, undermine culture.

The traditional point of view presumes that the child is inherently disposed to misbehave (a biblical view; therefore, antithetical to postmo-dernity) while the progressive point of view maintains that the child is inherently disposed to be good. The former presumes that the child can be turned from his original nature only through a combination of power-ful love and equally powerful discipline (not physical, necessarily, but compelling nonetheless); the latter posits that the child can be reasoned, rewarded, distracted (redirected), and gently prodded into behaving prop-erly. The traditional point of view is realistic; the postmodern view is ide-alistic, romantic. Symptomatic of the psychological paradigm are ineffectual discipline practices, the most glaring example being time-out, the most ineffectual discipline method ever conceived. From the traditional point of view, there is nothing as tragically absurd as a mom making a five-year-old who has just hit her sit in a chair for five minutes and "think about it." The traditional point of view predicts that under those circumstances, the child will almost certainly hit his mother again. And he does. (He is later discovered to have ODD and EOBD.)

The traditional paradigm emphasized the discipline of the child's behavior with the goal of teaching self-control. When a child misbehaved, he was punished. The psychological paradigm stresses the prominence of the child's feelings. When today's child misbehaves, his parents are likely to try to understand *why* he did what he did. Today's parents tend, therefore, to talk instead of punish, to engage in what I call "yada-yada discipline," which is sufficient to explain why so many of today's kids just keep right on misbehaving.

In the traditional family, children were expected to make regular contribution, mostly in the form of daily chores. In the postmodern family, children are primarily consumers. Today, few children have daily household responsibilities. The typical modern child is on a never-ending family entitlement program. He is not, therefore, a good citizen of his family. From day one, and through no fault of his own, he takes from the family without giving. He learns to *expect* from others, which is contrary to developing *respect* for others.

Having a regular routine of chores from an early age also trains a child to sustain focus and effort until a task is completed. The typical child growing up in the pre-ADHD era, whether he lived in a rural, suburban, or urban setting, was doing chores from an early age. Furthermore, these chores were challenging. Before I was four, my mother had me washing floors. A year later, I learned to wash my own clothes in my mother's "washing machine"—a galvanized tub with hand-operated rollers bolted to it that sat on our side porch during favorable weather. Family responsibilities of this sort trained baby boomers to focus on and finish tasks, accept responsibility, delay gratification (chores had to be done before the child could go outside and play), and develop organizational skills. By and large, today's children are not receiving this training. To assert, as the ADHD Establishment does, that the lack of such training does not influence the development of behavior diagnostic of ADHD is foolish.

The traditional family was adult-centered, meaning that children were expected to pay attention to their parents. In the postmodern family, children are at the center of attention. It is reasonable to predict that children raised within this context will be inattentive to adult authority figures, disrespectful, oppositional, demanding, petulant, and ungrateful. Indeed, those adjectives describe the typical American child. And how do today's parents deal with these problems? All too many of them just talk. More accurately, they talk until they are blue in the face. Then they yell. Then they feel guilty, for which they atone by dispensing favors, at which point they are right back at square one.

The pre-1960 parent understood, intuitively, that the most advantageous time to deal with antisocial behavior—tantrums, belligerent defiance, disrespect, dishonesty, and destructiveness—was when it first began to emerge, during toddlerhood. This early intervention was called "nipping it in the bud." Between the pre-1960 child's second and third birthdays, he or she was disciplined in a way that recognized the need to subordinate his powerful will to prosocial norms. In so doing, the parents led the child out of toddlerhood and into creative childhood, redefining themselves to the child in the process. By age two, he had every reason to believe his parents were his personal servants for life, there to do his bidding and to cater to his every whim. By age three, he saw them as commanding, formidable (yet loving and approachable—take it from two people who were there) authority figures. He felt completely secure in his parents' presence, but he also knew that when either one of them drew a line in the proverbial sand, he stepped over it at his peril.

Simultaneously, his parents made it clear to him that their relationship with each other trumped their relationship with him—they were husband and wife first, mom and dad second. The child was slowly but surely taken out of the center of parental attention as his parents established themselves at the center of *his* attention. From that point on, it was *his* job to pay attention to *them*. Everything about his life, his parents' roles in his life, and the very nature of the family unit changed during that critical twelve-month (or so) transitional period, and those changes effectively cured the child's toddlerhood.

Postmodern psychological parenting does not and cannot cure toddlerhood. Compelling cultural and peer pressures encourage today's mother to perform as a servant to her child for the whole of his or her tenure at home (which goes a long way toward explaining why the average age of emancipation in America has increased significantly since the early 1970s). The message on today's "mother bar"—the modern standard of good mothering—reads: *The Mother Who Does the Most for Her Child Is the Best Mother.*

The last fifty years have also seen a dramatic change in the father's role as well. In times gone by, the father was a paragon of masculinity—a responsible, hard-working guy who was dedicated to providing for and protecting his family. He was a husband first, a dad second. He did not come home from work to get down on the floor and play with his children. He came home to spend the evening with his wife. When it came to discipline, his rule was law, and he had no problem enforcing it. Today's father, by contrast, aspires to be his child's best buddy. When he comes home from work, his attention is on his kids, not his wife. He justifies this by pointing out that he's been away from them all day. Apparently, it does not occur to him that he has not seen his wife since breakfast either.

All of this has conspired to subordinate the husband-wife relationship to the parent-child relationship. Based on polls I take of parent groups, it appears that married couples with children spend around 90 percent of their time in the roles of father or mother; thus, only 10 percent in the roles of husband and wife. The American marriage is becoming lost in the near-constant parenting shuffle.

Quite simply, *you cannot raise children in two entirely different ways and expect to arrive at the same outcome.* Two diametrically opposed parenting styles arising from two diametrically opposed parenting philosophies will produce very different parenting outcomes (Figure 6.1). And indeed they have. Premodern, traditional child rearing reliably "cured" toddlerhood by age three. Postmodern psychological parenting perpetuates toddlerhood indefinitely. Fifty years ago, when five- and six-year-olds came to school, they were not just chronologically five and six; they were emotionally and behaviorally five and six years old as well. They had been trained to sit still,

TRADITIONAL CHILD REARING	POSTMODERN PSYCHOLOGICAL PARENTING
Emphasizes treating others with respect (e.g., good manners, doing for others)	Emphasizes acquiring high self-esteem (e.g., personal achievement)
Powerful disciplinary consequences	Talking ("yada-yada") discipline
Children contribute to family (chores)	Children are consumers
Parents at center of attention	Children at center of attention
Husband/wife roles predominate	Father/mother roles predominate
OUTCOME ↓	OUTCOME ↓
Child moves beyond toddlerhood by age three	Child becomes "stuck" in toddlerhood

Figure 6.1

to pay attention to adults, and to do what adults told them to do (irrespective of IQ, the keys to success in school). Today, significant numbers of children who are still emotional and behavioral toddlers come to school in five- and six-year-old bodies. They are inattentive, distractible, oppositional, petulant, and so on. This is not ADHD, ODD, or EOBD. This is toddlerhood in perpetuity, or TIP. A popular myth illustrates the point.

Since the 1960s, the Education Establishment has bombarded America with the "smaller class size leads to better learning" mantra. The success of this propaganda is attested to by the fact that increased education spending has diminished the teacher-pupil ratio in public elementary schools by more than half during that same time. But has student achievement improved? Quite the contrary. As class size has shrunk, American student achievement has deteriorated commensurately and continues to do so. This is not the consequence of ill-trained teachers. This is the consequence of children coming to school who are ill-prepared to sit still, pay attention to teachers, and concentrate on assignments; children, in other words, who are inattentive and lacking in self-control and respect for adult authority. This is the consequence of improper discipline during the preschool years—which is to say, this is the consequence of dysfunctional parenting that has become endemic.

Russell Barkley has stated, "Rearing environment makes no contribution to [ADHD]. So let's just get over the idea that AD/HD comes out of the family."[3] In one of his books, he writes, "Theories of causation of AD/HD can no longer be based solely or even primarily on social factors, such as parental characteristics."[4]

Psychiatrist David Goodman of Johns Hopkins University School of Medicine, who serves as a consultant for pharmaceutical companies that make ADHD drugs, told the *Boston Globe* in 2006 that ADHD is not "caused by bad parenting." Rather, he asserted, "It is a neurological condition validated by medical research whose impairments can be reduced by effective treatment."[5]

Members of the ADHD Establishment argue that any dysfunction noted in parents of ADHD kids is due to the stress of living with a child with these behavioral characteristics. From the historical perspective we have developed in this chapter, this argument falls flat.

SAME OLD, SAME OLD

Objective researchers—people with no ties, past or present, to pharmaceutical companies and/or who have not built their reputations as apologists for the medical model—studying the same issue have come to radically different conclusions. A 2005 Finnish study, for example, found parenting style was a definite predictor of the sort of problem behaviors that define ADHD, ODD, and EOBD. More specifically, this study found that mothers who tended to be highly involved (controlling) and highly affectionate (in overly close relationships with their children) were most likely to raise children with pronounced behavior problems.[6] The fascinating aspect of these findings is that the type of mother described—an overly involved micromanager whose primary relationships are with her children—is generally regarded as the epitome of good mothering today. Another study done the same year found that parenting style predicted the degree to which children were able to exercise self-control.[7]

The foremost researcher into the effect parenting style has on child behavior is psychologist Diana Baumrind of the Institute of Human Development, University of California, Berkeley. She has found that the children of parents who adhere to a traditional model score significantly higher on scales of adjustment than children of parents whose style is more attuned to modern norms. Specifically, Baumrind has found that children of permissive parents tend to have difficulty in four key behavioral areas: (1) "emotional regulation" (self-control); (2) rebelliousness and defiance toward adult authority, especially when given instructions or when they don't get their way; (3) ability to stick to and finish challenging tasks; and (4) antisocial behavior patterns. By contrast, children of authoritative parents—that is, parents who tend to be more traditional in their style—are happier, more self-confident, have better social skills, and much better self-control.[8,9] In short, Baumrind has found that modern parenting practices are far more likely than traditional attitudes and practices to produce the behaviors associated with ADHD, ODD, and EOBD. These findings are but three among dozens that contradict the ADHD Establishment's contention that parent behavior has nothing to do with ADHD.

On numerous occasions, members of the ADHD Establishment have accused me of "blaming parents" of ADHD children for their kids' problems. This is a convenient way of creating a red herring, a distraction from the fact that there is no good science to support the notion that ADHD is a biological phenomenon, and the same is true of the "science" behind the same contention regarding ODD and EOBD. As for parents being to blame, we want to make it perfectly clear that the blame for the epidemic of child behavior problems in America, of which ADHD and its diagnostic cousins are but the tip of the iceberg, lies with the poor parenting advice that mental health and child development professionals have been dispensing for the last forty years. Parents have every right to believe that people with capital letters after their names know what they're talking about, that they are giving good guidance. In this case, however, the faith was and is misplaced. "Experts" persuaded America to change its approach to child rearing. The symptoms of this sea change in parenting practice are ADHD, ODD, and EOBD—children who, well past their third birthdays, still behave like toddlers. It is nothing less than ironic, furthermore, that American parents believe they can obtain relief from these problems by seeking help from the very profession that created these problems, especially when the "help" being prescribed almost always includes powerful psychotropic drugs.

PLUG-IN DRUGS

Establishment spokespersons have repeatedly dismissed the notion that watching television can contribute to the development of ADHD, a dismissiveness that seems to border at times on sarcasm. To cite one example, in a 2000 speech in San Francisco, after correctly identifying my belief that television contributes to ADHD behavior, Russell Barkley referred to me and Scientologists in the same sentence, the not-so-subtle implication being that I am to be taken no more seriously than one takes Tom Cruise pontificating on the subject of psychiatry.[10]

In 1979, I wrote a fairly lengthy newspaper article in which I put forth the hypothesis that the act of watching television was infinitely more destructive to a child's cognitive development and learning style than the nature of programs the child watched. Noting that because all television programs "flicker" every few seconds (the sole exception then being *Mr. Rogers' Neighborhood*) as the viewer sees the action from one perspective, then another and another, through close-ups and flashbacks and scene changes and commercials and so on, a child watching a one-hour television program isn't watching any *one* thing for longer than a few seconds (the average length of any single camera perspective on a television program is around 3.5 seconds, children's programs included). This experience, multiplied by thousands of hours of watching during the formative years, must be having a deleterious effect on the development of attention span, I surmised. In subsequent writings, I proposed that a short attention span is unfavorable to being able to think before acting; therefore, the shorter a child's attention span, the more impulsive the child will be. Solid research has since confirmed both hypotheses.

The formative environment—a preschool child's social, material, and informational "ecosystem"—exerts tremendous influence on not just what, how, and how much a child learns, but on how the brain actually develops. As research psychologist Jane Healy has pointed out in

Endangered Minds, a rich formative environment, one that presents a variety of opportunities for hands-on exploration, creativity, and problem solving, "fertilizes" the growing brain, resulting in one that is healthier, more adaptable, and more intelligent.[11] A primary feature of good brain health is the ability on the part of a child, by age five, to stay focused on an age-appropriate task for whatever length of time it takes to finish it. Good brain health is a birthright, Healy says, not a matter of genetic luck. The fact that more and more school-age children are having problems sustaining attention and focusing on age-appropriate tasks implicates deficiencies in their environments. More specifically, since children in the not-so-distant past had relatively little difficulty in this area, the short attention span epidemic implicates a deficiency or deficiencies in the typical childhood environment that is unique to recent history. Without doubt, the most glaring difference between the environment of a young child fifty years ago and the environment of today's child is the prominence of electronic media—television, video games, and computers. Despite the dismissiveness of the ADHD Establishment, the possibility that electronic media are playing a primary role in the development of ADHD symptoms is worth serious consideration. In fact, recent research has elevated that possibility to the level of certainty.

One finding involves the connection between attention span and self-control. In keeping with the second of my original hypotheses, researchers have found that a short attention span and impulsivity go hand in hand.[12] In this regard, it's interesting to note that the DSM-IV identifies three distinct types of ADHD: one characterized primarily by inattention, another characterized primarily by impulsivity, and a third type in which inattention and impulsivity are equally prominent.[13] It now appears that these are not different types at all. Instead, whether an ADHD child seems primarily inattentive, primarily impulsive, or both, his problems begin with a short attention span.

As regards brain development, it's important to realize that the brain of a newborn child possesses all of the neurons it's ever going to have. As the child interacts with the environment, neural pathways begin to develop that connect and allow for the flow of information between different sectors of the brain. The more information that flows along a certain neural pathway and between brain sectors, the stronger that pathway and the more robust and resilient those sectors become. As the child grows, pathways begin to intersect and the brain—effectively, a biocomputer—begins to assign tasks to those parts of itself that can most effectively handle them. "Such efficiency," says Healy, "is developed only by *active practice in thinking and learning* which, in turn, builds increasingly stronger connections."[14] Television watching does not provide or involve active practice at anything. It is not even an *activity* by any stretch of the term; it is a *passivity* and therefore adverse to the needs of the growing brain. Allowing a growing child to watch television is to put a stumbling block in the path of the development of the most important organ in the child's body. In television's early days, people intuitively recognized this and dubbed it the "boob tube" and the "idiot box."

Consider that the average American child has watched more than five thousand hours of television before coming to kindergarten! That's roughly one-fifth of his or her waking time during those critical formative preschool years, meaning that television has become a primary environment for the American child. Add in the time preschoolers are now spending playing video and computer games and that fraction goes up to nearly one-fourth. These are not natural environments at all; they are not "normal" in any but the statistical sense of the term. They do not involve exploration, creativity, language, social interaction, or thoughtfulness—the growing brain's essential fertilizing ingredients. The question, therefore, is no longer *whether* electronic media are interfering with normal brain development, but to what degree.

Until recently, the ADHD/television link was speculative, but those days are behind us. A 2004 study published in the esteemed journal

Pediatrics found that each hour of television watched on average per day between the first and fourth birthdays increased by nearly 10 percent the risk of serious attention problems at age seven.[15] Dr. Dimitri Christakis of Children's Hospital in Seattle points out that because most programs watched by children—including supposedly "good" children's programs—jump unpredictably and hyperactively from one perspective, scene, and time frame to another, what's known as the "orienting response" is in a constant state of alert. The orienting response is activated whenever a person—for our purposes, a child—suddenly sees something unfamiliar. This would occur when a child watching television suddenly is confronted by dancing animals, a camera zoom, a sudden change of scene or perspective, and so on. The novelty of the event or thing will cause the child to focus intently until he understands what is happening. Christakis believes that continued exposure to high-paced, unrealistic action sequences on television conditions a child's brain to that level of stimulation. (The authors think it is reasonable to assume that the same sort of conditioning takes place in response to video games. In this regard, researchers at the National Institute of Mental Health speculate that large amounts of television and video games "may promote development of brain systems that scan and shift attention at the expense of those that focus it."[16] In other words, electronic media may well strengthen the orienting response at the expense of attention span.)

Christakis doesn't use the term, but his research strongly suggests that television's constant activation of the orienting response is every bit as addictive as a drug like cocaine. A child conditioned to a high level of stimulation will strive to maintain it. He will become preoccupied and even obsessed with watching television and playing video games (commonly reported to us by parents of children displaying ADHD behaviors). Without the "calming" effect of electronics, his behavior will take on features that also characterize a drug addict in need of a fix. He will appear driven, hyperactive, purposeless, and impulsive (symptomatic of

ADHD); he will resist and even openly defy attempts to limit or direct his behavior (symptomatic of ODD); and he will become agitated to the point of explosiveness when he doesn't get what he wants (symptomatic of EOBD).

Within the fixed boundary of a classroom, we can reasonably predict that this child will be either a behavior problem or frequently inattentive and "off task" (or both). If he's an extrovert, he will be disruptive. If he's an introvert, he will often look like he's "off in his own little world." In either case, he will lose his place during reading exercises, fail to finish class assignments, and not seem to know what's being discussed when he's called upon.

Eventually, his teachers tell his parents (who, remember, are having their share of problems with him at home) they think he has ADHD and give them the name of a psychologist who has built a reputation diagnosing and "treating" children who supposedly have this false disorder. After administering a very expensive but largely superfluous battery of tests, the psychologist tells the parents that the teachers' suspicions were on target. He asks the child's pediatrician or a psychiatrist to start him on an attention-stimulating drug and begins seeing parents and/or child in regular therapy sessions during which the issue of the child's preoccupation with television and video games is probably never discussed.

Christakis's research is borne out by a growing body of testimonies from parents who have seen the light and turned off the television. On my website, I answer questions from parents and stay in touch with many of the parents I counsel through this venue. Over the years that I have provided this service, quite a number of parents have shared stories of children diagnosed with ADHD or identified by teachers as candidates for diagnosis whose behavior and school performance improved quickly and dramatically when television and video games were removed from their lives. In almost every case, these kids are described as going through a period of withdrawal during which they exhibit predictable symptoms:

moodiness, irritability, obsessing about watching television (getting a fix). Typically, and depending on the age of the child and the strength of the addiction, after a withdrawal period of one to three weeks, parents begin seeing the signs of recovery, and within two or three months the child is better behaved at home and doing much better academically in school.

The experience my wife and I had with our son, Eric, parallels these accounts. Midway through the third grade (1977–78), Eric's teacher described him as disruptive, inattentive, and unfocused. She had to virtually stand over him, she said, to get him to finish his work. In addition, he was a behavior problem in class, unable to tolerate losing in playground games, and equally unable to admit that anything he did was wrong. She was already recommending, in January, that Eric be retained. This came as no real surprise to my wife and me, as Eric was a major handful for us as well—oppositional, petulant, and still prone to major tantrums when he didn't get his way. In short, Eric was a textbook case of ADHD, ODD, and EOBD.

Three months later, an amazed teacher reported what she called a "miracle." Eric was now one of the best-behaved children in the class, he never failed to finish work on time, and his reading skills had increased one grade level in three months. He finished the year in fine form and was promoted to the fourth grade, where his improvement continued. Needless to say, no drugs were involved in Eric's turnaround. My wife, Willie, and I attribute it to two primary changes we made in our household: (1) we began parenting according to the traditional model w' learned as children (but rejected as young parents) and (2) we completel' removed television from our children's lives. For five years, Eric and Ar watched virtually no television at all. When it was reintroduced, a stric limit of no more than five preapproved hours a week was enforced. Other than occasional minor infractions or slips, Eric never had any other school problems. Today, he's a respected corporate pilot, and he and his wife, Nancy, and their four well-mannered boys live three miles from us.

These stories represent the good news. Because of the brain's plasticity—its ability to actually "rewire" itself in response to features of the environment (for better *and* worse)—which is greatest during the first twelve years of life, a child whose attention span has been disabled by electronic media can recover fairly quickly. The story of Eric and many other testimonies from parents of children whose attention spans rebounded after electronic media were eliminated from their lives attest to that. So an attention span lost is not necessarily lost forever.

The problem is that the drugs used to treat what's known as ADHD will bring about a significant improvement in attention span within thirty minutes, an improvement that lasts three to twelve hours depending on the type of drug administered, whereas it takes the brain of a school-age child two or three months following the elimination of electronic media to recover an adequate attention span. Even though the latter approach makes infinitely more sense, the fact that the drugs provide instant gratification seduces many parents into subscribing to them. In a very real sense, the almost immediate relief obtained causes the parents themselves to become "addicted" to giving their kids these medications (as described in chapter 5).

Some years later, I wrote a column in which I recounted our experience with Eric and reiterated my belief that television is a major culprit in the growing ADHD epidemic. I subsequently received a letter from the president of CHADD, who said that if proper discipline and no television cured Eric of ADHD, then he didn't have it in the first place. ADHD, she said, was a neurobiological disorder that required medical treatment, as in drugs. This sort of circular reasoning—only drugs cure ADHD; therefore, a person who meets DSM criteria for ADHD but is cured without drugs didn't really have ADHD—is the refuge of people who are living in a house of cards. This is analogous to claiming that only drugs can cure pneumonia; therefore, a person who survives a medically verified episode of pneumonia without drugs didn't have pneumonia to begin with. Similarly, a leading member of the ADHD Establishment once told me during a phone conversation that watching too much television could cause children to develop behaviors that mimicked ADHD; nonetheless, these kids don't have "real" ADHD. I'm certain the fellow did not feel himself being hoisted on his own petard. If a child exhibits a sufficient number of ADHD symptoms as listed in the DSM but doesn't *really* have ADHD, then what good are the DSM criteria? Answer: they are worthless. Furthermore, if one child who qualifies for the ADHD diagnosis doesn't *really* have ADHD, that calls into question whether any child so diagnosed *really* has ADHD.

In a 1980 study of half a million school-age children, the California Department of Education found that the more time a child spent watching TV, the lower his test scores regardless of IQ, social background, or study habits.[17] Since then one study after another, including a follow-up study by Christakis, has found that television watching is associated with underachievement. Ask any teacher what single behavior makes the critical difference between a student whose classroom achievement is commensurate with his or her IQ and a child who is a consistent underachiever and the answer will be "paying attention in class."

Christakis's research is also corroborated by cross-cultural findings. Interestingly enough, one does not have to leave America to find a culture that eschews electronic media: the Amish, who are well known for their rejection of most modern indulgences. In Amish communities, ADHD is virtually nonexistent. One 1999 study found that among two hundred Amish children followed prospectively and compared with the population at large, symptoms of ADHD and ODD were highly unusual.[18] Indiana pediatrician Michael Ruff is a member of a small-group private practice that serves more than eight hundred Amish families. In a 2005 article published in the journal *Clinical Pediatrics*, he reported that "not a single child in this group has been referred to us by the schools for evaluation or recognized by us as having [ADHD]."[19]

Considering that the average number of children born to an Amish couple is seven, that's remarkable. Even if the pediatricians in Ruff's practice have only seen, on average, three of those seven children per family, that's not one case of ADHD in 2,500 children. The ADHD Establishment says there ought to be between 75 and 250 ADHD kids in that population. The only thing that can account for the difference between the non-prevalence of ADHD among the Amish and its prevalence in the world at large is lifestyle. Notable in this regard is the fact that Amish children grow up with next to zero exposure to televisions or video games. Amish also adhere to traditional, biblically based child-rearing practices. From an early age, Amish children are expected to perform physically demanding chores and entertain themselves. If the weather permits, they play outdoors, as did almost all American children in the pre-ADHD age. As Ruff points out, both physical chores and active outdoor play promote attention span. The ADHD Establishment would be hard-pressed to explain how, of all the American cultural groups that share a common European heritage, only the Amish have managed to not become infected with the elusive ADHD gene.

It should not be surprising that evidence to the effect that electronic media can bring on ADHD symptoms, however compelling, does not impress members of the ADHD Establishment. In March 2008, one could still find the following statement on Russell Barkley's website: "Research has not supported popularly held views that ADHD results from . . . excessive viewing of television or poor child management by parents."[20]

Commenting specifically on Christakis's findings, Dr. David Rabiner of Duke University said, "At this point, there's a compelling body of evidence that suggests that it's genetics that plays the biggest role in ADHD, not bad parenting."[21] Since 1997, Rabiner has published a newsletter, "Attention Research Update," that promises to "provide parents, educators, and health care professionals with a convenient and economical source to stay informed about the latest research on ADHD."[22] He is a past member of the professional advisory board of CHADD. On his website, he promotes the use of medication in the treatment of ADHD, saying that according to numerous studies ". . . stimulant medication provides significant benefit to between 70 and 80% of children [with ADHD]."[23] In other words, he is a bona fide member of the ADHD Establishment. For prominent members of the Establishment to deny that a growing body of evidence is linking television and other electronic media to ADHD symptoms suggests that they have blinders on with respect to any evidence that runs contrary to a medical model of ADHD. On the one hand, it's fine for them to believe ADHD can be explained medically. On the other hand, their objectivity is called to question when they dismiss evidence that might refute their point of view.

NUTRITION AND DIET

Although the role of nutritional and dietary factors is downplayed, even ridiculed in mainstream ADHD circles, too many parents attest to certain foods bringing about profound changes in their children's behavior for diet to be ignored as a possible contributing factor, for some children at least. Establishment spokespeople characteristically dismiss such reports, explaining away the differences parents plainly see as "not supported by research." They mean *their* research, which is designed and interpreted so as to support *their* point of view. In fact, as is the case concerning electronic media, a growing body of evidence strongly suggests that diet does affect how the brain works; therefore, it follows that nutrition must affect behavior. For example:

- Researchers at Purdue University found significant
  improvement in children with inattention, hyperactivity, and

other disruptive behaviors after their diets were supplemented by essential fatty acids (EFAs).[24]

- Over the past twenty years, one expert in nutritional medicine claims to have successfully managed *hundreds* of ADHD children without medication.[25] On his website, he makes available a user-friendly survey with which parents can assess the degree to which diet might be a factor in their children's ADHD behaviors, along with specific recommendations for diet therapy.

- In England, a researcher found significant positive behavioral and learning effects as a result of administering omega-3 fatty acids to disruptive, inattentive children.[26] Although the children in the study did not have a formal ADHD diagnosis, 31 percent of them would have qualified according to DSM criteria. After three months of treatment, 44 percent of these children no longer qualified as compared with only 6 percent in a placebo group. Furthermore, the benefit of this nutritional intervention over six months compares favorably with improvement obtained from methylphenidate. In addition, the effects from omega-3 are found to be longer-lasting.[27] Needless to say, omega-3 is far cheaper than prescription medication.

- A study of children in Australia with ADHD-related learning and behavioral problems compared the effects of an EFA supplement with those obtained from a placebo. The supplemented group made significant gains in behavior and attention over the placebo group.[28]

- A study found significant improvement in behaviors defining ADHD and ODD following eight weeks of daily supplementation with a high dose of two important omega-3 fatty acids, EFA, and DHA concentrates.[29]

The most famous dietary approach to the treatment of ADHD behavior is the Feingold Diet, developed by allergist and pediatrician Dr. Benjamin Feingold (1899–1982). After serving as chief of pediatrics at Cedars of Lebanon Hospital in Los Angeles, Feingold established a number of allergy centers for Kaiser-Permanente and served as the chief of allergy at the Kaiser-Permanente Medical Center in San Francisco. He is not, as some in the ADHD Establishment have implied, a maverick operating on the fringe of medical science.

Feingold began exploring diet-based therapy in 1956, having noted that eliminating certain food colorings and preservatives not only eliminated allergic symptoms in certain patients but also brought about positive changes in behavior and mood. He named his regimen the K-P Diet, for his employer. Later, when Feingold's dietary prescription became well-known as a means of treating hyperactive and learning disabled children, the media gave it its popular name.

Initially, Feingold eliminated artificial food colorings and flavorings from the diets of hyperactive children who had not responded well to drug therapy. He found that one-third of children on the K-P Diet improved significantly and one-third improved slightly, with the other one-third showing no improvement at all. When he began eliminating the preservatives BHA and BHT, however, his success rate jumped to over 70 percent. After eight years of research involving hundreds of children, Feingold presented his data to the 1973 annual conference of the American Medical Association. Shortly thereafter, a group calling itself the Nutrition Foundation published statements claiming that Feingold's approach lacked valid scientific support. The general public was unaware that the Foundation's membership included Dow Chemical, Coca Cola, and other companies who made, used, and distributed the additives Feingold was targeting. In their zeal to discredit Feingold and his work, NF subsequently funded several research studies designed to "prove" what it wanted the public to believe—that Feingold's approach was worthless. A 1983 review of these studies published in the *Journal of the American Dietetic Association* concluded that Feingold's claims were overblown and that there was no need for further research into the possible effect of artificial additives on behavior and no need for improvements in food labeling.[30] Around that same time, however, toxicologist Bernard Weiss and autism expert Bernard Rimland published studies favorable to Feingold's methods in the *Journal of the American Academy of Child Psychiatry*[31] and the *Journal of Learning Disabilities*,[32] respectively. The controversy has since settled down, but research continues to explore the efficacy of Feingold's approach, and there is growing reason to believe that Feingold was onto something of value.

In 2004, for example, researchers analyzed fifteen ideally structured trials that studied the impact of artificial food colorings (AFC) on hyperactivity. Their data and methodological review confirmed that AFCs have a significant effect on behavior and concluded that "this study is consistent with the accumulating evidence that neurobehavioral toxicity may characterize a variety of widely distributed chemicals."[33]

Perhaps the most convincing evidence in favor of Feingold's approach are the testimonies from tens of thousands of parents who claim that what is now called the Feingold Program brought about dramatic improvements in their ADHD children's behavior; in many cases, improvements that were far better and more long-lasting than those resulting from medication. Although these parent reports are dismissed by the ADHD Establishment as nonscientific, the issue boils down to one fundamental question: why would these parents lie?

Although the majority of published studies concerning the effect of sugar on children's ADHD behaviors or learning do not support the idea that sucrose causes major, ongoing behavior problems, one group of researchers has discovered that a significant sugar load can lead to hyperactivity and impaired learning.[34] In the most ambitious study of this nature ever performed, the academic performance of more than a million

New York City school-age children was studied from 1978 to 1986. Average standardized test scores rose 8 percent when sugar was restricted and two synthetic food coloring agents were removed from their diets.[35]

On his website, Russell Barkley states unequivocally that diet and nutrition treatments "do not have a sound scientific basis" and "have been disproven in research."[36] As we've seen, that's not exactly the case. As with the electronic media–ADHD link, the Establishment is reluctant to admit the possibility that inexpensive nutritional therapy (which can be managed by parents) may offer significant long-term advantages over very expensive pharmaceutical therapy (which requires ongoing professional oversight and management).

WE'RE NOT BLAMING PARENTS . . . WE'RE *EMPOWERING* THEM

It's very simple, really. If the behaviors that define ADHD, ODD, and EOBD are a function of biology, then diagnosis and treatment rightly belong to the medical profession and its allies in psychology and the pharmaceutical industry. If, on the other hand, those problem behaviors result from endemic parenting dysfunctions, formative environments that are saturated with electronic media, and poor nutrition, then parents can correct them without the help of doctors, psychologists, and drugs. That's very threatening to the ADHD powers-that-be. No wonder they exaggerate the significance of research that seems to confirm their point of view. No wonder they dismiss and deny the significance of research that clearly disconfirms their point of view. Their problem is that they've built a house of pseudoscientific cards that's not going to stand much longer.

In *The Myth of the A.D.D. Child*, psychologist Thomas Armstrong writes, "[ADHD] appears to exist largely because of a unique coming together of the interests of frustrated parents, a highly developed psycho-pharmacological technology, a new cognitive research paradigm, a growth industry in new educational products, and a group of professionals [teachers, doctors and psychologists] eager to introduce them to each other." He calls ADHD a myth and says that with close inspection "we discover that—as with the disappearing Cheshire cat in Lewis Carroll's classic children's tale—all we're really left with in the end is the smile, if that."[37]

RECOMMENDED READING

For more on the psychological parenting revolution that swept America in the late 1960s and early 1970s and its effects on the behavior of parents and children, we recommend:

Rosemond, John. *Parenting by The Book*. West Monroe, LA: Howard, 2007.

For more on the ill-effects of electronic media on the cognitive and behavioral health of children:

Healy, Jane, EdD. *Endangered Minds: Why Children Don't Think and What We Can Do About It*. New York: Simon & Schuster, 1999.

Healy, Jane, EdD. *Failure to Connect: How Computers Affect Our Children's Minds—For Better and Worse*. New York: Simon & Schuster, 1998.

Postman, Neil. *The Disappearance of Childhood*. New York: Vintage, 1994.

Winn, Marie. *The Plug-In Drug: Television, Computers, and Family Life* (25th Anniversary Edition). New York: Penguin, 2002.

For more on the connection between ADHD behaviors and nutrition:

Bell, Rachel, and Howard Peiper. *The A.D.D. and A.D.H.D. Diet! A Comprehensive Look at Contributing Factors and Natural Treatments for Symptoms of Attention Deficit Disorder and Hyperactivity.* Sheffield, MA: Safe Goods Publishing, 1998.

Feingold, B. F. *The Feingold Cookbook for Hyperactive Children.* New York: Random House, 1979.

Feingold, B. F. *Why Your Child Is Hyperactive.* New York: Random House, 1985.

Stevens, Laura. *12 Effective Ways to Help Your ADD/ADHD Child: Drug-Free Alternatives for Attention-Deficit Disorders.* New York: Avery, 2000.

CHAPTER 7

WHY JOHNNY CAN'T SIT STILL, PAY ATTENTION, DO WHAT HE'S TOLD, AND LEARN TO READ

SEA CHANGES IN EDUCATIONAL POLICY AND PRACTICES TOOK PLACE in the United States in the twentieth century. Making education a publicly funded mandate and requiring parents to enroll their children in school and keep them there until midadolescence produced a number of profound societal shifts. These included extending the various benefits and advantages of an education to expanding segments of the population, most significantly the underclass. After government (public) education became universal, illiteracy rates dropped dramatically for several decades. Interestingly enough, however, illiteracy has been rising since the 1940s, coincident with significant changes in how reading is taught in most American schools, public and private. Not coincidentally, as illiteracy rates have risen, so too has the incidence of inattention, distractibility, and hyperactivity in children.

WHOLE LANGUAGE AND RISING ILLITERACY

In 1930, the Bureau of the Census documented an illiteracy rate of 4.7 percent among persons fourteen years of age and older. This represented a dramatic decrease from rates in preceding decades. By 1947, the illiteracy rate had dropped to 2.7 percent, but a large part of this apparent decrease was attributable to the gradual dying off of an older generation that had not received the full benefit of public education and in which, therefore, illiteracy was more common.[1] Up until the 1950s, most American schools used a phonics-based approach to reading instruction. Children were taught to read by first learning the sounds of each letter of the alphabet, then learning how those sounds blended into syllables, and finally learning how those syllables combined into words.[2] But that was about to change.

In the 1930s, progressive professors of education at Harvard and Columbia declared that phonics, involving as it did the rote memorization of sounds and symbols, was inefficient drudgery. They claimed children could learn to read as naturally as they learned to talk, if taught to peruse whole words in context. This so-called whole-language philosophy was the basis of the Dick and Jane readers that gradually began to replace the traditional McGuffey series. The whole-language movement generated tremendous controversy and was attacked in the 1950s by Rudolph Flesch in *Why Johnny Can't Read*.[3] Notwithstanding the growing evidence that reading problems and illiteracy were on the rise, whole language was steadfastly defended by mainstream educators as well as the International Reading Association. Reading "experts" of the time went into a collective state of denial as literacy levels began to steadily slip following World War II, and many children who did learn to read struggled in their efforts.

The new approach—also known as "holistic" instruction—gained considerable traction after the war years, and by the 1960s, the whole-language revolution had succeeded at replacing phonics instruction in America's schools. Illiteracy rates have steadily risen ever since. By 1966, forty-two million adult Americans could not read at a functional level; this in spite of a huge commitment of taxes for literacy-related programs, numbering seventy-nine administered by fourteen federal agencies.

Robert Sweet Jr., cofounder and former president of The National Right to Read Foundation, points out that prior to whole-language instruction, teachers did not even think there was such a thing as a child of reasonable intelligence who could not be taught to read.[4] Indeed, until the shift to whole-language instruction, remedial reading classes were rare.

The correlation between wholesale changes in reading instruction and the epidemic rise of reading problems since 1950 strongly suggests that the former has contributed to, if not caused, the latter. In fact, researchers have recently discovered that problem readers, when individually tutored in phonics, make substantial gains over children tutored using whole language. Furthermore, it has been established that phonics-based instruction enriches and strengthens the brain's reading pathways. It also appears that the ability to recognize whole words is the *consequence* of first being able to decipher them phonetically.[5] In other words, whole-language instruction bypasses an essential step in reading skills. It's a prime example of putting the cart in front of the horse.

In the meantime, phonics received a boost when a study sponsored by the National Institute of Child Health & Human Development (NICHHD) at the University of Houston contended that not only did phonics work, it was the best way to teach reading. In June 1996, *Forbes* called the findings "a slap in the face of the education establishment." The magazine reported that in California, where the whole-language approach had enjoyed a long history in public schools, parents "were shocked by recent test results that placed their kids last among the nation's students, tied with Louisiana."[6]

Reid Lyon, a specialist in reading and language with NICHHD, says that recent scientific evidence clearly shows poor readers need to be remediated using phonics-based instruction.[7] The authors contend that if phonetic instruction is the most appropriate approach with poor readers, it is logical to propose that phonics is the most appropriate approach for *all* children.

The bottom line: whole language is a shortcut teaching method that is producing problem readers, and as we will see, students who have trouble reading also tend to have attention and behavior problems and are often "diagnosed" with ADHD. Ironically and absurdly, most public schools respond to this problem by providing problem readers with remediation based substantially on the whole-language method. Not surprisingly, reading problems are becoming increasingly commonplace. Although scientific support of phonics-based instruction is overwhelming, America's public schools show no sign of changing their dysfunctional approach. This dysfunction stems back to university teacher-education programs that train future teachers in whole-language instruction, meaning that very few of today's reading teachers even know how to teach phonics (compounded further by the fact that most of today's teachers, as children, were taught to read with the whole-language approach). Topping things off, there's the antiphonics propaganda disseminated by the National Education Association.

The NEA, the lobby that provides the drumbeat for many, if not most, current education practices, cleverly waffles on the issue of phonics versus whole language. One of their spokespersons says that "effective" teachers recognize that phonics is a "useful tool" for teaching reading but are also "aware of the dangers of overreliance on one method of word recognition."[8] Note the subtle implication that teachers who teach reading according to the scientifically validated phonics method are not effective. One might also ask what danger phonics poses to children when, according to one research team, brain-imaging studies show that the brain's reading pathways are substantially normalized through intensive phonics instruction.[9] Said NEA spokesperson cleverly sidesteps the issue by not defining the nature of the danger in question. This is nothing but demagoguery and reveals that America's public education bureaucracy is resistant to what is clearly in the best interest of America's kids. Why? Because phonics-based instruction would solve problems (and, as we will see, not just reading problems, but attention and behavior problems as well), and in so doing, would require the total overhaul of an education system that is currently being rewarded for inefficiency.

A significant portion of today's education dollar goes to support remedial reading instruction, provided in various forms and through various programs. Those funds not only provide jobs for teachers but administrators as well. Solving America's reading problems would mean public schools would need fewer administrators, fewer special education teachers, fewer regular classroom teachers (fewer problem readers would mean the teacher-pupil ratio could increase significantly), fewer classrooms, smaller buildings, and therefore a whole lot less taxpayer money than is currently being allocated for public education in federal and state budgets. That prospect is the Education Establishment's worst nightmare. Therefore, the "danger" that phonics poses is not to America's children, but to education bureaucrats.

THE NEA: HOOKED ON WHOLE LANGUAGE

In the mid-1980s, entrepreneur John M. Stranahan investigated the problems his son was having learning to read and discovered that the school his son attended was using whole language rather than the phonics approach he'd been taught as a child. Deciding to take matters into his own hands, Shanahan created a phonics study tape for his son, and in no time the boy was on par with his classmates. Shanahan recognized a business opportunity and in 1986 started Gateway Educational Products in Orange, California, to market "Hooked on Phonics."

In its first full year of operation, Gateway generated $100,000 in revenues. That number began growing by leaps and bounds as Shanahan began advertising heavily on radio and television. In 1991, the company's total radio and television budget topped $41 million. In 1992, Gateway began producing thirty-minute infomercials and within no time, "Hooked on Phonics" was a household name. By 1994, the company's total annual revenues had reached $150 million.

As his business boomed, Stranahan made improvements to "Hooked on Phonics" and brought out a number of new products including "Hooked on Math," the "Hooked on Phonics Writing Kit," an audio-driven program to introduce children to the classics, a "We the People" history and civics program, and foreign language programs. In addition, Shanahan established the Gateway Prison Literacy project to teach reading to California prison inmates, most of whom were illiterate. But trouble lay ahead for this successful, civic-minded entrepreneur. According to an article published in *Success* magazine ". . . his success earned Shanahan some powerful enemies in the education establishment," most notably the National Education Association, a reliable supporter of the Democratic Party."[10] (Between 1990 and 2002, nearly 95 percent of NEA's political contributions went to support Democratic candidates. According to the Center for Public Integrity, the NEA gave almost all of its campaign contributions during election year 2003–2004 to Democratic Party committees.[11]) Simply, the success of "Hooked on Phonics" raised the distinct possibility that American parents would begin to see through the whole-language fiasco and demand a return to phonics-based instruction.

The authors of the *Success* article suggest that the NEA may have complained to the Clinton administration, which, in turn, asked the Federal Trade Commission to begin investigating Gateway's products and advertising. Ultimately, the FTC claimed that Gateway did not provide statistical evidence to back their claims concerning "Hooked on Phonics." In 1994, Shanahan agreed to a consent order stipulating that his advertising could no longer make claims that were not supported by scientific evidence (notwithstanding that the reading method used by today's public schools is not supported by scientific evidence!). Absent from the consent order was any admission of wrongdoing, and the FTC did not levy a fine against the company. Both Gateway and the FTC agreed to not discuss the details of the order.

On the eve of the FTC announcement of the agreement in December 1994, *Dateline NBC* aired a segment that promised "the real story behind 'Hooked On Phonics.'" According to *Success*, the FTC had violated the agreement not to discuss the resolution of its investigation. Moreover, *Dateline* maintained that the FTC had charged Gateway with deceptive and misleading advertising, a mischaracterization that was then repeated by other news outlets.

The fallout was immediate and devastating as many "Hooked on Phonics" customers began to return their products. Many people, especially conservative politicians, saw the affair as an attack on home-based education. Although the backlash forced an FTC spokesperson to announce that the agency challenged the basis for Gateway's advertising *claims* and not for the product itself, the admission offered cold comfort for Shanahan, whose business was rapidly drying up. He ultimately sold Gateway to a venture capital group, who sold it again. Today, "Hooked on Phonics," largely due to partnerships with Wal-Mart and Sylvan Learning Centers, is again becoming a player in the educational products marketplace.

PUSHING ACADEMIC INSTRUCTION DOWN

Another policy response to America's reading problems has been to push reading instruction down from first grade, where it was traditionally introduced, to kindergarten and even before. What is commonly termed the "push-down curriculum" has gradually forced out "softer" subjects and activities such as arts, music, gym, and recess as elementary schools succumb to ever-increasing pressure to achieve higher scores on standardized testing.

As was the case with both authors, many children in the 1940s and 1950s came to first grade not knowing their ABCs. Notwithstanding, first-grade graduates in both decades were reading at a level that is significantly higher than is the case for today's first-graders (when other variables, such as parent education level, are held constant), and yet many if not most of today's kids come to first grade—even kindergarten—knowing their ABCs and already possessing fundamental reading skills. Obviously, the push-down curriculum isn't working and, as is the case with whole language, may well be adding to the problem. Even a program as highly touted as Head Start has consistently failed to demonstrate any long-term academic benefits. Whereas Head Start graduates do indeed enter kindergarten slightly ahead of kids of equivalent background who haven't attended Head Start, within a few years both groups are performing at the same level.[12]

Commenting on the push-down trend, psychologist and author David Elkind (*The Hurried Child*) points out that it was driven by a simplistic mind-set: if America's kids are having reading problems, and many children entering first grade have not acquired basic reading skills, then teaching reading before first grade would solve the problem.[13] But pushing down the curriculum has failed to solve anything. Furthermore, the push-down curriculum is probably making the problem worse by expecting of very young children what their brains are not ready to handle. Says Elkind: "[The push-down curriculum] doesn't make sense from what we know about human development. We are biological beings who grow in stages, able to do some things at some ages and not at others."[14]

South African education expert Dr. Jan Strydom has developed a remedial program, "Audiblox," that has been highly successful in helping children overcome learning disabilities. The program, described in his book, *The Right to Read* (coauthored with his daughter, Susan du Plessis), is based on the simple, intuitive premise that effective learning depends upon certain foundational skills and concepts. When, as is the case with whole language and the push-down curriculum, learning is expected of a child who has not developed the prerequisite foundations, the child's natural "learning schema" is disrupted, often resulting in learning disabilities. In other words, most children who fail to learn to read adequately have never been taught the basic foundational skills upon which the ability to read must be built. Strydom also insists that effective learning of any new subject area initially requires repetitious drill (e.g., the flash-card approach to learning such things as phonetic sounds and multiplication tables), yet another traditional education practice that progressive educators have all but forced out of America's schools.

Along these same lines, in a position statement adopted in 1990 and revised in 1995, the National Association for the Education of Young Children had this to say:

> Today, not only do many kindergartens and primary grades focus on skill acquisition in the absence of meaningful context, but the expectations that are placed on children are often not age-appropriate. Whether the result of parental pressures or the push to improve student performance on standardized tests, curriculum expectations of older children have been pushed down to earlier grades. *Children entering kindergarten are now typically expected to be ready for what previously constituted the first grade curriculum. As a result, more children are struggling and failing.*[15] (Copyright held by the National Association for the Education of Young Children)

A major part of the rationale behind the push-down curriculum is the growing gap between U.S. student achievement and student achievement in other industrialized countries. Ironically, however, in countries like France, Germany, and Japan, where a traditional, nonacademic kindergarten curriculum has been retained, students consistently outpace American students in all academic areas. In Finland, where student achievement outstrips that of American children at all grade levels, reading instruction does not begin until age seven. Those same countries, furthermore, are not dealing with epidemics of reading disabilities and ADHD.[16]

THE MISEDUCATION OF AMERICA'S CHILDREN

The accumulating evidence strongly suggests that when young children are force-fed educational expectations for which they are not developmentally prepared, certain compensatory responses—including boredom, inattention, distractibility, and various task-avoidance strategies (including outright defiance and other behavior problems)—are predictable. These behavior problems, stemming from the miseducation of America's children, are directly linked to the "diseasing" of our children with ADHD and related "disorders."

The notion that dysfunctional teaching methods and developmentally inappropriate instruction are contributing to attention problems in young children is strengthened by the work of James Campbell, a practicing pediatrician in Fulton, New York. Dr. Campbell has worked extensively with children with reading problems, many of whom also fulfill DSM criteria for ADHD. He has found that by simply providing these kids with phonics-based tutoring, as reading skills improve, problems of attention and behavior diminish considerably, often to the point of insignificance.[17]

Research done by psychologist Gretchen LeFever further reinforces that introducing academic instruction premature to the establishment of certain essential developmental foundations can contribute to attention problems. In a population of students in Tidewater, Virginia, LeFever found that the youngest students in any elementary grade were the kids most likely to be identified as having ADHD. In one of the two communities she studied, an astonishing 62 percent of children who were young-for-grade were taking methylphenidate during school. Since an earlier study had found that 21 percent of students taking stimulant medication for ADHD did not take their medication during school, one can reasonably assume that more than 70 percent of all young-for-grade students in the community in question were being treated.[18]

Another researcher has discovered that children exposed to child-centered preschool programs that do not stress academics fared better when they got to elementary school than children who were in more academic preschools. The children in the former group displayed less school-related anxiety, were less dependent upon help from parents, and had more confidence in their abilities. Although not specific for behaviors comprising ADHD, these findings are consistent with the notion that younger children are more likely to fare well if formal, didactic instruction is delayed beyond preschool age.[19]

Developmental psychologist and university professor Rebecca Marcon conducted a similar study of economically disadvantaged minority children who had three different preschool (including kindergarten) experiences ranging from nonacademic (what she termed child-initiated) to academically driven. Consistent with Elkind's hypothesis, Marcon found that the children who attended child-centered, nonacademic preschools had the best outcomes by grade four, while children who had attended more didactic, teacher-centered preschools had the worst outcomes. Elementary teachers later rated the children from the latter group lower in conduct and work/study habits, and perceived them to be *more distractible, less willing to follow directions, and less prosocial.*[20] In other words, the more developmentally favorable the preschool environment, the less likely it is that a child will exhibit the behaviors associated with ADHD, ODD, and EOBD in elementary school.

Despite the evidence discussed above, there is little reason to expect wisdom to prevail in educational circles. University-based educational elites and professional "experts" appear unwavering in their commitment to educational practices that either fail to improve outcomes or contribute to adverse ones. A representative example is the North Carolina Standard Course of Study, which outlines educational requirements for all public schools in the state, one that prides itself on being on the cutting edge of education reform. Competency requirements proposed for NC *kindergarten* students include being able to identify and discuss common features and functions of computer software, knowledge and skills in the use of computers and other technologies, the ability to use graphing software to organize and display data, and the ability to demonstrate the use of standard units of measure as compared with nonstandard units of measure.[21]

Not only are such expectations for children in kindergarten unrealistic, the emphasis on computer learning indicates that educational policymakers in the proud state of North Carolina (and most other states) have no regard for research by the likes of Jane Healy (see chapter 6) that spells out the dangers to brain development and learning style posed by early exposure to computers. When it comes to new technologies, America's schools, with rare exception, public and private, have a "damn the torpedoes, full speed ahead!" mentality. Here we see a state education department *requiring* an educational experience that is certain to increase the number of inattentive and distractible children, as well as the number of children who develop significant reading problems. It's as if the research is in one universe, and America's schools are in another.

North Carolina also proposes to advance the academic achievement of at-risk four-year-olds through a program called More at Four. This voluntary pre-K program describes its mission as preparing "children for school success through high-quality early education."[22] Mind you, when preschool and kindergarten were places where children simply learned to play cooperatively, strengthening creative and social skills in the process, America's kids had fewer problems in elementary school when it came to either academics or behavior. Programs similar to More at Four are springing up across the U.S. At present, they are voluntary, but the authors propose that the intent is to eventually extend compulsory public education to children as young as three—an education the government has already proven itself ill-suited to provide.

CLASSROOM PRACTICES

In the late 1960s and early 1970s, American educators became infatuated with education experiments such as the Summerhill School in England, where students determined what they studied and set their own pace, the teacher-student relationship was egalitarian, and grades were nonexistent. By the mid-1970s, "open" schools modeled loosely after the Summerhill experiment were the rage in the U.S.

Open schools were, as the name implies, absent walls or any other clear boundaries between classrooms. Children could wander freely from one learning center to another, making their own choices as to what they learned. Instead of assigned seats, children sat where they chose, usually around tables where they could share what they were learning with one another. Theoretically, this autonomy would result in children discovering their natural strengths and experiencing education as a self-satisfying, even joyous, process. Education would become rewarding unto itself, and children so gratified would want to learn more and more.

Unfortunately, but predictably, after a waste of millions of taxpayer dollars, the experiment bombed. Children who attended open schools were found to lag significantly behind their peers in basic skills. By the early 1980s, most open schools had been retrofitted with walls and individual desks. Nonetheless, the experiment left an indelible mark on American education. In many of today's elementary classrooms, children sit at tables instead of desks and are allowed to engage at various learning stations in the classroom once their seatwork has been done. Grades have largely fallen out of favor in American education. Children are often rated based on individual instead of group standards. Furthermore, a child who performs poorly on a test is often given a second chance to do better. Teachers often see themselves as "facilitators" rather than instructors, and when they do teach, they are expected to do so with great appreciation for "individual differences." So, if Johnny would rather sit on the floor when he reads and does classwork, he is allowed to sit on the floor. These innovations have not invaded every public school in the country, but teachers who embrace these sorts of new methods regard themselves as elite and are increasingly looked to as role models by and for younger teachers.

Obviously, today's all-too-typical classroom is a place where the need to sit still and pay attention is not paramount. Why pay attention, for example, when you're going to be given a second chance anyway? And why pay attention in class when your mother is expected to reteach anything you didn't get the first time around?

PARENT INVOLVEMENT

In the late 1970s, educators became intrigued by the fact that Vietnamese children, two years after arriving in America with no command of English, were usually functioning close to if not at the top of their classes. Investigators discovered that homework was a group exercise in the Vietnamese home, involving parents, grandparents, aunts and uncles, and siblings. This was interpreted to mean that parent involvement in homework improved student achievement, and American parents were told to get involved. Apparently, no one thought to consider that a practice that was functional in one culture, under one set of circumstances, might not be functional in another culture, under other circumstances.

Today, the parent-involvement ethic is firmly entrenched in American education. Teachers routinely export teaching responsibilities to the home in the form of daily and weekly assignments that obligate parents to sit with their children nearly every evening, reteaching, helping with projects, making sure homework is completed (without blemish), and helping children study for tests. Especially in the lower elementary grades, teachers even send work home that children cannot possibly do on their own, virtually forcing parents (mothers, almost always) to become teachers-by-proxy. Under the circumstances, mothers are caught between the rock and the hard place. Even those who realize that children should not become dependent upon parental help where school achievement is concerned feel compelled to participate in these counterproductive exercises for two reasons, both having to do with fear:

1. Fear that if they don't, other children will begin to outperform their kids; ultimately, or so the apocalyptic prophecy goes, their children will be left hopelessly behind.
2. Fear that if they don't, they will be judged bad moms.

And thus the mental health of women is sacrificed on the altar of educational correctness. And thus children have one less reason to pay attention in class.

I often tell my audiences the story of the time my mother, a PhD research scientist, mathematician, and statistician, refused to help me with a math assignment, telling me that if she could figure it out when she was a child, I could too. In the face of my protests to the contrary, she held firm. Ultimately, I figured out the assignment on my own. The point of the story is that I survived this "rejection" and grew up to be a capable, competent human being. In fact, my mother's attitude of "you have to learn to paddle your own canoe" helped me to become resilient and tenacious, both of which will more than compensate for an IQ that is not in the "gifted" range.

Once, upon telling this story, a woman asked, "What if you hadn't figured it out? Would your mother have helped you then?"

"Probably not," I answered. "She was perfectly willing, as were most mothers of her generation and before, to let the chips of her child's strengths and weaknesses fall where they may."

"Oh, I could never do that!" the woman exclaimed.

This mother has submitted to the whip of involvement. She deems it her responsibility to make sure her child gets everything, that he develops exemplary abilities in every subject area. She will help her child with his homework every night, perhaps even through high school. And she will send to college a child who has no appreciation for his strengths versus his weaknesses and perhaps thinks he is good at everything. Not knowing he does not really possess any significant aptitude in math, he may register as a math major. One can imagine where the story goes from there.

This simply isn't fair. It isn't fair to lead children to become dependent upon their mothers for their school achievement (or anything else, really). It isn't fair to create in women the sense that the measure of a mom is her child's accomplishments. It isn't fair for America's schools to virtually force women to become enablers of their children. It isn't fair to create a situation that deprives children of full incentive to pay attention in class. It isn't fair to prevent children from learning how to paddle their own canoes and come to grips with the immutable fact that some paddle better than others, but if you try hard and long enough, you'll eventually find a stream that's suited to your skills.

FEEL-GOOD EDUCATION

Since its introduction into the Zeitgeist in the 1960s, high self-esteem has become the holy grail of American education. Current educational philosophy, founded on a fallacy, puts priority on teachers and schools doing everything in their power to make sure every child develops and maintains a "good feeling about himself" and enjoys an educational experience that is free from stress, frustration, and failure. To accomplish this touchy-feely goal, grades have become all but meaningless. From 1991 to 2001, high school grade-point averages climbed from 3.09 to 3.26 (out of a possible 4.0) even as achievement scores as measured by such tests as the SAT went down. The practice of grade inflation has impacted colleges as well. In school year 2000–2001, 51 percent of Harvard's undergraduates held A or A-minus averages.[23] It is irrefutable that one cannot become proficient at a task without honest, objective feedback, so it is not surprising that more and more employers are complaining that even college graduates come to the workplace lacking in fundamental writing, spelling, and math skills.

Maureen Stout, PhD, assistant professor of educational leadership at California State University, says the self-esteem movement has had a devastating effect on students. In *The Feel-Good Curriculum: The Dumbing Down of America's Kids in the Name of Self-Esteem*, Stout argues convincingly that a preoccupation with how students feel about themselves has turned schools into *quasi*-mental health clinics and teachers into counselors, creating a generation of children and young adults who are self-absorbed, arrogant, disrespectful of authority, and ignorant.[24] The problem begins in university teacher-training programs, where future teachers are brainwashed with an egalitarian philosophy that holds that effort, not achievement, is what counts and that every student ought to be evaluated according to a standard that is unique to him- or herself, based on an intuitive assessment of the child's ability level. Where behavior is concerned, "Don't do that because it is wrong" is replaced with "Don't do that because you will feel bad if you do." In other words, moral standards have been replaced with a pseudotherapeutic ethic in which the child's feelings become the final arbiter of right versus wrong. If Billy doesn't feel bad when he bullies Johnny (in fact, he feels good!), then why should he stop bullying Johnny?

Along this same line, a primary feature of the new therapeutic school philosophy is the New Age notion that children don't really *mean* to misbehave; rather, they do so only because they have either (1) "issues" they need to express and don't know how to go about doing so in functional ways or (2) brain-based psychiatric disorders over which they have no control. The former include boredom (the most often given reason for why gifted children misbehave in class), teacher-student personality conflicts, peer relationship problems, family problems, situational problems (e.g., death of a pet), or long-standing self-esteem issues (brought on by yet other unresolved issues). The psychiatric disorders in question are the subject of this book. Whether a child's misbehavior is caused by theoretical issues or fictitious disorders, the child is magically transformed from a perpetrator to a victim. Punishment, therefore, is out of the question.

The ubiquitous phrase "bad choices" reflects the new therapeutic philosophy. Instead of a child doing something bad, he has simply made a bad choice, as if whether one behaves well or not is a constant shell game in which one sometimes picks the right shell and sometimes not. If not, then again, the child is not punished. Instead, the child's teacher or counselor or principal talks to the child, explaining why the choice was a wrong one and how to pick the right shell next time. After gaining assurances from the child that he will never make the wrong choice again, he is released to go back to class or recess and make the wrong choice again. If despite numerous therapeutic sessions with teachers, counselors, and principals, the child continues to make bad choices, then he is usually assumed to have a disorder that prevents him from making good choices. At that point, he is referred to a specialist who will almost surely agree with the school's take and see to it that the child begins taking the "appropriate" medication so that he will stop making so many bad choices and begin developing better self-esteem. The problem, however, is that high self-esteem is highly associated with bad choices.

FEELING GOOD, ACTING BADLY

Beginning in the late 1960s, parenting writers such as psychologist Thomas Gordon (*Parent Effectiveness Training*) and family counselor Dorothy Briggs (*Your Child's Self-Esteem*) argued that children misbehaved, did poorly in school, and developed emotional problems because of low self-esteem. Both best-selling authors maintained that low self-esteem was endemic to America's kids because the traditional American family was adult-centered rather than child-centered and authoritarian rather than democratic. In *Teacher Effectiveness Training*, Gordon made the same charges concerning the American classroom. The antidote to the supposed epidemic of bad mental health (mind you, neither Gordon nor Briggs presented any objectively obtained hard evidence to support their contentions) was a revolution in American family and school culture. With self-appointed experts like Gordon and Briggs leading the charge, the revolution happened, and it failed miserably. It is interesting, to say the least, that every indicator of positive mental health in America's kids has been on the decline since 1970.

In *Learned Optimism*, Martin Seligman, PhD, professor of psychology at the University of Pennsylvania, proposes that three factors have converged to depress the mental health of America's children: rampant individualism; an erosion of faith and reliance on God, community, nation, and the large extended family; and the self-esteem movement.[25]

Social scientist Roy Baumeister has been studying the effect of self-esteem on behavior since the early 1990s. His research, without question the best in the field, finds that high self-esteem is associated with antisocial behavior. Self-esteem is unusually high, for example, among gang members and prison inmates. Baumeister refers to the widespread acceptance and promotion of high self-esteem by researchers, clinicians, teachers, and parents as an *"article of faith."*[26]

Research done by Baumeister and others strongly suggests that the goals of the post-1960s self-esteem movement have succeeded. Self-esteem in America is, generally speaking, high, certainly much higher than in countries like Korea and China that have adhered to a traditional ethic of humility and modesty (which, up until the psychological parenting revolution of the 1960s and '70s, were valued character traits in America as well). America's kids have higher self-esteem than children from nearly every other country.

Unfortunately, the promises of the self-esteem movement have not panned out. For example, the mental health of America's children has worsened considerably over the past forty years. The gurus of self-esteem promised that high self-esteem would improve school performance, yet academic achievement scores began going down in the 1960s and the downward trend, with occasional upticks, continues. It appears that people with high self-esteem believe that anything they do is worthy of merit; therefore, they consistently underperform. In the final analysis, and no matter how one looks at it, high self-esteem is not a desirable, functional attribute. It leads to antisocial behavior, disrespect of others, irresponsibility, low motivation, and underachievement. People with high self-esteem also have greater-than-normal problems dealing with frustration. Obstacles that cause a person with a well-moderated self concept to rise to the challenge often cause people with high self-esteem to give up.

A 2001 meta-analysis (review of all the published studies at the time) documents the failure of twenty years' worth of school programs designed specifically to increase child self-esteem. The researchers conclude with the following comment: "During the time that self-esteem has increased, few positive changes have occurred in children and young adults' behavior. Indeed, most of the relevant behavioral indicators have worsened. From the 1970s to the 1990s, SAT scores decreased, adolescent crime rates skyrocketed, teen suicide rates rose, and depression and anxiety increased."[27]

The postmodern, nontheistic religion of self-esteem has spawned a host of problems for America's children, many of which—low tolerance for frustration, demands for instant gratification, lack of respect for interpersonal boundaries, violent outbursts when denied, disrespect of authority, and mood swings from elation (when things are going one's way) to depression (when things are not)—connect directly to the diagnostic criteria for ADHD, ODD, and EOBD.

The typical institutional response to a child with already high self-esteem who is exhibiting one or more of the aforementioned "symptoms" in school is to send the child to a therapeutic program that—you guessed it!—attempts to raise his level of self-esteem. And around, and around, and around we go.

At this point, the reader has every right to ask, "So what's the solution?" That is the subject of the next two chapters.

PART 3

Empowering Parents to Take Back Control

CHAPTER 8
NIPPING "ADHD" IN THE BUD

As we've pointed out, the "symptoms" comprising ADHD, ODD, and EOBD are nothing more than a laundry list of typical toddler behavior. In a child between eighteen and thirty-six months, they are called the "terrible twos." In a child who has passed his or her third birthday, they are indications that toddlerhood has not been resolved and are therefore more accurately termed "toddlerhood in perpetuity" (TIP). Although the TIP child will certainly create disorder, he has no disorder—there's nothing "wrong" with him. Rather, he's in grave danger of becoming what people once called a spoiled brat.

If ADHD and its diagnostic offspring are manifestations of unresolved toddlerhood, the "terrible twos" ad infinitum, then parents should take action between a child's eighteenth and thirty-sixth month to prevent future disorder and to give their children the incomparable and priceless gift of emotional, cognitive, and behavioral health. Helping children develop that state of feeling right, thinking right, and behaving right is not rocket science. We already know how to do it because up until relatively recently, most children who came to first grade fit that description. They came to school having already learned good self-control; having already learned to pay close attention to and obey adult authority figures, complete assigned tasks, and do their best; and having already learned to behave with respect toward others. Yes, there were exceptions, but they were not significant enough in number to justify cultural angst, psychologists and social workers in schools, or prescriptive books on how to deal with them.

As a consequence of the psychological parenting revolution of the late 1960s and early 1970s, parents stopped doing what their elders had done to resolve the terrible twos before it became the even more terrible threes, fours, fives, and so on. The bad news is that barring a cultural earthquake, American parenting is never again going to resemble what the raising of children looked like fifty-plus years ago. Ah, but the good news is that any parents today who so choose can raise their kids in accord with the same principles their great-grandparents adhered to in raising theirs. The world is different, yes, but the principles are as valid today as they ever were. There are basically three:

1. The family is adult-centered, not child-centered.
2. From an early age, children are good citizens of their families, because that is where good citizenship begins.
3. Beyond their third birthdays, children are accountable and are expected to be responsible, but they are allowed to be children.

Here are fifteen practical things today's parents can begin doing when their children are two years old (or even, in some cases, slightly before) to translate those three simple principles into action. This is the only prescription parents will ever need to cure the "terribles" and set their children on the right track.

CREATE AN ADULT-CENTERED FAMILY

For the first two years or so of a child's life, it is necessary that the child be the center of his parents' attention. By age three, however, the parents should be the center of the child's attention. At this point, he needs to be paying more attention to them than they are paying to him. Between the second and third birthdays, it is imperative that parents assume the mantle of leadership and begin exercising a firm, loving authority.

Creating and maintaining an adult-centered family simply requires that the husband-wife relationship be more active than the relationship either parent is having with the child or children. Husband and wife have a weekly date night that doesn't include the kids. For every family vacation they take a marriage vacation of equal length. They talk to one another more than they talk to their kids. They do more for one another than they do for their kids.

If the family does not include a husband and a wife, then the single parent takes lots of time out for just herself or himself. She has more active relationships with other adults than she does with her children. She puts her kids to bed early so that she can enjoy time to herself in the evening. Because she is much more than simply their mother, she becomes a person of interest to her children. They pay attention to her. They want to know about her life.

When parents occupy the center of attention in the family, the children learn to pay attention to adults, and believe me, paying attention to adults will bring them more success in school than having high IQs. The most successful students are not those with the highest scores on intelligence tests; rather, they are the ones who best pay attention to their teachers.

EXPECT YOUR KIDS TO OBEY

The proper discipline of a child is not accomplished by manipulating reward and punishment. It is accomplished through the conveyance of proper leadership. Leaders act like they know what to do and that what they are doing is right and proper. They act with dignity, grace, bearing, and confidence. Leadership is not about manipulating consequences; it is about effective communication, what I, in *Parenting by the Book*, call "leadership speech." Such speech is straightforward, characterized by an economy of words and little if any explanation, and leaves nothing to the imagination of the child. Therefore, he knows exactly what the parent expects.

Leadership speech is, "It's time to pick up these toys and get ready to go to the dentist."

Leadership speech is *not*, "We really need to start getting ready to go to the dentist, okay? And I'd really like these toys up off the floor before we go, okay? So how about if we start picking up these toys, okay?"

If you didn't recognize yourself just now, then you recognized another parent you know; probably more than one, in fact. All too many of today's parents plead, bargain, bribe, cajole, encourage, reason, explain, promise, and then, when none of that works, they threaten and scream. Then they feel guilty. Then they apologize and go right back to pleading and bargaining and so on. And 'round and 'round they go. Then they say, "My child won't do what I tell him to do."

Wrong! Your child will do what you tell him to do, but you first have to *tell* him. *Telling*, as in the example three paragraphs ago, is the same as *expecting*. Anything less is *wishing*, and children do not grant adult wishes. When adults wish that children would obey, children respond with constant testing. Today, that's called oppositional defiant disorder.

If you can accept that whether your children obey you or not is primarily a matter of how you give instructions, define boundaries, and convey expectations, and not a matter of the level of serotonin in their brains, then you have just taken the first step toward claiming your leadership of your children and liberating them from the need to test your authority 24/7.

ENCOURAGE INDEPENDENCE FROM AN EARLY AGE

Boundaries are important in any relationship, which means they're important in the parent-child relationship. Boundaries define what parents will and will not do for a child and place limits on a child's ability to access his parents. It's impossible (and impractical) to create such boundaries before a child is at least eighteen months of age, but past that point, boundaries can be put in place slowly but surely. The point is to help a child develop skills that foster responsibility and independence.

The earlier a child learns to do things for himself, the better for all concerned. Early responsibility equates to early independence. Furthermore, responsibility begets responsibility. So, for example, toilet-train your child before he's two years old. If your great-grandmother toilet-trained her kids before they were two, so can you. It's no different, really, from teaching a child to eat with a spoon, and approached calmly and purposefully (like you approach spoon training), your child will be using the toilet on his own within a couple of weeks.

Your child will enjoy the independence gained from no longer having to wear diapers (or those other evil garments, pull-ups). He will want to learn to do more, so the next step is to teach him to dress himself. Make things easy for him so that learning isn't frustrating, so that he will look forward to the next responsibility you offer him, and the next, and the next, so that eventually, when he goes to school, he will welcome the responsibilities his teachers give him.

Boundaries that clearly separate the world of childhood from the world of adulthood help children look up to adults with respect and admiration. They are also important to helping a child develop independence and responsibility. Along these lines, two of the most common mistakes today's parents make, and they are made out of the goodness of their hearts, is to (1) sleep with their children and (2) make a habit of playing with their children.

We cannot overstress the importance of children sleeping in their own beds, in their own bedrooms. Forget the psychologically correct hogwash about bonding problems and attachment disorders (there is no compelling evidence that even adopted children are at high risk for attachment disorders). Parents who read books of this sort don't neglect their children's fundamental emotional needs. A child who relies on sleeping with his parents to go to sleep peacefully is going to have difficulty with self-help in other areas. Both of the authors have found that children who sleep with their parents have a generally low tolerance for frustration of any sort. These are children who tend to give up easily; likewise, these are parents who tend to solve problems for their children that their children are actually capable of solving for themselves. Success in school, not to mention life itself, requires the ability to persevere in the face of frustration.

Today's parents seem to feel that a big part of good parenting is getting down on the floor every day and playing with one's child. This is a new thing. Baby boomers do not remember their parents playing with them on any regular basis, and remember, baby boomers were generally more emotionally resilient than today's kids. Whereas occasional adult-child play sessions can be fun, when they become the norm they prevent a child from acquiring what psychologist Burton White (*The First Three Years of Life*) has said is one of the most important of all developmental milestones: the ability to play on his own for sustained periods of time by his third birthday.[1]

Yes, parents should provide appropriate play materials for a child, ones that strengthen imagination and creativity like clay and building blocks, but helping a child learn the potential that lies within a certain play material and playing with him are two different things. A child who learns to play on his own is learning not to depend upon adults to solve problems for him. He's learning to create goals (e.g., build a block wall, form an animal out of clay) and stay with a task until it's finished. He's strengthening his attention span, developing organizational skills, learning trial-and-error, learning "stick-to-itiveness," and so on.

ELIMINATE CLUTTER IN YOUR CHILD'S ENVIRONMENT

Parents of young children frequently ask, "How can I get my child to pick up his toys?" Invariably, the child who resists picking up his toys is a child who has too many toys to pick up. A two-year-old can and should be expected to pick up after himself, but the typical child this age has already acquired more than fifty toys (that's actually a very conservative estimate). Expecting a toddler to pick up even ten toys is unrealistic. It's the equivalent of scattering one thousand thumbtacks over a one-acre surface and telling an adult to pick them up. Faced with instruction, a toddler will engage in all manner of avoidance behaviors: ignoring, dawdling, whining, and outright refusing. The parent responds by attempting to bribe the child into picking up his toys. When that doesn't work (and it usually doesn't), the parent becomes more insistent, then threatening, then punitive, and often ends up reluctantly (and angrily) picking up the toys. This "go nowhere fast" power struggle is a breeding ground for oppositional behavior that gets ever worse over time. The child also learns that by acting like a task is too much, his parent will do it for him.

The solution to this vexing problem involves neither play nor punishment, but managing the situation such that the task is doable. That can mean only one thing: giving the toddler access to only the number of toys he can, and will, pick up. And how many is that? No more than one, to begin with at least.

I recommend that parents of toddlers operate a "toy library," restricting the number of toys the child can "check out" to one. The library ought to be maintained in some relatively secure place, at least until the child understands the routine and the rule.

The child selects a toy to play with. When he's done, he simply brings it to the parent in charge and exchanges it for another one. When the child has "gotten it," the number of toys checked out can increase to two. But until the child is at least three, two toys should be the limit.

Parents who use this approach also discover that a toddler needs very few toys. Ten, in fact, is more than enough to keep a toddler occupied throughout the day.

The "toy library" approach promotes longer periods of independent play, meaning, of course, that Mom and Dad are able to enjoy relatively long periods of uninterrupted time. It's certainly paradoxical, but a toddler can play imaginatively with one or two toys much longer than he can play with ten. At three toys, a toddler's ability to make choices begins to become overwhelmed, and he begins to whine and do other annoying things that are more a function of his circumstances than his personality.

PROMOTE GOOD FAMILY CITIZENSHIP WITH CHORES

If preparing children for citizenship is important, and Grandma was right that good citizenship begins at home, then it follows that children should learn the service ethic within their families. Children do not serve the greater good of their families by making good grades or acquiring sports trophies. The only way they can do so is by performing chores.

Furthermore, children should *not* be paid for doing chores. An adult performs community service because he is a member of the community. Likewise, a child should perform chores because he is a member of the family. Paying children for chores undermines their value as citizenship lessons. It also leads to children not doing their chores whenever they don't need any money. Besides, parents are not compensated for cooking meals, doing the laundry, or tending to the yard. Under the circumstances, paying children for doing chores implies that children have privileged status within the family, that they are free of obligation.

Three is the most advantageous age at which to begin assigning chores to children. This age child has a strong need to identify with his parents and expresses that need, in part, by following them around the house, wanting to get involved in the things he sees them doing. If he can't get directly involved, he imitates. If Dad's repairing a leaky faucet, he wants to help. When Mom cooks, he gets out a few pots and pans and plays on the kitchen floor. This interest should be capitalized upon by giving the three-year-old a few minor chores around the house. In order to become routine, they should take place at the same time every day. A three-year-old can help make his bed in the morning, help set the table at lunch, and pick up and return the two toys he's been able to check out of the toy library before his bedtime story. A few simple yet meaningful chores at this age set the stage for increasing responsibilities as the child grows older. Chores assigned before age three—during the "terribles"—are likely to be met with resistance. Likewise, a child's "chore readiness" begins to wane if parents wait much later than the fourth birthday to begin this important citizenship lesson.

Fours and fives should be responsible for keeping their rooms orderly. That job should not be overwhelming, which means they shouldn't have a lot of things in their rooms to begin with. Besides, the fewer playthings a child has, the more creatively and imaginatively the child will play, and the longer he will play on his own. In addition to being responsible for their order and cleanliness in their rooms, fours and fives should be doing one or two chores per day in common areas of the home. A simple vacuum cleaner can even be purchased especially for the child and he can even learn to vacuum. By the time a child goes to first grade, he should even be well acquainted with what's involved in top-to-bottom cleaning of a bathroom. And most definitely, if a child doesn't do a chore properly the first go-'round, he should do it again, and again, as many times as it takes for him to get it right.

Chores are not only a medium for citizenship training, but they also set the stage for success in school. They train children to accept daily assignments, stay on task, do one's best, and (if not paid for) do one's best simply because it's the right thing to do. For more on chores, see my book *The New Six-Point Plan for Raising Happy, Healthy Children* (Andrews McMeel, 2006).

KEEP ELECTRONIC MEDIA TO A MINIMUM
(AND PROMOTE LOTS OF EXERCISE)

If you say, "We already limit electronic media in our home," then consider that parents tend to underestimate the average amount of time their children spend per week focused on various electronic screens—television, video games, computers, handheld gaming devices—by half. There is nothing that will drain a child's motivation; nothing that will destroy a child's attention span for anything other than what's on a screen (e.g., a book, which does not read itself to you and the pages of which do not move); nothing that will interfere more with the development of imagination, creativity, and proper problem-solving skills than many a child's first addiction—electronic media. In chapter 3, we covered the dangers to their developing brains of exposing young children to plug-in drugs, which leaves only our recommendations, which are based on sound scientific evidence.

First, don't allow a child any exposure (understanding that one cannot control a child's life 24/7) to electronic media until age seven or until he has learned to read fairly well, whichever occurs last.

Second, after introducing electronic media, and for as long as a child lives under your roof, do not allow more than a combined total of five hours of screen time per week. That's a bit less than one hour a day.

Third, the moment a child begins having attention problems in school, or for children who are already having attention problems, pull the plug on everything and keep it pulled until the child's attention span fully recovers, and then some. A child who isn't allowed to spend a great deal of time sitting in front of an electronic screen will soon start using his God-given initiative, resourcefulness, and imagination to invent creative ways of passing time.

To make this explicit, let's just say that your child, age eight and in the second grade, is a fairly good reader and having no problems in school. On Sunday evening, let him peruse a television schedule for the coming week and select three hours of programs. Make a rule that at least one of those hours must be educational in nature—wildlife or historical documentaries, how-to programs, docu-dramas, et cetera. The child selects, you approve, and those become the programs—the only programs—he is allowed to watch that week. Programs missed cannot be made up, but he can substitute one program for another, as long as the substitution is requested and approved in advance. To avoid arguments over what was selected, have him write down his choices and post them on the refrigerator, right alongside his list of weekly chores.

Needless to say, by keeping electronic media to a bare minimum in your child's life, you promote exercise. Children who are not lulled into electronic stupors (by television) or lulled into electronic hyperactivity (by video games) will do what children naturally do—they will be active. Proper exercise is part of a well-rounded and healthy lifestyle, and studies have shown that the earlier in life good exercise habits are established, the more long-lasting they will be, and the more healthy the individual is going to be throughout his life. It isn't necessary that you enroll your child in a structured exercise program (although for some kids, especially those who need a jump-start in the exercise department and those who live in areas where outdoor play opportunities are limited, that may be a good idea). It's only necessary that you encourage lots of outdoor time. Exercise comes naturally to a child. Riding a bike, running, kicking a ball, climbing a tree, walking—natural activities make for the best exercise for a child. Remove electronic hindrances, and exercise will take their place.

MAINTAIN SOUND NUTRITIONAL HABITS
(AND PROMOTE LOTS OF EXERCISE)

On average, American children consume a diet that is worse by far than that of children in any developed nation, which is why the incidence of obesity and type 2 diabetes among America's kids is growing by leaps and bounds. This is bad for children, and what's bad for children is eventually bad for America, because a viable, competitive economy depends on healthy, motivated workers. A growing body of evidence links a diet high in noncomplex carbohydrates (white rice, white flour, refined sugar) and low in fiber and protein to listlessness, inattention, irritability, erratic mood swings, surliness, forgetfulness, and other behaviors associated with ADHD, ODD, and EOBD. Other studies implicate food additives and preservatives to similar problems.

Make sure your children have a diet that is balanced and as natural as possible. In that regard, forget about the traditional "food pyramid" you were probably exposed to in school. That was based primarily on dietary myths as opposed to sound scientific research. A good diet isn't rocket science; it's common sense. Every day, a child should eat three or four servings of fresh (not processed and canned) fruits and vegetables, two servings of food high in protein (meat, beans, tofu), and drink at least forty-eight ounces (four to six glasses) of water. Not flavored, carbonated water, mind you, but plain old water. The "water" today's children consume more often than not comes in the form of soft drinks, fruit-flavored drinks, sports drinks (the value of which, even during periods of strenuous physical activity, is dubious), and energy drinks, most of which combine a small amount of vitamins with carbonated water, sugar, and caffeine.

Children who are allowed to choose what they eat and don't eat almost always choose foods that are high in sugar and other refined carbohydrates and fat; foods, in other words, that not only are of little nutritional value but also are most likely to bring on behaviors and mood states associated with the "disorders" under discussion. It follows that parents should not cater to a child's food preferences, especially at mealtimes. At family meals, everyone's plates should contain the same items. When a child is catered to at family meals, he is automatically defined as having special status within the family, and other, increasingly outrageous demands for preferential treatment are sure to come.

Sometimes parents cater out of anxiety that if they do not, the child in question "won't eat." Dr. Ravenel has been practicing pediatrics for nearly forty years, eleven years of which he spent teaching pediatrics in a university-affiliated pediatric residency training program. He is not aware of any young child who has expired or even suffered significant medical consequences because he didn't want to eat what was put on his plate at family mealtimes. Yes, there are children who have starved themselves to death (known as *anorexia nervosa*), but this problem almost always develops during adolescence and the authors are aware of no studies linking it to parents who refuse to cater to food preferences in earlier childhood.

Children who have enjoyed such catering are not going to immediately begin eating roast beef, mashed potatoes, and green beans, washed down with water, when they have become accustomed to hot dogs, French fries, and a soft drink. The transition can be made by adhering to a program I developed in the mid-1980s that according to parent reports has resulted in the "cure" of many a finicky eater since then. At family meals, the child is served one teaspoon of each of the food items (e.g., pork tenderloin, mashed sweet potatoes, spinach) prepared and told that when he eats everything on his plate, he can have seconds of any single item, in any quantity. Initially, these kids "hold out" by only eating the one or two items that do not cause them attacks of food revulsion disorder, but after significant hunger develops (usually no more than a few days), they begin eating all three teaspoons of food, gagging dramatically the entire time, of course. At that point, parents should increase the per-item amount to a tablespoon. When the child is consistently consuming everything on his plate at that level, the per-item amount should be increased to one-quarter cup, and so on. Eventually—and I have received not one report of failure in the twenty years I've been recommending this approach—the child is eating a normal diet and even asking to try new things.

Oh, and one more thing: make sure your child gets lots of healthy exercise. It aids in digestion.

PUT THE KIBOSH ON TANTRUMS

Full-blown tantrums, usually in response to "no," generally begin around the second birthday, but some children begin throwing them earlier, some much later. If your child is still in a crib when tantrums first appear, take him immediately to his crib, put him inside, tell him, "You can scream here," and walk away. Let him cry it out. Tantrums are not life-threatening even if they last more than an hour, which is sometimes the case. As time goes on, consistency on your part will result in tantrums of shorter and shorter duration. Needless to say, you should never give in to a tantrum, even if you immediately realize that you made an arbitrary decision. Children should learn to live with arbitrary decisions.

If tantrums start or are continuing past the point where the transition has been made to a big-boy or big-girl bed, then define a certain area of the home as a "tantrum place" where the child can throw tantrums to his or her heart's content. The child's room will suffice (remember, it shouldn't be overflowing or even moderately flowing with toy clutter), but some children will not stay in their rooms. In that case, you may have to use a baby gate in the doorway to keep your child confined. If he is capable of knocking it over or climbing over it, then it will be worth the time and expense to cut down the child's bedroom door so that both parents can see over it but the child can't climb over it, and rehang it with the door lock reversed. At the first sign of a tantrum, put the child in his room, close the door, and lock it. This will not result in any psychological trauma. The child simply won't like the fact that when he throws a tantrum, he is confined to his room. Eventually, tantrums will stop.

If the child will stay in a designated area until a tantrum has run its beastly course, any relatively isolated area of the home can be used as the tantrum place. With our daughter Amy, who did not begin throwing tantrums until she was three years old, my wife and I selected the downstairs bathroom, explaining to Amy that its soft carpet was ideal for thrashing around upon, and that the bathroom provided her the opportunity to fuel her tantrums with water and relieve any bowel or bladder stress that her tantrums might induce. Slowly but surely, her tirades reduced from "bipolar" to insignificant levels and then stopped altogether, although relatively quiet fits of pique continued to occur into adolescence.

MAKE PRUDENT EDUCATIONAL DECISIONS

In today's educational climate, we recommend against putting a child into any public school other than one located in a very small town or rural area where accountability to community standards tends to trump "educational correctness." We generally, and strongly, recommend schools that adhere to a traditional educational model including, but not limited to, phonetic reading instruction, drilling on basic facts, merit-based grading, and teacher-centered classrooms. That describes few schools these days, but one can now and again find a traditional paradigm still being practiced in schools that are religious-affiliated (Catholic, Episcopal, Lutheran, Hebrew, and nondenominational Christian) and some charter schools.

If you can't find or afford a school that fits the above description, then consider homeschooling. A variety of homeschool curricula are available these days, and support and networking are available to homeschooling parents through state and local affiliates of the American Homeschool Association (www.americanhomeschoolassociation.org). The overwhelming majority of homeschooling parents report positive outcomes for both themselves and their children. They also report greater confidence in the quality of their children's education and a greater sense of security; they find that homeschooling doesn't take up much more time than the daily assignments today's schools, especially public, send home to parents. As a group, homeschooled kids not only score above the norm on standardized achievement tests[2] but score as well as students from conventional school in most areas of college-entrance tests except in English, where they sometimes score higher.[3]

It is a myth that homeschooled children suffer social disadvantages. First, homeschooling rarely takes place in isolation. Most homeschooling takes place in the context of homeschool cooperatives that involve several teaching parents and five to seven children. Second, a homeschooled child can legally participate in any curriculum areas (art, music) or extracurricular activities (sports, special interest clubs) offered through the local public schools. Needless to say, homeschooled kids are not exposed to the same level of social risk as children who attend public or even private schools. Studies of social adjustment indicate that home-educated students are likely to be socially and psychologically healthy.[4] Homeschooled students tend to have a broader age-range of friends than their schooled peers, which may foster maturity and leadership skills.[5] In college, they tend to have fewer adjustment problems.

One college professor noted that top universities are beginning to aggressively recruit homeschooled kids because they "tend to make fantastic college students ... mature and self-motivated. . . . The high school 'herd' environment does not prepare kids for the self-reliance required for success in college."[6]

RESTRICT AFTER-SCHOOL AND WEEKEND ACTIVITIES

Many of today's parents seem to think parenting is taking a child to a soccer game and watching from the stands. That's not parenting. Parenting is not a spectator sport. It's hands on! It's a verb!

Today's parents are likely to expend a lot of energy doing things that have little if any long-term value to a child, and little energy doing things that are of lasting value (and would, in fact, make their job a whole lot easier in the long run). Like taking the time to teach a child—by explaining and rehearsing, for example—how to be recognized when two adults are engaged in conversation.

Instead of filling your family's discretionary time with organized activities that reduce parents to onlookers, fill it with truly *family* activities like going on picnics, to museums, to live theater productions, on hikes in state parks, and the like.

HELP YOUR CHILD DEVELOP HOBBIES

One of the questions I occasionally ask my seminar audiences is "How many of you, as children, had a hobby?" Nearly everyone raises a hand.

I then tell them to keep their hands up if at least one of their children has a hobby, defined as an activity or interest pursued independently, of the child's own initiative, and in which the child is actively involved on a regular basis. That distinguishes a hobby from an organized, adult-directed, after-school activity.

Almost every hand goes down.

Why is it that so few of America's children have hobbies? Fifty-odd years ago, nearly every one of the kids in my suburban Chicago neighborhood had one. Collecting and trading baseball cards was a popular pastime, as were coin and stamp collections. Some were into photography, others into building radios.

At various times, I collected baseball cards, rocks, newspapers from cities around the country, coins, and stamps. I also played mad scientist with my chemistry set. I guess you could also say that, up until high school, when I started playing on the school team, golf was a hobby.

Our hobbies were expressions of individuality. We took pride in them and loved to show them off. Collecting newspapers set me off from the kid next door, who collected coins. Hobbies were tangible expressions of personal accomplishment that built not only self-respect, but respect for one another. Hobbies involved setting goals and reaching for them. In other words, they were catalysts for growth.

When our kids were still young, my wife and I made three big changes in their lives. First, we took the television out of the home and kept it out for several years. Second, we reduced their toy inventory to pre-1960 levels. Third, we no longer allowed more than one after-school activity at a time.

After they got over their shock and adjusted to our new old-fashioned lifestyle, each developed a hobby. Eric began building models of World War II military equipment and, later, airplanes. That got him interested in flying. After hanging around the local airport, he began taking flying lessons during the last year of high school. He is now a corporate pilot.

Amy asked for piano lessons, which led to an interest in musicals and songwriting. She began trying out for community theater productions, working her way up from the chorus in *Annie!* to the female lead in *Oliver.* Today, as a thirty-something wife and mother of three, she is still active in community theater.

For want of some time, a hobby can be lost. For want of a hobby, a talent may never develop. For want of talent, a life is less rich.

CHOOSE A NONACADEMIC PRESCHOOL (OR NONE AT ALL)

As pointed out in chapter 7, nearly all of the studies done by independent, objective researchers confirm that the preschool years (through kindergarten) should be nonacademic. In Finland, where achievement at every grade is higher than in the U.S., children do not begin learning how to read until they are seven. That, by the way, is the way it was in America until fairly recently, when policymakers decided that one way to raise sagging achievement was to push the traditional first-grade curriculum down into kindergarten. The propaganda accompanying this policy change caused parents to believe that if learning to read in kindergarten was better than learning to read in first grade, then learning to read in preschool was better yet! Preschools—especially commercial preschools and preschools serving upscale populations—began competing for students by promising all manner of academic advantages. In other words, teaching children such things as their ABCs and number facts at earlier and earlier ages is driven by market pressures, not solid research. The best research, in fact, clearly says that while it's possible to teach a four-year-old to read, the risk of later learning problems and boredom in school is greatly increased in the process.

It's still possible to find preschool programs that eschew academics in favor of teaching social skills (including taking direction from adults), fostering responsibility, and nurturing creative processes. That does not include most commercial, chain preschools, or preschools attached to private schools. One is most likely to find a nonacademic preschool being run as a church ministry. Preschools that seek accreditation from the National Association for the Education of Young Children also tend to be nonacademic.

Numerous red flags should go up whenever television or computers are prominent features of a preschool classroom. Good teachers don't need television to keep children under control, and preschools that are truly in tune with the cognitive needs of children don't bother with computers.

ALLOW FAILURE

Learning to fail is critical to success. No one who has developed outstanding competency in a certain skill area has done so without first failing and learning from his mistakes. Whether failure is a negative or positive experience for a child depends on the manner in which adults respond. Do they act disappointed in the child's performance, or do they take the time to help the child understand why he failed and improve his performance? Obviously, criticizing a child who has not "measured up" is not going to be helpful unless the criticism is constructive and accompanied by positive coaching.

Relevant to this topic is the tendency of today's parents to praise anything and everything their children do. I remember an occasion when I was talking to a neighbor on his front lawn, close to where his five-year-old son was kicking a soccer ball. At one point, the child asked the father to watch him kick. The child held the ball in the air, dropped it, and kicked at it with enthusiasm, but the ball barely glanced off the side of his foot and after wobbling for a few seconds, came to a stop only a few feet from where the boy stood. My neighbor clapped and exclaimed, "Good job!" Parent behavior of that sort is more common today than it was when I was a child because of concerns over self-esteem. My thought was that if almost missing the ball is a good job, then nothing this child does justifies providing him with corrective instruction. In fact, a child who is praised indiscriminately may come to even resent adult attempts to correct.

It would have been better for the boy's father to say, "Nice try," and then later take the time to help his son develop the timing and coordination necessary to kick a ball that's being dropped from three feet. In other words, this was a teaching opportunity wasted for the best of intentions.

TEACH MANNERS FROM AN EARLY AGE

In *Toward a Meaningful Life: The Wisdom of the Rebbe,* the late Rabbi Menachem Mendel Schneerson—leader of the Lubavitcher movement of Chassidic Judaism for most of the last half of the twentieth century—states unequivocally that a child's character education should take priority over his academic education.[7] In fact, the esteemed Rebbe (pronounced reb'-be) says all other educational efforts are basically meaningless unless built on the solid foundation of good character.

In the movie *Blast from the Past,* one of the characters finally realizes, as he puts it, "Good manners are a way of showing respect for others" and not, as he'd previously thought, a means of calling attention to oneself. He's also discovered, he says, that the most important of all manners is that of doing all you can to help the people around you feel comfortable.

As attested to in both of the above examples, character and manners are inseparable. Good manners are symptomatic of good character, and the linchpin of good character is respect for others, as reflected by good manners, which consist simply of efforts to make other people feel comfortable.

Today's parents would certainly say they want their children to possess good character, but how many actually take the time to teach proper manners? Modeling the correct behavior is not enough. Teaching manners requires instruction, and instruction—whether reminding, explaining, correcting, or rehearsing—takes time. The world would definitely be a better place if parents would take even half the time they spend driving their children to various extracurricular pursuits and taught proper manners instead.

Teaching manners to preschool children—the earlier the better—pays off in numerous ways. I have nothing but personal experience to support what I'm about to say, but I'll bet my life savings that good manners go hand in hand with obedience and respect for adults, doing one's best in school, and good relationships with siblings and friends. Not to mention that the well-mannered child's parents receive lots of positive feedback from other parents, teachers, neighbors, and so on. For all those reasons, the child in question will be much happier than he or she otherwise would have been.

The first manners a child should learn, by his or her fourth birthday, are (in no particular order):

- Saying "please," "thank you," and "you're welcome" when appropriate.
- Saying "I'm sorry" when he's hurt someone physically or emotionally.
- Saying "excuse me" when appropriate (but see below for when it's not appropriate).
- Sharing toys and other possessions freely with playmates.
- Saying "Yes ma'am/sir" and "No ma'am/sir" when appropriate (I'm betraying my Southern roots here).
- Not complaining about food prepared by someone else (even your mother!) and set in front of you.
- Not interrupting adult conversations, even with, "excuse me."

I assign a lot of weight to that last one for several equally good reasons. First, in learning not to interrupt, a child learns patience; he learns how to wait, to tolerate delays. Second, not interrupting requires and strengthens self-control. Third, learning not to interrupt strengthens a child's sense of interpersonal boundaries and, therefore, respect for adults.

It would appear that many, if not most, of today's parents teach their children it's perfectly all right to interrupt two adults in conversation, and for any reason at all, by simply walking up and saying, "Excuse me!" I gather this because when a child simply walks up and starts talking, it's usually the case that the child's parent will stop talking to me, look down at the child, and say, "What have I taught you to say?" At which point the child says, "Excuse me." At which point the parent withdraws from conversation with me and begins paying attention to the child.

After a recent talk I gave in southern California, a gentleman from South Africa introduced himself and remarked that he, too, was annoyed and amused by parents who tolerated their children's interruptions. He told me that in his country, one of the first things a child is taught is how to be recognized when he wants to say something. Specifically, the child walks into the general area where the adults are talking and stands a respectful distance—at least eight feet—away. When the adults reach a point where a pause in their conversation feels natural, one (the child's parent, usually) will turn to the child and say, "Yes?" at which point the child will speak.

The fellow from South Africa had the right idea. Teach your child to stand a respectful distance from adults who are talking and wait, silently and still, until he is acknowledged. And, when it comes right down to it, gradually increase his wait until he's learned to be silent and still for upwards of five minutes.

So what's the child to do if there's a genuine emergency? I suggest you give your child a hand signal to use in such circumstances. And, let's face it, what a child considers an emergency is not always an emergency or even close to it.

What should you do when your child interrupts, even after you've taught him the art of waiting? I really don't think there's a formula for that one, other than to say make sure he learns that misbehavior has consequences. Put him to bed early that evening. Cancel a sleepover that's to take place later in the week. Whatever you do, do something he'll remember!

The mother of a five-year-old recently remarked to me, somewhat apologetically, that her child was "bad" about interrupting conversations. I thought, *No, your child isn't bad about interrupting; rather, you and your husband have been "bad" about teaching him not to interrupt.* They would no doubt disagree. My experience with parents leads me to believe these folks would respond defensively, even indignantly, to my accusation. They would say, "But every single time she interrupts we tell her it's not right!" That's not teaching. That's nagging, which is how most parents try to "teach" their children manners, and nagging does nothing but breed even more nagging. Eventually, nagging breeds contempt or, at the very least, a lack of respect. So, what should these parents—and by extension, any parent who wants to properly instruct a young child in proper social decorum—do about this nagging not-so-little problem? They should do six things.

Get in touch with reality. Reality is that proper manners are not natural human behaviors. They are contrary to our nature. Think about it! It is not human nature to share, say thank you, or wait your turn. It is natural to be selfish, take other people for granted, and want to be first in line. It follows that children do not "outgrow" bad manners, nor do they simply absorb them by social osmosis. They must be taught! Furthermore, because replacing human nature with proper behavior is akin to paddling upstream, face it: it is not easy to teach a child manners. It requires work!

Make it a project. Whenever you teach a child something new, whether the something is using the toilet or not interrupting conversations, like using a spoon or making his own bed, you must make it a project. You can't teach these sorts of skills haphazardly, on a "catch as catch can" basis, and expect success. Willie and I recently took Jack, our then five-year-old grandson, with us on a cruise, during which we made a project of proper table manners. Before each meal, we sat down with Jack and reviewed the ins and outs of proper table etiquette. We kept to the basics: waiting until everyone has their food and the blessing has been said, asking someone to pass instead of reaching, and asking to be excused instead of simply getting up. If he slipped during a meal—and because of the review, he only slipped once in three days!—we gently reminded him of the proper behavior. Afterward, we made sure to tell him how proud we were of him. In other words, we kept table manners "in front of him" for three days. Because Jack already knew his proper table manners and just needed a bit of polish, three days was all it took. When teaching a manner that's never been learned, expect the project to last from one to two weeks.

Teach one manner or one set of manners at a time. The younger the child, the more important this becomes. At age five, we could reasonably expect Jack to remember a set of three table manners, all of which applied to one specific situation. If Jack had been a year or so younger, however, we'd have only made a project of one table manner at a time. More than one would be overwhelming for a child younger than five, and that translates to lots of frustration for parents and child.

Rehearse important manners before occasions when they will be needed. Let's say you're trying to teach your four-year-old to look people in the eye and say hello when spoken to. Immediately before each situation in which that behavior will be called for, give your child practice.

Remind on the spot, but gently. Quite simply, it is bad manners to sternly, much less loudly, reprimand a child when other adults are present. Remember that good manners are intended to make those around us feel comfortable. Listening to an adult reprimand his or her child in an angry tone of voice is decidedly discomforting, so don't do it. If your child needs a reminder, take him aside and/or whisper in his ear. If you've been successful at making a project of learning the manner in question, whispering will do the trick.

Remember to praise. When your child uses manners appropriately, be sure to praise his or her effort. And remember, in giving praise, the most sincere praise is low-key and matter of fact. You don't need to jump up and down and applaud when your child does something right. A simple acknowledgment, as in, "You did a good job with your manners tonight, and we're very proud of you" will suffice.

William of Wykeham (1324–1404), the founder of both Winchester College and New College, Oxford, thought manners were so important to education that he coined and used "Manners maketh man" as the motto for not one, but both of these venerable institutions. (I'm certain, by the way, that William also valued good manners in women.) Indeed, it is the grace of good manners that separates the men from the boys and the women from the girls, not soccer, piano, or gymnastics. Not even good grades! So if you want your children to grow up graceful and charming and all those mannerly things that "maketh" maturity, put the majority of your parenting eggs in the basket that will ultimately count for more than any other basket your children will carry with them into adulthood—the good manners basket!

USE NO-TOLERANCE DISCIPLINE

When a child misbehaves, the child should hear that the behavior in question will not be tolerated. That message needs to be as clear as possible, which requires that the adult delivering the message do so calmly. It should go without saying, the more agitated and angry an adult is, the less well the child is going to hear the adult's message.

Effective child discipline is not a matter of using right methods; rather, it's a matter of *presentation*, of how effectively adult authority is communicated to the child. From this point of view, which is in keeping with traditional understandings of discipline, methods are less important than attitude.

Whenever I conduct a workshop in discipline for parents or teachers, I make the point that without a proper attitude, no method is going to work for long; with the right attitude, however, just about any method will work. That right attitude can be described in terms of five "C" words: *calm, confident, consistent, commanding*, and *compelling*.

Being calm and confident conveys to the child that you are responding to his misbehavior not because it troubles *you* but because in the long run, it's going to be increasingly troublesome for *him*. The child needs to hear the message, "I'm going to discipline you because if I don't, then what you just did is going to become more and more of a problem for *you*, and it's my responsibility to do everything I can to prevent that from happening."

It's the difference between an exasperated parent saying, "How many times do I have to tell you not to interrupt conversations? Huh? What's it going to take? Tell me!" and a calm parent saying, "You obviously have not yet learned that interrupting people who are talking to one another is rude. I don't want you to grow up to be rude, so when you interrupt, I'm going to send you to your room and put you to bed early." Needless to say, the second message is going to have a more positive impact than the first.

Being consistent doesn't mean that every time a child interrupts, you send him to his room and to bed early. It's not a good idea, in fact, to use the same consequences over and over again because a child so punished will eventually "immunize" to the same old, same old. An example is a child who is spanked nearly every time he misbehaves. In short order, spankings come to mean nothing to the child. That sort of consistency can backfire. The sort of consistency that never backfires is consistency of *attitude*, meaning that even though your consequences vary from misbehavior to misbehavior, your attitude does not. You are calm; therefore, your message of intolerance comes across more clearly, more commandingly.

Intolerance means not threatening, giving second chances, or making deals. It means you accustom your child to an important fact of life in your home: you are going to tell him to do something once, and once only. Expecting and enforcing first-time obedience from an early age makes for much less wear and tear on both parent and child. It's far easier to teach a child first-time obedience than to teach second-, third-, or who-knows-how-many-times? obedience. Any policy other than first-time obedience forces a child to constantly test in order to determine where the parent is now drawing the line in the sand. When the line is drawn in the same place, forever, children stop testing and that makes for a much happier childhood (not to mention a much happier parenthood).

If you tell your child to pick up his toys, and you come back into the room five minutes later, and the toys still aren't picked up, don't say, "I told you to pick up these toys five minutes ago. I didn't mean pick them up when you feel like it. I meant pick them up now!" To teach self-control, you must be a paragon of self-control. When you find that the toys haven't been picked up, simply tell the child that since he didn't feel like picking up the toys, he is excused to his room where he will remain for the rest of the day. You will pick up the toys. If he protests that he was going to pick them up, simply say, "You are welcome to help me, but you are going to spend the rest of the day in your room whether you help me pick them up or not. I'm only going to tell you something once. Your life is going to be a lot easier when you learn that."

Note again that the benefit of obedience is to the child, not the parent. Being cool, calm, and collected is not a matter of personality. It's a matter of self-training. It's a matter of understanding that your discipline must be *disciplined*. If it is, then it will be compelling, the last of the five characteristics of good discipline.

For more on this important subject, I refer the reader to the "Leadership Discipline" chapter in my book, *Parenting by the Book* (Howard, 2007).

CHAPTER 9
NIPPING "ADHD" IN FULL BLOOM

THE NAKED CITY WAS A POPULAR TELEVISION SERIES OF THE 1950s, inspired by the 1948 detective film of the same name. Every installment ended with the somber-voiced narrator saying, "There are eight million stories in the naked city. This has been one of them."

Dr. Ravenel and I have not heard millions of stories of children diagnosed with or who met criteria for ADHD who were cured without drugs, but we have heard hundreds. Not remarkably, many of the children in question were not cured until they *stopped* taking drugs. The stories that follow in this chapter are a representative sample of the hundreds we could tell. Some of these stories concern children who qualified for diagnoses other than ADHD, but they illustrate our approach, which rests on the belief that these childhood behavior disorders are manifestations of dysfunctions of discipline and lifestyle that are endemic to today's family culture. Once identified, these problematic circumstances are easily corrected, and once corrected, the behavior of the ADHD/ODD/EOBD child usually recovers to a state of normalcy within a relatively short period of time.

Our approach is not rocket science. It's a commonsense combination of good, old-fashioned discipline, removing electronic media (or minimizing their significance), and restoring a healthy lifestyle in terms of good nutrition and exercise. Unlike the case with a pharmaceutical approach, no one could argue that any aspect of our "prescription" involves risk.

The ADHD Establishment acknowledges these cures. They have no choice. But they deny that they have any bearing on their point of view. They maintain that if a child whose behavior fits DSM criteria for one or more of the diagnoses in question is cured without medical means, the child didn't really have the disorder. As we've already pointed out, the reasoning behind this position is circular. Either the criteria are meaningful or they are not. If children who qualify for a diagnosis don't really have the disorder at issue, then the diagnostic criteria are meaningless. Furthermore, the validity of a diagnosis does not depend on the method of cure. A person with cancer who is cured by holistic medicine still had cancer. For traditional medical doctors to say that the individual didn't really have cancer is absurd. Likewise, for the ADHD Establishment to say that a child cured by nonmedical means of what by virtue of their own diagnostic criteria is called ADHD "didn't really have ADHD" is absurd.

In a sense, however, we agree. These children didn't really have ADHD or any other childhood behavior disorder. They "had" nothing; rather, they *needed* something. If a woman in an abusive relationship becomes depressed, it doesn't mean she "has" a brain disease. Her depression speaks to *need*—in this case, the need to remove herself from a relationship that's bad for her mental health. Likewise, we see no proof or compelling evidence that ADHD (et cetera) kids *have* anything. They need. Our approach meets what we believe to be that need. That our approach almost always works when parents work at it says we're on the right track.

So, with no further ado, let's take a look at some of the hundreds and hundreds of stories in the ADHD city.

PARENTS CURE ADHD WITH COMORBID ODD IN A WEEK!

The current generation of mental health professionals has given parents the impression that time-out, properly used, will end any discipline problem. I was at one time an avid time-out pusher myself. I used it with my son, Eric, during his younger years and recommended it often to parents. Belatedly, I came to the conclusion that time-out works with children who are already well-behaved. It does not work—not for long, anyway—with children who have developed behavior problems that are outrageous either in kind or frequency. To mix my metaphors, using time-out to deal with the "outrageous" child is like trying to stop a charging elephant with a flyswatter. Fact is, outrageous behavior requires equally outrageous consequences.

Today's parents are reluctant to employ outrageous consequences—and by this I do not mean hurtful, cruel, or mean—because professional psychobabblers have intimidated them into believing that outrageous discipline is psychologically harmful; it will harm self-esteem. (Heaven forbid!) By outrageous discipline I mean any consequence that serves to prove, once and for all, that parents mean business—permanently. To illustrate the concept, I offer the following true-life drama.

A certain young fellow had major behavior problems both in school and at home. He was disruptive, disrespectful, and disobedient and had been since the first grade. At the frequent conferences that were held with his teachers (he was in the fifth grade when he came to my attention), principal, counselor, and school psychologist, they repeatedly suggested that the young man had ADHD. Indeed, his behavior fit the DSM criteria to the proverbial T. To top things off, he also qualified for a diagnosis of ODD.

The school folks reassured the young fellow's parents that ADHD is genetic; therefore, his behavior wasn't their fault. Because ADHD involves a biochemical imbalance, they said, he needed medication to help him control his impulses. The parents had resisted this well-intentioned hog-wash for several years.

"Finally," the mother told me, "we reached the limit of our tolerance for his shenanigans. He came home from school one day to discover a padlock on the door to his bedroom, which houses his television, computer, video game unit, sports equipment, models, and so on. We told him he'd be allowed in his room for fifteen minutes in the morning to dress for school and for fifteen minutes in the evening to get ready for bed, which was going to be seven thirty every night, seven nights a week. His bed was going to be the sofa in the living room—most comfortable, if you ask me."

Needless to say, the boy was stunned. He threatened to report his parents for child abuse, to which they simply reminded him that he would be properly fed, properly protected from the elements, and sleeping in a bed that was much safer than his own. After all, he could only roll out of one side of it!

"But please!" they said. "Tell whomever you like how abused you are."

This would last at least six weeks, they told him. During that time, he would not be allowed to participate in any after-school activity, have friends over, use the phone, watch television, or go anywhere except to accompany his parents. Furthermore, every single incident of misbehavior at school or home would add a week to his "exile," and no amount of good behavior would shorten it.

"It was amazing," his mother continued. "His teacher called us several days later to tell us he'd become a completely different child. She'd never seen so much improvement so quickly. He became a model child at home as well—polite, cooperative, talkative, a general pleasure to be around."

Six weeks later, the padlock was removed from his door with assurances it would be reattached at the first hint of relapse. I followed them for a year, during which time the young fellow's behavior and school performance continued to improve.

With more parents like that, the makers of ADHD drugs might have to go into the sleeper-sofa business.

MOTHER TAKES A SHORTCUT TO HEAD OFF ADHD

At the beginning of the school year, a seven-year-old girl had long, flowing tresses that she prized and also twirled in her fingers constantly during class. Her second-grade teacher became concerned because the little girl was inattentive, seemed to be daydreaming a lot, and wasn't getting her work done. As a consequence, she was making poor grades and was falling rapidly behind the rest of the class.

The teacher and school counselor told the mother that her daughter probably had ADHD and recommended that she be tested by a local psychologist who specialized in the "disorder." The mother was skeptical. Something didn't sound right.

Acting on her intuition, she went home, took a pair of scissors, and cut the child's hair short. This wasn't done in anger, mind you, and the child was only mildly upset.

"If you're going to sit in school and twirl your hair all day," she told her daughter, "then you won't be allowed to have long hair. When your grades are good again, I'll let you grow your hair back out."

In no time, the child's school behavior and performance was back up to par, and six months later she was making nearly straight As on her own. She was no longer inattentive. She no longer sat for long periods of time staring off into a personal universe. In six months, she went from "probably having ADHD" to being one of the best students in the class. And her hair is growing longer by the day. In short, her "attention deficit disorder" was cured in one day by a mother with a pair of scissors and equal amounts of determination and common sense.

The story is fascinating for several reasons, the first of which concerns the mother's nonpsychological solution. This sort of straightforward, no-nonsense approach to a child-rearing problem is almost unheard of these days. Today's typical parent has been led to believe that any downward deviation from a behavioral or academic norm on the part of a child has psychological import. As a consequence, children with problems are often treated with kid gloves when, as this story indicates, tough love is often called for.

This mother's "take the bull by the horns" approach was decidedly old-fashioned. Mental health professionals have contributed significantly to the myth that yesterday's child-rearing was psychologically harmful. In that light, I wouldn't have been at all surprised had someone reported the mother to the local social services agency for child abuse.

In the 1990s, the Office for the Study of the Psychological Right of the Child and the National Association of School Psychologists released a collaborative document that purports to define "psychological maltreatment." The examples include "spurning," which includes "gestures or other convenient symbols to debase . . . the child," and "terrorizing," which includes "violence or threats directed to the child's loved ones or objects."

According to a liberal, but by no means outrageous, interpretation of this definition (which is nothing more than a covert attempt to demonize traditional parenting), the child in question was both spurned and terrorized. Yet there is every indication that she not only did not suffer, but also benefited immensely from her mother's "psychological maltreatment."

Finally, there is the issue of ADHD. The girl obviously did not suffer from this "illness," for which no cause has ever been isolated; nonetheless, had her mother taken her to a professional for evaluation, there is a fairly good chance the girl would have been so diagnosed. If so, she probably would have been medicated, and her teacher probably would have been instructed to grade her according to lowered standards.

One has to wonder how many ADHD children are there who could have been cured in short order by something as old-fashioned and commonsensical as this mother's psychological incorrectness.

GETTING TO THE ROOT OF A PROBLEM

The "scientific" name is trichotillomania (TTM). Simply speaking, it is the acquired compulsion to pull one's own hair out by the roots. For some trichotillomaniacs the habit begins developing in early childhood; in others, later in childhood; in still others, not until adulthood. Some professionals theorize that TTMs are punishing themselves for some imagined offense. Others, including a pundit on one TTM website, think it's due to a "grooming gene gone haywire."

Explanations of this sort are in keeping with the dominant postmodern, pseudosocio-psycho-medical paradigm currently embraced by much of Western civilization. This paradigm holds that an individual who behaves in some persistently aberrant fashion is not responsible; rather, the behavior is caused by either societal pressures (e.g., poverty, peer pressure), a psychological conflict (e.g., guilt over masturbation, unresolved issues due to bad parenting), or a physiological malfunction (e.g., a gene, a biochemical imbalance, an allergy, a brain abnormality), or a combination thereof. The usual array of treatments—drugs, behavior modification, psychotherapy, and group therapy—are tried with TTMs. In a rare case, a therapy will succeed, but no therapy works reliably. This hair-pulling "disease" (what TTM websites call it) is a stubborn one.

I have long maintained that where children are concerned, patterns of antisocial and/or self-defeating behaviors that the medical and psychological establishments call "diseases" or "disorders" are just plain old problems of self-control. Where medical doctors and psychologists recommend drugs and therapy, I usually recommend old-fashioned discipline. I am convinced, in fact, that medical/psychological approaches to a child's misbehavior can, and often do, make the problem in question worse rather than better. The attention and explanation a therapist gives a problem can be deadly. The therapist's serious concern causes the child's parents to begin tiptoeing around the child and deferring to the behavior in question. Contributing to this is the fact that the therapist mystifies the problem by recasting it in medicobabble. Tantrums become early onset bipolar disorder. Belligerent rebellion against parental authority becomes oppositional defiant disorder. Irresponsible behavior in school becomes attention-deficit/hyperactivity disorder or a learning disability.

In addition, a therapist gives the behavior an explanation that externalizes the problem (posits that the cause lies outside the child's realm of control), and therefore, in effect, gives the child permission to continue having the problem. In effect, the child becomes a victim, and one cannot, with clear conscience, discipline a victim. In no time, the child is sitting at the center of a cyclone of concern and attention. Why give up a problem, why get control of it, when the payoff is so powerful?

The parents of a four-year-old girl asked me what to do about their daughter's hair-pulling, which had been going on for six months. They had tried "everything," they said, and then taken her to a psychologist. "After four months of seeing the psychologist, the hair-pulling is only worse," they wrote. "The psychologist thinks that this began when I learned that I was pregnant with our second child, and that she is stressed."

See? The child is pulling her hair out by the roots because she is in psychological distress over the fact that she will soon have a competitor. Given that sort of completely speculative, unscientific explanation, what were the parents to do? Postpone the second child's arrival? Psychological explanations of misbehavior—and make no mistake about it, this child's hair-pulling was most definitely a *mis*behavior—often have the unintended effect of paralyzing parents' ability to act authoritatively. And when a child senses a vacuum of authority, the child's problems, whatever their source, will surely worsen. Wisely, before asking my advice, the parents decided to stop wasting their money on this babble-therapy.

They had read on my website a story about a mother who had cured her school-age child's incessant nose picking by—when he picked—making him stand in the bathroom and pick in front of the mirror, for the alleged purpose of becoming a "champion nose picker." In no time, the child stopped picking. The mother of the four-year-old hair-puller asked if a similar procedure might work with her daughter.

I immediately thought about otherwise normal children whose tantrums take the form of banging their heads against the floor or other hard objects while screaming at the top of their lungs (symptoms of EOBD). My stock advice: Draw a circle on an out-of-the-way wall and tell the child, "This is your new head-banging place. If you want to bang your head, stand here and bang in this circle. It's the best head-banging spot in the whole house!" I've never, in the twenty-five years I've been proffering this, heard of it failing.

So, with miraculous nose-picking and head-banging cures in mind, I responded, "Go ahead and try it. One thing is certain: You absolutely must stop giving this problem attention. It has obviously become the center of a cyclone in your family . . . and as long as it occupies that vaunted position, your daughter will continue doing it. This is not to say that her hair-pulling is manipulative, mind you, but simply the way it is. Children don't think these things through. You need to, yes, limit it to a certain unseeable area of the home, as in, 'You can pull your hair in the bathroom only. If we see you doing it elsewhere, you will have to go to the bathroom for ten minutes, during which we encourage you to pull and pull and pull so as to get it out of your system.'"

A day later, the mother wrote back: "John, thank you so much for your response. I think you must have been able to feel my exhaustion and stress! When she began pulling her hair during lunch today, I calmly led her to the bathroom and told her that this was the new hair-pulling place . . . from now on, the only place where she could pull her hair. I told her that she should, from now on, go ahead and pull as much as she wanted. 'Will you watch?' she asked me. I told her no, I was going to finish my lunch. I shut the door and returned to the table. Fifteen minutes later she returned and finished her lunch. Her dad is reading to her as I type this, and we have not made one mention of hair all evening (I clued him in via an e-mail so she wouldn't hear our conversation). I can't say that she is 'cured' so quickly, but after being in the bathroom just that once and my not flipping out about it seems to be helping already. This has been the calmest evening we've had in half a year. I'll keep you updated."

Note that the parents, as I had instructed, did not even tell their daughter that they were proud of the fact that she hadn't pulled her hair in a few hours. Well-intentioned praise of that sort just might be all the trigger the behavior needs to reemerge with a vengeance. If and when a particular misbehavior suddenly goes into hiding, don't mention it. Calling its name might just bring it back!

A week later, the mother gave me another update: "It was eight days ago that we began putting our daughter in the bathroom to pull her hair. We have totally stopped discussing it. For several days after her first time in the bathroom, she didn't pull her hair once. Then her grandparents came for a visit. They had been clued in to what we were doing, so there wouldn't be a scene if she started to pull her hair. Which she did! I calmly led her to the bathroom, and she promised to stop, but her grandpa, whom she adores, told her, 'We'll still be here when you're done.' She returned a few minutes later, with no evidence of having actually pulled her hair out! The rest of the day was uneventful.

"The next day, my mom and I went shopping, and we were purchasing some new things for her. When we noticed her pulling her hair out (we've come to realize it is simply attention-seeking behavior), we left the counter and returned her new things to the shelves and prepared to leave. She wanted to know why, and I just told her, 'We need to go home now.' She knew why, and knew that a tantrum would bring other unpleasant consequences!

"Since then, she hasn't pulled her hair once. A friend who told me that she thought we were being 'mean' and 'hard-hearted' about this said that (the daughter) couldn't help it. I kept that in the back of my mind, and observed her at play, rest and during the one video a week she is allowed. There was no unconscious pulling. She did it only where she thought it would bring her attention. I think this is working!"

So much for "not being able to help it," "grooming genes gone out of control," "stressed over the anticipation of a new sibling," biochemical imbalances, brain abnormalities, conflicts, anxieties, unresolved psychological issues, attachment problems, failure to bond, self-punishment for secret bad thoughts, repressing traumatic memories, obsessive-compulsive disorder, and so on. So much as well for drugs, psychotherapy, and for people with capital letters after their names who know a lot of stuff the common folk don't know but don't haven't a clue when it comes to what the common folk have known, especially about children, for thousands of years: to wit, children aren't complicated. Therefore, child rearing is relatively easy. If it's not, then you're doing something wrong . . . *bad wrong*, as we Southerners say. Someday, hopefully, parents will once again realize that when children do things they shouldn't, they don't need a psychologist. They need discipline . . . firm, calm, and loving discipline.

When I told this story in my nationally syndicated newspaper column, a firestorm of controversy ensued. Among dozens of critical letters and e-mails from TTMs all over the U.S. was one from the executive director of the Trichotillomania Learning Center (TLC) in Santa Cruz, California, accusing me of dispensing harmful, misleading information. She said that sending the little girl to the bathroom to pull her hair amounted to "shaming" and also chastised me for not mentioning the name of the disorder in the original column.

How, pray tell, is being told that you can pull all the hair you want, as long as you pull in the bathroom, going to result in shame? Being permitted to do something within certain benign boundaries is not shameful. It is liberating. In this case, it liberated the little girl from the habit of hair-pulling. Unfortunately, it is certainly the case that too many parents of hair-pulling children do try to shame and/or scare their kids into stopping by telling them how awful they look, spanking them, telling them their hair will never grow back, and so on. It is axiomatic that shaming a person who is engaging in compulsive behavior will only exacerbate the problem. But as this case illustrates, shame is not the only alternative to professional treatment.

I did not mention TTM by name because a valid disorder does not disappear in response to calm, authoritative instruction. Since the little girl in question stopped her hair-pulling after being told to pull in the bathroom only, she clearly "had" nothing. She was, however, developing a habit that conceivably could have developed into a compulsion and might have eventually resulted in a diagnosis. I was told by another TLC associate that the little girl might have stopped only temporarily. Indeed, the symptoms of a truly diagnosable disorder may wax and wane, but in the long run are much, much more persistent than was the case here.

Nearly one year later, the girl's mother sent me this update: "My daughter is a much happier little girl these days, not to mention that our family is much calmer. She even laughs about it now. One day, she put her hand up to scratch her head and said, 'Don't worry, Mom, I'm not pulling my hair out, I'm just scratching an itch.'"

The fact is, there is no proven biological state that defines TTM any more than there is one that defines the compulsion to change one's clothes numerous times a day (not unheard of in children, by the way). To say, however, as do the folks at TLC, that TTM "strikes" people is to imply that it is an invasive disease. This may serve to relieve guilt, but it also may send parents running to professionals when, as in this case, a little creative discipline might have done the trick.[1]

As I told my critic, "Behavior alone does not a disorder make." Nonetheless, one must wonder how many "disorders" have been manufactured out of nothing more.

"THE DOCTOR" CURES EARLY ONSET SCHMIPOLAR DISORDER

In 2007, the parents of a six-year-old boy asked my advice concerning his daily, sometimes violent tantrums that had been ongoing since he was three. They had removed nearly everything from his bedroom including his dresser and lamp because they were often the objects of his destructive rages. When he threw one of his fits, they confined him to his room for the day, but if he tried to hurt one of them when being escorted there (e.g., digging his nails into his mother's arm), or he kicked the walls or some article of furniture along the way (he had done considerable damage to his bedroom walls), they confined him to his room for a week other than church and school. When his mom e-mailed me, she said he was "currently upstairs kicking his walls and screaming his head off." She asked if one week of confinement was unreasonable, adding, "I have put up with this for far too long."

Whether "reasonable" or not by whatever standard, one week of confinement in a spartan but otherwise pleasant room was obviously accomplishing nothing. More of the same was surely destined to accomplish more of the same. I told them to sit down with their son at the first calm moment and tell him that "the Doctor" had said they were going about this all wrong (passing the disciplinary "buck" to an absent, third-party authority figure is often strategic). He was old enough, the Doc said, to go to his room on his own. So, from then on, when he pitched one of his fits, that's what they were to do: simply tell him to go to his room. If he obeyed, right away, he only had to stay there until he'd gotten himself back under control. When he came out, however, he had to apologize to everyone who witnessed the outburst.

If, however, he refused to go to his room, requiring that one of his parents take him, he had to remain there the rest of the day and go to bed immediately after supper. If a tantrum occurred after supper, and he refused to go on his own to his room, then he had to go to bed immediately.

The Doctor also told the parents that until they were able to fix—spackle, paint—all damage to his room they could not buy him anything other than what was absolutely necessary.

I recommended that they finish the conversation on a upbeat note, as in, "So, we promise to do what the Doctor says from now on!"

A month later, this update: "He has had three tantrums in the last month—a huge change from one to three per day. He is more helpful at home, is reading to his little brother, and has a much sunnier attitude." The repairs to his room were almost finished, and the return of his dresser was imminent.

It's a fairly safe bet that Janice and Demitri Papolos, authors of *The Bipolar Child*, would have said this child was in the throes of early onset bipolar disorder. The parents' description of his often erratic behavior fit the Papolos' description like hand-in-glove. According to them, EOBD is caused by as-yet-unknown physiological abnormalities, as in the still-theoretical (but widely thought to be established beyond question) "bio-chemical imbalance." Suffice to say, my general take on this latest childhood behavior disorder amounts to "bipolar, schmipolar." I may someday be proven wrong, but until there is as much proof that things like wild tantrums at age six are caused by biochemical glitches as there is that bacterial pneumonia is caused by identifiable bacteria, I'll stick with schmipolar.

At this time, I'll simply point out that physical anomalies capable of sustaining violent emotional upheavals and a generally surly attitude for three years cannot be cured by simply telling the child in question that when such an upheaval occurs, he can either go to his room on his own or be taken there, that his choice determines his length of stay, and that he must apologize afterward. Yet this "therapy" worked, so one can only conclude that this little boy's physiology is without defect.

CHILD CURED OF EOBD AND ODD AND TOILET TRAINED IN ONE DAY!

Through my website, I received an e-mail from the exasperated mother of a four-and-one-half-year-old girl who refused to use the toilet. She insisted on wearing disposable diapers and did not care that she would not be allowed to attend school if she had not accepted that the toilet is where civilized persons put their "business." It is perhaps needless to point out that this child refused to do just about anything her parents told (pleaded with) her to do. In addition, she was prone to wild tantrums when her parents did not accede to her oft-outrageous demands. She most definitely fit the DSM description for ODD and was presenting EOBD characteristics as well.

The mother told me she had tried everything. "No, you haven't," I responded. I persuaded her to take a week off from her job, telling her that I doubted the cure would take longer than that.

"Can we wait until after her dance recital at the end of next month?" she asked, to which I pointed out that I had reserved the next week to work with her. Politely, but firmly, I told her I wasn't willing to give her my time according to *her* whim. I also knew that this mom was in great conflict. On the one hand, she wanted her daughter to use the toilet. On the other, she didn't want to do anything to upset her daughter, an only child who was obviously in complete control of their small family. Mom needed a resolute push. I gave it to her.

One day, while the daughter was visiting a relative, her parents stripped her room of all possessions, including favorite clothing, and put everything in the attic. They also removed all diapers, pull-ups, and anything else that was associated with wearing them from the home.

When she returned home, her parents handed her a pair of panties and said, "You are never again going to wear a diaper or a pull-up, but you can go poop and pee in these new panties all you want."

Then they showed her to her room and told her that this was the state of her life—no favorite clothing, no toys, no dolls, no special privileges—until she decided to begin using the toilet. Furthermore, they said they were never going to tell her to use it again. She had to use it on her own (which she knew how to do, of course).

If she used the toilet properly for three days, she would receive one item back—her least favorite item. Every three days of perfect toilet hygiene would result in the return of another item. If she had an "on purpose" (they were not "accidents" by any stretch of the definition), she would clean herself in the bathroom and wash her clothes in a bucket in the bathroom while her parents stripped her room back to square one.

"We will then make you stay in your room until you ask us, politely, if you can please come out to use the bathroom," they said. "If you use the bathroom properly, then you can stay out of your room until bedtime."

The princess began to wail piteously, made a face, and promptly "purposed" on herself. Equally promptly, and doing their best to act unruffled, her parents took her through the routine. As she screamed hysterically, Mom put a washcloth in her hand and made her wipe herself down. Then Mom stood over her, holding her hands and making them move properly, while the princess washed her soiled clothes in the bucket. Then her parents took her to her room, where she continued to scream and sob for three hours.

Finally, she stopped, composed herself and called, "I want to use the bathroom!"

The next day, I received this e-mail from the mother: "She has been using the bathroom properly since yesterday afternoon. I never in my wildest dreams thought this problem could be solved so quickly. What do I do now?"

I simply told her to stay the course. To make a short story shorter, the child never had an "on purpose" again. About six months later, the parents came up to me at a speaking engagement and introduced themselves.

NIPPING "ADHD" IN FULL BLOOM

They told me that not only was their daughter using the toilet like a normal child her age, without prompting, but she was also obeying them the first time they told her to do something. Furthermore, she was a much happier child, which was the best news of all.

Isn't it amazing how quickly brain chemicals can be brought back into balance with nothing more complicated than proper discipline?

CURED! SIXTH GRADE BOY WITH ADHD, DEPRESSION, AND ANXIETY

Brad, an eleven-year-old boy in the sixth grade, was finally referred for evaluation after a longstanding history of behavior and learning problems. His pediatrician diagnosed ADHD and then referred him to a specialty clinic where a psychiatrist confirmed ADHD as well as depression along with some anxiety features. Although oppositional defiant disorder was never diagnosed, Brad was not by any means a compliant child, and he was becoming noticeably more defiant of authority as he approached his teen years.

Brad was treated first with a stimulant, and then an SSRI antidepressant was added into the mix. Nonetheless, he continued to present significant problems both at home and at school, so his pediatrician increased the daily dose. At that point, his parents learned of Dr. Ravenel's work with ADHD children and sought his help. When Dr. Ravenel first became involved, Brad was having great difficulty sleeping, was acting out in class, and continued to underachieve.

Brad was heavily engaged in video games and watched copious amounts of television. In addition, his diet was heavy on junk food and deficient in fresh vegetables and fruits. None of the professionals involved in his prior evaluations had ever inquired about his exposure to electronic stimuli or about his eating habits. Why would they? After all, the ADHD Establishment steadfastly maintains that neither electronics nor poor nutrition has anything to do with ADHD.

By their own admission, Brad's parents had reached the point of exhaustion in their efforts to help him succeed in school. Almost every night, they orchestrated a homework session around the kitchen table that took a toll on everyone's emotional health. The parents were not comfortable with the kind or quantity of medication Brad was taking, but they didn't know what else to do.

Dr. Ravenel started by having Brad's parents and teachers fill out a commonly used behavior assessment questionnaire. Brad more than met criteria for ADHD, ODD, depression, and anxiety. Following a more comprehensive evaluation (but no testing), and with the cooperation of his primary pediatrician, Brad was slowly weaned off his medications. Within four months, he was drug-free and has remained so for more than two years as of April 2008. Meanwhile, Brad's parents sharply reduced his exposure to electronic media and significantly increased his intake of fresh fruits and vegetables.

Dr. Ravenel's parent-coaching involved helping Brad's parents begin to see him as capable of developing self-control and doing well in school as opposed to a child with a neurological handicap. This was essential to helping them—and especially the mother—stop micromanaging (i.e., enabling).

Three months into a therapeutic regimen that was medication-free, Brad's mother reported that she had been successful at backing out of the homework business. Brad was on his own in school. Granted, he continued to struggle to some degree, but his most recent report card showed six Bs, two As, and one C. Once in danger of failing the sixth grade, he was now functioning independently and responsibly in school. Perhaps most important, he was learning how to struggle, and that struggle paid off.

One year later, Brad's parents and several teachers again completed separate copies of the original behavior questionnaire. Their answers clearly indicated that all diagnostic behaviors had been resolved. Brad no longer showed any significant symptoms of ADHD, ODD, depression, or anxiety. Most telling was the fact that his parents spontaneously observed that he had changed his self-concept from being handicapped to one of being capable of controlling himself and of being successful from his own efforts.

One of the more interesting features of Brad's case was that during his rehabilitation, the parents were dealing with another crisis and were not able to be consistent with the disciplinary measures Dr. Ravenel recommended. Basically, Brad was cured of ADHD, ODD, depression, and an anxiety disorder by parents who cut back the influence of electronics, improved his diet, and elevated their expectations, saving themselves thousands of dollars in the process.

CURED! DEPRESSED EIGHT-YEAR-OLD WITH ADHD AND ODD

Randall began receiving frequent demerits for bad behavior during three- and four-year preschool. His problems with inattention and impulsivity continued, and worsened, through kindergarten and first grade. To say that he was disruptive in class would be an understatement.

In the second grade, at the suggestion of the teacher, Randall's parents involved their pediatrician. On the basis of verbal reports obtained from the parents and Randall's teachers, the pediatrician diagnosed ADHD and started Randall on a time-release stimulant. After a period of improvement, Randall's parents reported feeling that the drug's effectiveness had diminished, so the pediatrician increased the dose. Almost immediately, side effects such as poor appetite, headaches, and moodiness became an issue, so the pediatrician did what most would do under the circumstances: he changed from one stimulant to another. That brought on sleep problems, so yet another medication was added.

After nearly a year of ups and downs with medications, Randall's parents became disturbed over what they accurately perceived as a treatment plan that relied exclusively on drugs, so when they heard, through the parent grapevine, that Dr. Ravenel offered a nonmedical approach to ADHD, they sought his advice. Sure enough, Dr. Ravenel's first step was to stop Randall's medications. According to his parents' and teachers' responses to standard behavior questionnaires, Randall easily qualified for ADHD and ODD.

When his parents informed Randall's third-grade teacher that they were going to deal with his behaviors without the use of drugs, the teacher told them she felt their decision was naive and unlikely to succeed. She put considerable pressure on the parents to continue the original treatment approach. Nonetheless, and to their credit, the parents moved ahead with the new plan.

Dr. Ravenel recommended significant restrictions on parent participation in homework. Effectively, Randall was now expected to do his homework on his own and accept the consequences thereof. As is the case with most boys these days, Randall was overinvolved with television and video games, so Dr. Ravenel obtained a commitment from the parents to take Randall off all electronics cold-turkey for the time being.

Dr. Ravenel then began helping the parents put in place a home-based discipline plan called "Three strikes, you're out!" with which to deal with Randall's oppositional and disrespectful tendencies. Misbehaviors were clearly defined and posted on the refrigerator. They included "Becoming loud and argumentative when we tell you to do something," "Calling us names when we don't give you or let you do what you want," and "Ignoring us when we talk to you." On any given day, Randall could misbehave twice without significant consequence. On those two occasions, he was simply assigned to fifteen minutes of time-out. On the third occasion, he was confined to his room for the remainder of the day, a room which had been stripped of electronic entertainment as well as most of Randall's favorite playthings. In addition, his bedtime was moved up one hour. If the third misbehavior took place after supper, his parents sent him immediately to bed. Over the course of two forty-five-minute parent coaching sessions, Dr. Ravenel emphasized to the parents the need to be both consistent and dispassionate in their enforcement of the new system.

Two weeks following completion of the parent training, Randall's teacher reported being amazed at the dramatic improvement she saw in his classroom behavior and academic performance. A teacher who had given Dr. Ravenel's nonmedical approach little chance of succeeding began referring other children to his practice. She further confided that had she known that ADHD could be successfully treated without drugs, she would have gone in the same direction with her now-adult child.

Four months after Dr. Ravenel began working with the parents, follow-up questionnaires and verbal reports showed complete resolution of behaviors diagnostic of ADHD and ODD. His teacher used the word "dramatic" to describe Randall's improvement at school.

After three years of no contact with Randall or word of his status, Dr. Ravenel phoned the parents to ask how he was doing. They were happy to report that he was continuing to do well both at home and at school. In the sixth grade, he was making all As and Bs. His teachers described him as a conscientious, well-rounded student who loves to learn. Obviously, Randall's self-image had improved considerably since discovering that he could control himself and do well in school without drugs.

CURED! ELEVEN-YEAR-OLD BOY WITH ADHD

Caleb's parents had homeschooled him from day one. They contacted Dr. Ravenel when Caleb was in the sixth grade, seeking assistance with ongoing learning and attention problems. Specifically, he continued to struggle with reading and writing assignments and had great difficulty sitting still, paying attention during instruction, and completing work within defined deadlines.

His parents subscribed to a traditional parenting approach, which probably goes a long way toward explaining why this otherwise inattentive child was well-behaved. According to Dr. Ravenel's assessment, Caleb met criteria for a diagnosis of ADHD. Not surprisingly, he was overinvolved with electronic media and his diet was high in refined carbohydrates, low in protein, and almost devoid of fresh ingredients.

Dr. Ravenel began by recommending sharp restrictions in Caleb's exposure to television and video games along with dietary modifications that included virtually eliminating refined carbohydrates, increasing protein consumption, and omega-3 fatty acid supplements. Two months later, his parents noted that Caleb's ability to concentrate had markedly improved, and he was making substantial progress with his reading and writing. Sure enough, according to the parents' responses to a standard questionnaire approved by the Establishment, he no longer met ADHD criteria. Caleb himself offered that he felt more alert and efficient after eating a high-protein breakfast.

The Establishment vehemently denies that either electronic media or poor nutrition can cause ADHD. Yet here's a story, one of many in fact, in which removing electronics and implementing a healthy diet cured ADHD. One is moved to ask: if changing certain aspects of a child's lifestyle can cure ADHD (as determined by DSM-IV criteria), then does it not make sense that those aspects were the cause of the problem in the first place?

A COMMONSENSE APPROACH

In each of the above real-life cases, behaviors diagnostic of ADHD, ODD, EOBD, depression, and anxiety were cured with nothing more than an approach based on common sense. It is common sense that effective discipline is the way to deal with misbehavior. It is common sense that assaulting the developing brain with electronic stimulation can compromise attention span and self-control; therefore, it is common sense that in order to recover its potential, the brain needs to be electronics-free. It is common sense that problems in a person's diet can cause changes in mood, productivity, energy, and attention; therefore, it is common sense that a healthy diet makes for a more functional behavior.

The Establishment deals in rocket science—genes, chemical imbalances, prefrontal dysfunctions, "wiring" issues in the brain, and the like. The approach used by Dr. Ravenel and myself is not rocket science. It's simple and inexpensive. Most important, it brings results. Having "been there, done that" as one-time members of the Establishment, we are convinced that our approach is vastly superior to a medical approach based on the disease model. It produces results without undesirable side effects, results that are longer-lasting and that produce improvements not just in behavior but also in self-concept. Children who have benefited from this approach come to believe in themselves. They develop a confidence in their abilities that cannot be compared to believing that one is capable only when under the influence of a chemical compound. Dr. Ravenel and I also submit that if our experience is not enough, the evidence is on our side. Stated simply, the research does not validate the Establishment's approach. It validates ours.

Our approach teaches self-control. What are ADHD, ODD, and EOBD if not failures of self-control? One prominent practitioner has compared self-control to a muscle that can be strengthened through exercise and observes that "Self-control is a psychological skill whose development could potentially prevent, or aid in the treatment of, vast amounts of psychopathology."[2]

Our approach makes unnecessary the ADHD Establishment's expensive testing, long-term (expensive) therapies, and potentially harmful (and expensive) medications. It's so simple that once learned, parents can teach one another, which is truly back to basics, not to mention truly threatening to an industry that has persuaded parents, primary care physicians, therapists, educators, insurance companies, and the media that where such things as ADHD are concerned, nothing is simple, nothing is basic, and nothing is common sense.

The Establishment has one thing right: Dr. Ravenel and I are rabble-rousers. We aim to rouse. We hope we succeeded with you.

NOTES

INTRODUCTION
1. Personal pronouns in this book always refer to John Rosemond.

CHAPTER 1: FIVE SLIPPERY WORDS
1. Wylie, M.S. (2005, September/October). Visionary or voodoo? Daniel
    Amen's crusade has some neuroscientists up in arms. *Psychotherapy
    Networker*.

CHAPTER 2: REDEFINING CHILDHOOD
1. Smoller, J. W. The etiology and treatment of childhood. Developmental
    Psychology.org (devpsy.org). Retrieved May 28, 2008 from
    http://www.devpsy.org/humor/childhood_as_disease.html
2. American Psychiatric Association. (2000). *Diagnostic and statistical manual
    of mental disorders* (4th ed., text revision). Washington, DC: Author.
    (Emphasis added by the authors.)
3. Ibid.
4. Committee on Quality Improvement, Subcommittee on Attention-
    Deficit/Hyperactivity Disorder. (2000). Clinical practice guideline:
    Diagnosis and evaluation of the child with attention-deficit/hyperactivity
    disorder. *Pediatrics, 105,* 1158–1170.
5. Jensen, P. S., & Cooper, J. R. (2002). *Attention deficit hyperactivity disorder:
    State of the science—best practices* (Introduction, p. xxii; chapter 1, p. 14).
    Kingston, NJ: Civic Research Institute.
6. Diller, L. H. (1998). *Running on Ritalin* (chapter 9). New York: Bantam.
7. Angold, A., Erkanli, A., Egger, E., & Costello, J. (2000). Stimulant
    treatment for children: A community perspective. *Journal of the American
    Academy of Child and Adolescent Psychiatry, 39,* 975–994.

8. Rosenhan, D. L. (1973). On being sane in insane places. *Science, 179*(70), 250–258.

9. Rappley, M. D., Eneli, I. U., Mullan, P. B., Alvarez, F., Want, J., & Luo, M. S., et al. (2002, February). Patterns of psychotropic medication use in very young children with attention-deficit hyperactivity disorder. *Journal of Developmental and Behavioral Pediatrics, 23,* 23–30.

10. Conrad, P. (2004, August). Prescribing more psychotropic medications for children—what does the increase mean? Archives of *Pediatric and Adolescent Medicine, 158,* 829–830. Copyright © 2004 American Medical Association. Reprinted with permission.

11. Quinn, P. O. (1996). *Attention deficit disorder: diagnosis and treatment from infancy to adulthood* (Basic Principles into Practice Series, Vol. 13). New York: Routledge.

12. Caplan, P. J. (1995). *They say you're crazy: How the world's most powerful psychiatrists decide who's normal* (p. 205). Reading, MA: Addison-Wesley.

13. American Psychiatric Association. *Diagnostic and statistical manual.*

14. Caplan, P. J. *They say you're crazy* (pp. 213–214). (Emphasis added by the authors.)

15. Papolos, D., & Papolos, J. (2006). *The bipolar child* (chapter 1, pp. 4, 7, 33). New York: Broadway Books.

16. Ibid. (chapter 1, p. 32).

17. Ibid. (chapter 2, p. 54).

18. Ibid. (chapter 1, pp. 7, 8).

19. Ibid. (chapter 8, pp. 252–253).

20. Ibid. (Preface, p. xviii).

21. Juvenile Bipolar Research Foundation. [Homepage]. Retrieved May 28, 2008 from http:www.jbrf.org

22. Papolos, D. (2002). Child bipolar questionnaire—version 2.0. Juvenile Bipolar Research Foundation. http://www.jbrf.org

23. Healy, D., & Le Noury, J. (2007). Pediatric bipolar disorder: An object of study in the creation of an illness. *International Journal of Risk and Safety in Medicine, 19,* 209–221.

24. Papolos & Papolos. *Bipolar child* (chapter 2, p. 40).

25. About.com. Bipolar disorder. Retrieved May 28, 2008 from http://bipolar.about.com/cs/fr.htm

26. About.com. Parenting special needs. Retrieved May 28, 2008 from http://specialchildren.about.com/od/booksonmentalhealth/gr/bipolarchild.htm

27. Moreno, C., Laje, G., Blanco, C., Jiange, H., Schmidt, A., & Olfson, M. (2007, September). National trends in the outpatient diagnosis and treatment of bipolar disorder in youth. *Archives of General Psychiatry, 64,* 1032, 1034.

28. Ibid.

29. Center for Autism and Related Disorders. What is autism? Retrieved May 28, 2008 from http://www.centerforautism.com/whatisautism/

30. American Academy of Pediatrics. Children's health topics; Autism. Retrieved March 27, 2008 from http://www.aap.org/healthtopics/autism.cfm

31. National Dissemination Center for Children with Disabilities. (1998, resources updated October 2003). *Pervasive Developmental Disorders.* http://www.nichcy.org/pubs/factshe/fs20txt.htm#cause

32. Healy & Le Noury. Pediatric bipolar disorder, 219.

33. Reitman, D. (2003). A modest proposal for a new diagnostic classification: Intrinsic motivation deficit disorder (IMDD). *The Behavior Therapist, 26,* 310–311.

34. Levine, M. (2004). *The myth of laziness.* New York: Simon & Schuster.

35. Willis, D. W. (2004, January). *Pediatric News.*

36. Paul, R. (2005, February 1). Psycho feds target children. LewRockwell.com. http://www.lewrockwell.com/paul/paul232.html

CHAPTER 3: BIOLOGY IN WONDERLAND

1. Baughman, F. A., & Eakman, B. (2003, June). Making a killing. *Chronicles Magazine,* 44–45. http://www.beverlye.com/200306302032.html

2. Kendler, K. (2005, March). Toward a philosophical structure for psychiatry. *American Journal of Psychiatry, 162,* 433–440.

3. Smalley, S. L, et al. (2002). Genetic Linkage of Attention-Deficit/Hyperactivity Disorder on Chromosome 16p13, in a Region Implicated in Autism. *American Journal of Human Genetics, 71,* 959–963.

4. Norton, A., & Reuters Health Service. (2002, October 22). Online interview with Fred Baughman, Jr., MD. http://www.adhdfraud.org/commentary/102502-2.htm

5. British Broadcasting Company Radio. (2007, August 23). Transcript of "ADHD" on BBC Radio 4. http://www.bbc.co.uk/radio4/science/checkup_20070823.shtml

6. Gross, M. A. (2007). The cause of ADD/ADHD is genetic. The ADD Medical Treatment Center of Santa Clara Valley. http://www.addmtc.com/cause

7. Brown, K. (2003, July 11). New attention to ADHD genes. *Science, 301*(5630), 160–161.

8. Gatten, K. J. Researcher investigates source of ADHD. *The Catalyst Online.* Retrieved May 28, 2008 from http://www.musc.edu/catalyst/archive/2003/co3-7researcher.htm

9. Barkley, R. A. (2007, November 1). Attention-deficit/hyperactivity disorder: Nature, course, outcomes, and comorbidity. ContinuingEdCourses.Net. Copyright 2004–2007, Russell A. Barkley. http://www.continuingedcourses.net/active/courses/course003.php

10. Barkley, R. A. About ADHD—a fact sheet. Russell A. Barkley, Ph.D.: The Official Site. Retrieved May 28, 2008 from http://www.russellbarkley.org/adhd-facts.htm

11. ADHDrelief.com. Famous people and attention deficit disorder. Retrieved May 28, 2008 from http://www.adhdrelief.com/famous.html

12. Hallowell, E. M., & Ratey, J. J. (2005). *Delivered from distraction: Getting the most out of life with attention deficit disorder* (p. 149). New York: Ballantine.

13. Lewontin, R., Rose, S., & Kamin, L. (1985). *Not in our genes.* New York: Pantheon.

14. Ibid.

15 Hallowell & Ratey. *Delivered from distraction* (pp. 123–124).

16. Barry, R. J., Clarke, A. R., & Johnstone, S. J. (2003, February). A review of electrophysiology in attention-deficit/hyperactivity disorder: I. Qualitative and quantitative electroencephalography. *Clinical Neurophysiology. 114*(2), 171–183.

17. Cigna HealthCare. (2007, November 15). Cigna HealthCare coverage position statement. http://www.cigna.com/customer_care/healthcare_professional/coverage_positions/medical/mm_0239_coveragepositioncriteria_quantitative_eeg_qeeg.pdf

18. Hallowell, E. M. & Ratey, J. J. (1995). *Driven to distraction* (pp. 191–194). New York: Touchstone Books.

19. Massachusetts General Hospital. Biography of Stephen V. Faraone, Ph.D. Retrieved May 28, 2008 from www.massgeneral.org/pediatricpsych/staff/faraone.html

20. Joseph, J. (2003). Genetics and antisocial behavior. *Ethical Human Sciences and Services 5,* 41–44.

21. Lewontin, R., Rose, S., and Kamin, L. *Not in Our Genes.* New York: Pantheon, 1985. p. 115.

22. Shire, U.S. Inc. (2005). *Normalization—the ultimate goal for treatment success* [Brochure]. Florence, KY: Author.

23. NIH Consensus Development Panel. (2000). National Institutes of Health Consensus Development Conference statement: Diagnosis and treatment of attention-deficit/hyperactivity disorder (ADHD). *Journal of the American Academy of Child and Adolescent Psychiatry, 39,* 182–197.

24. Jensen & Cooper. *Attention-deficit hyperactivity disorder* (Introduction, p. xxii; Part 2, p. 1).

25. Ibid. (Part 2, p. 1).

26. Product manager for Shire, U.S. Inc. (2005, March 30). E-mail message to Dr. Bose Ravenel in response to his question.

27. Jensen & Cooper. *Attention-deficit hyperactivity disorder* (chapter 3, pp. 2, 7).

28. CBS News. (2007, November 13). Brain maturity may lag in kids with ADHD. Retrieved May 28, 2008 from http://www.cbsnews.com/stories/2007/11/12/health/main3492746.shtml?source=search_story

29. Ibid.

30. Jackson, G. E. (2005). A curious consensus: "Brain scans prove disease"? *Ethical Human Psychology and Psychiatry, 8*(1), 55–60.

31. CBS News. Brain maturity may lag in kids with ADHD.

32. Baughman & Eakman. Making a killing.

33. Ibid.

34. Ibid.

35. Castellanos, X. F., et al. (2002). Developmental trajectories of brain volume abnormalities in children and adolescents with attention-deficit/hyperactivity disorder. *Journal of the American Medical Association, 288,* 1740–1748.

36. Wylie, M. S. (2005, September/October). Visionary or voodoo: Daniel

Amen's crusade has some neuroscientists up in arms. *Psychotherapy Networker.*

37. American Psychiatric Association, Division of Research. (2005). The clinical use of SPECT: Single photon emission computed tomography. *Psychiatric Research Report, 21*(2), 9–13.

38. Lacasse, J. R., & Leo, J. (2005, December). Serotonin and depression: A disconnect between the advertisements and the scientific literature. *PLoS Medicine, 12*(12), 35–45.

39. Leo, J., & Lacasse, J. R. (2008, February). The media and the chemical imbalance theory of depression. *Society, 45,* 35–45.

CHAPTER 4: THE POLITICS OF DIAGNOSIS

1. Carroll, L. (1865). *Alice's Adventures in Wonderland.* The Literature Network. http://www.online-literature.com/carroll/alice/12/

2. Crichton, M. (2003, January 17). Aliens cause global warming. Speech given at the California Institute of Technology, Pasadena, CA, and available on Crichton's website. http://www.crichton-official.com/speech-alienscauseglobalwarming.html

3. David, B., & Oakley, N. (2008, February). Cutting through the fat. *Delta Sky.* http://www.delta-sky.com/2008_02/starbooks/

4. Coulter, A. (1999, June 18). Justice O'Connor creates hostile environment. *Human Events.* Retrieved from http://findarticles.com/p/articles/mi_qa3827/is_199906/ai_n8876614

5. *Science Daily.* (2008, March 15). Adolescent girls with ADHD are at increased risk for eating disorder, study shows. http://www.sciencedaily.com/releases/2008/03/080314085032.htm

6. ADDvance.com. ADD (ADHD) checklist for girls. Retrieved May 28, 2008 from http://www.addvance.com/help/women/girl_checklist.html

CHAPTER 5: THE POLITICS AND PERILS OF PHARMACEUTICALS

1. Angell, M. (2004). *The truth about the drug companies: How they deceive us and what to do about it* (pp. 10–11). New York: Random House.

2. Ismail, M. A. (2007, April 1). Spending on lobbying thrives. Center for Public Integrity. http://www.publicintegrity.org/rx/report.aspx?aid=823

3. Angell, M. *The truth about the drug companies* (p. 104).

4. Moses, H., Braunwald, E., Martin, J. B., & Their, S. O. (2002). Collaborating with industry—choices for the academic medical center. *New England Journal of Medicine, 347,* 1371–1375.

5. Editorial. (2004, February 17). The "file drawer" phenomenon: Suppressing clinical evidence. *Canadian Medical Association Journal, 170*(4), 437, 439.

6. Kirsch, I. & Moore, T. J. (2002, July 15). The emperor's new drugs: An analysis of antidepressant medication data submitted to the U.S. Food and Drug Administration. *Prevention & Treatment. 5,* 1.

7. Whittington, C. J., Kendall, T., Fonagy, P., Cottrell, D., Cotgrove, A., & Boddington, E. (2004, April 24). Selective serotonin reuptake inhibitors in childhood depression: Systematic review of published versus unpublished data. *The Lancet, 363,* 1341–1345.

8. Kondro, W. & Sibbald, B. (2004, March 2). Drug company experts advised staff to withhold data about SSRI use in children. *Canadian Medical Journal, 170,* 783.

9. Jackson, G. E. (2005). *Rethinking psychiatric drugs: A guide for informed consent* (chapter 4, pp. 30, 31). Bloomington, IN: AuthorHouse.

10. Hearn, K. (2004, November 29). Here, kiddie, kiddie. *AlterNet.* http://www.alternet.org/story/20594/

11. Ibid.

12. Ibid.

13. Shire, U.S. Inc. (2002, June). *ADHD and the family: A blueprint for success* [Brochure]. Florence, KY: Author.

14. Rapoport, J., Buchsbaum, M., Weingartner, H., et al. (1980). Dextroamphetamine: Its cognitive and behavioral effects in normal and hyperactive boys and normal men. *Archives of General Psychiatry, 37,* 933–941.

15. Eli Lilly (sponsor). ADHD assessment questionnaire. WebMd. Retrieved June 28, 2005, from https://healthmanager.webmd.com/webmd/advhq/ADHDAssessPlus/report.aspx. (No longer on website.)

16. Hallowell, E. M., & Ratey, J. J. (1996). *Answers to distraction* (p. 128). New York: Bantam.

17. Children and Adults with Attention Deficit/Hyperactivity Disorder (CHADD). Mission and history. Retrieved May 28, 2008, from http://www.chadd.org/Content/CHADD/AboutCHADD/Mission/default.htm

18. Children and Adults with Attention Deficit/Hyperactivity Disorder (CHADD). Understanding AD/HD: How is AD/HD treated? Retrieved June 2, 2008, from http://www.chadd.org/Content/CHADD/Understanding/Treatment/default.htm. (Emphasis added by the authors.)

19. National Resource Center on AD/HD. Diagnosis & treatment: Treatment overview. Retrieved June 2, 2008, from http://www.help4adhd.org/en/treatment/treatmentoverview

20. National Resource Center on AD/HD. Diagnosis & treatment: Managing medication for children and adolescents with AD/HD (WWK3). Retrieved June 2, 2008, from http://www.help4adhd.org/en/treatment/medical/WWK3. (Emphasis added by the authors.)

21. Ibid.

22. Kern L., DePaul, G., Vope, R., Sokol, N., Lutz. G., Arbolino, L., et al. (2007). Multisetting assessment-based intervention for young children at risk for attention deficit hyperactivity disorder: Initial effects on academic and behavioral functioning. *School Psychology Review, 36*(2), 237–255.

23. Hearn, K. Here, kiddie, kiddie.

24. Children and Adults with Attention Deficit/Hyperactivity Disorder (CHADD). CHADD's 2006–2007 Annual Report. Retrieved March 28, 2008, from http://www.chadd.org/Content/CHADD/AboutCHADD/Reports/default.htm

25. Hearn, K. Here, kiddie, kiddie.

26. Ellison, P. A. (2003, June). Myths and misconceptions about AD/HD: Science over cynicism. (From *Attention* magazine.) National Resource Center on AD/HD. Retrieved June 2, 2008, from http://www.help4adhd.org/en/about/myths. (Emphasis added by the authors.)

27. Brooke, S., Molina, B., Flory, K., Hinshaw, S., Greiner, A., Arnold, L., et al. (2007). Delinquent behavior and emerging substance use in the MTA at 36 months: Prevalence, course, and treatment effects. *Journal of the American Academy of Child and Adolescent Psychiatry, 46*(8), 1028–1040.

28. BBC News. (2007, November 12). http://news.bbc.co.uk/2/hi/uk_news/7090011.stm

29. Schachter, H. M., Pham, B., King, J., Langford, S., & Mosher, D. (2001). How efficacious and safe is short-acting methylphenidate for the treatment of attention-deficit disorder in children and adolescents? A

meta-analysis. *Canadian Medical Association Journal, 165,* 1475–1488. (Emphasis added by the authors.)

30. McDonagh, M. S., Peterson, K., Dana, T., Thakurta, S. (2007, December). Drug class review on pharmacologic treatments for ADHD. Final report. Oregon Evidence-based Practice Center.http://www.ohsu.edu/ drugeffectiveness/reports/documents/ADHD%20Final%20Report%20Up date%202.pdf

31. Healy, M. (2008, January 28). Growing up with, and out of, ADHD. *Los Angeles Times.* http://articles.latimes.com/2008/jan/28/health/he-adhd28

32. American Academy of Pediatrics. (2004). *ADHD: A Complete and Authoritative Guide* (pp. 77–79). Elk Grove Village, IL: Author.

33. Cherland, E., & Fitzpatrick, R. (1999). Psychotic side effects of psychostimulants: A 5-year review. *Canadian Journal of Psychiatry, 44,* 811–813.

34. Breggin, P. R. (1999). Psychostimulants in the treatment of children diagnosed with ADHD: Part II—adverse effects on brain and behavior. *Ethical Human Sciences and Services, 1, 222, 225, 227.*

35. Kroutil, L. A., Van Brunt, D. L., Herman-Stahl, M. A., Heller, D. C., Bray, R. M., Penne, M. A. (2006, February 14). Nonmedical use of prescription stimulants in the United States. *Drug and Alcohol Dependence, 2,* 32.

36. Biederman, J. (1999). Pharmacotherapy of attention-deficit/hyperactivity disorder reduces risk for substance use disorder [Electronic article]. *Pediatrics, 104,* e20–30.

37. Lambert, N. M. & Hartsough, C. S. (1998). Prospective study of tobacco smoking and substance dependencies among samples of ADHD and non-ADHD participants. *Journal of Learning Disabilities, 31,* 533–544.

38. Barkley, R. A, Fischer, M., Smallish, L., & Fletcher, K. (2003, January). Does the treatment of attention-deficit/hyperactivity disorder with stimulants contribute to drug use/abuse? A 13-year prospective study. *Pediatrics, 111*(1), 97–109.

39. Hyman, S. E., & Nestler, E. J. (1996). Initiation and adaptation: A paradigm for understanding psychotropic drug action. *American Journal of Psychiatry, 153,* 151–162.

40. Jackson, G. E. *Rethinking psychiatric drugs* (chapter 6).

41. Ibid. (p. 267).

42. Barkley, R. A. (2002). ADHD—long-term course, adult outcome, and comorbid disorders. In P. S. Jensen and J. R. Cooper (Eds.), *Attention deficit hyperactivity disorder state of the science—best practices* (chapter 4, pp. 6, 7). Kingston, NJ: Wiley Publishers.

43. Jackson, G. E. (2005). *Rethinking psychiatric drugs* (chapter 9, p. 294).

44. Seligman, M. E. P. (2006). *Learned optimism: How to change your mind and your life.* New York: Vintage.

45. Bandura, A. (1997). *Self-efficacy: The exercise of control.* New York: Worth Publishers.

46. Cherland & Fitzpatrick. Psychotic side effects of psychostimulants.

47. Adderall XR package insert (2007). (Emphasis added by the authors.)

48. FDA News. (2007, February 21). FDA directs ADHD drug manufacturers to notify patients about cardiovascular adverse events and psychiatric adverse events. http://www.fda.gov/bbs/topics/NEWS/2007/NEW01568.html

49. Matochik, J., Mordahl, T., Gross, J., Semple, W., King, C., Cohen, R., et al. (1993). Effects of acute stimulant medication on cerebral metabolism in adults with hyperactivity. *Neuropsychopharmacology, 8*(4), 377–386.

50. Satterfield. J. H., Schell, A. M., & Barb, S. D. (1980). Potential risk of prolonged administration of stimulant medication for hyperactivity. *Journal of Developmental and Behavioral Pediatrics, 1,* 102–107. Cited in Jensen & Cooper, *Attention-deficit hyperactivity disorder* (chapter 10, p. 9).

51. Nissen, S. E. (2006). ADHD drugs and cardiovascular risk. *New England Journal of Medicine, 354,* 1445–1448.

52. Agency for Health Care Research and Quality. (2007, September 17). AHRQ and FDA to collaborate in largest study ever of possible heart risks with ADHD medications [Press release]. http://www.ahrq.gov/news/press/pr2007/adhdmedpr.htm

53. Poulton A., & Cowell, C. T. (1987). Slowing of growth in height and weight on stimulants: A characteristic pattern. *Journal of Paediatrics and Child Health, 39,* 180–185.

54. Lisska, M. C., & Rivkees, S. A. (2003). Daily methylphenidate use slows the growth of children: A community based study. *Journal of Paediatric Endocrinology and Metabolism, 16,* 711–718.

55. Swanson, J. M., Elliott, G. R., Greenhill, L. L., Wigal, T., Arnold, E., et al.

(2007). Effects of stimulant medication on growth rates across 3 years in the MTA follow-up. *Journal of the American Academy of Child and Adolescent Psychiatry, 46*, 1025.

56. Hearn, K. Here, kiddie, kiddie.
57. Jackson, G. (2005). Cybernetic children: How technologies change and constrain the developing mind. In N. Radcliffe & C. Newnes (Eds.), *Making and breaking children's lives*. Ross-on-Wye, Herefordshire, England: PCCS Books.

CHAPTER 6: A SIMPLE EXPLANATION
1. Wiener, D. N., & Phillips, E. L. (1971). *Training children in self-discipline and self-control*. Upper Saddle River, NJ: Prentice Hall.
2. Seligman. *Learned optimism* (p. vii).
3. Barkley, R. Dr. Russell Barkley on AD/HD: Excerpts from his lecture in San Francisco, CA, on June 17, 2000 (p. 14). In A parent's guide to helping kids with learning difficulties. SchwabLearning.org. http://www.schwablearning.org/pdfs/2200_7-barktran.pdf?date=4-12-05
4. Barkley, R. A. (1998). *Attention-deficit hyperactivity disorder: A handbook for diagnosis and treatment* (p. 176). New York: Guilford Press.
5. Foreman, J. (2006, June 26). Hyperactive adults need help too. *Boston Globe*.
6. Aunola, K., & Nurmi, J. (2005). The role of parenting styles in children's problem behavior. *Child Development, 76*(6), 1144–1159.
7. Eisenberg, N., Qing, Z., Spinrad, T. L., Valiente, C., Fabes, R. A., & Liew, J. (2006). Relations among positive parenting, children's effortful control, and externalizing problems: A three-wave longitudinal study. *Child Development, 76*(5), 1055–1071.
8. Baumrind, D. (1966). Effects of authoritative parental control on child behavior. *Child Development, 37*(4), 887–907.
9. Baumand, D. (1967). Child care practices anteceding three patterns of preschool behavior. *Genetic Psychology Monographs, 75*(1), 43–88.
10. Barkley. Dr. Barkley on AD/HD: Excerpts from his lecture in San Francisco.
11. Healy, J. M. (1999). *Endangered minds: Why children don't think and what we can do about it*. New York: Simon & Schuster.
12. Strayhorn, J. M., Jr. (2002, January). Self-control: Theory and research.

Journal of the American Academy of Child and Adolescent Psychiatry, 41(1), 7–16.

13. American Psychiatric Association. *Diagnostic and statistical manual.*

14. Healy. *Endangered minds.* Quoted in G. DeGaetano, *Visual media and young children's attention spans.* http://users.stargate.net/~cokids/VisualMedia/html. (Emphasis added by the authors.)

15. Christakis, D. A., Zimmerman, F. J., DiGiuseppe, D. L., & McCarty, C. A. (2004, April). Early television exposure and subsequent attentional problems in children. *Pediatrics, 113*(4), 708–713.

16. Jensen, P. S., Mrazek, D., Knapp, P. K., Steinberg, L., Pfeffer, C., Schowalter, J., et al. (1997, December). Evolution and revolution in child psychiatry: ADHD as a disorder of adaptation. *Journal of the American Academy of Child & Adolescent Psychiatry, 36*(12), 1672–1681.

17. Stone, P. (1986, January/February). TV addiction. *Mother Earth News.* http://www.motherearthnews.com/DIY/1986-01-01/TV-Addiction.aspx

18. Papolos & Papolos. *Bipolar child* (chapter 5, p. 151).

19. Ruff, M. E. (2005, September). Attention deficit disorder and stimulant use: An epidemic of modernity. *Clinical Pediatrics, 44,* 557–563.

20. Barkley, R. A. About ADHD—a fact sheet. Russell A. Barkley, Ph.D.: The Official Site. Retrieved March 27, 2008 from http://www.russellbarkley.org/adhd-facts.htm

21. Clayton, V. (2008). What's to blame for the rise in ADHD? Msnbc. http://www.msnbc.msn.com/id/5933775/page/2/

22. Rabiner, D. (2006). Background information on David Rabiner, Ph.D.: Senior Research Scientist, Duke University. Helpforadd.com. http://www.helpforadd.com/background/

23. Rabiner, D. (2006). Medication treatment for ADHD/ADD and attention deficit disorder. Helpforadd.com. http://www.helpforadd.com/medical-treatment/

24. Stevens, L., Zhang, W., Peck, L., Kuczek, T., Grevstad, N., et al. (2003). EFA supplementation in children with inattention, hyperactivity, and other disruptive disorders. *Lipids, 38,* 1007–1021.

25. Galland, L. Nutritional therapies for attention deficit hyperactivity disorder. Foundation for Integrated Medicine. Retrieved May 28, 2008 from http://mdheal.org/attention.htm

26. Richardson, A. J., & Montgomery, P. (2005). The Oxford-Durham study: A randomized controlled trial of dietary supplementation with fatty acids in children with developmental coordination disorder. *Pediatrics, 115,* 1360–1366.

27. Schachter, H. M., Pham, B., King, J., Langford, S., & Moher, D. (2001). How efficacious and safe is short-acting methylphenidate for the treatment of attention-deficit disorder in children and adolescents? A meta-analysis. *Canadian Medical Association Journal, 165,* 1475–1488.

28. Sinn, N., & Bryan, J. (2007). Effect of supplementation with polyunsaturated fatty acids and micronutrients on learning and behavior problems associated with child ADHD. *Journal of Developmental and Behavioral Pediatrics, 28,* 82–91.

29. Sorgi, P. J., Hallowell, E. M., Hutchins, H. L., & Sears, B. (2007). Effects of an open-label pilot study with high-dose EPA/DHA concentrates on plasma phospholipids and behavior in children with attention deficit hyperactivity disorder. *Nutrition Journal, 6,* 16.

30. Lipton, M. A., & Mayo, J. P. (1983, August) Diet and hyperkinesis—an update. *Journal of the American Dietetic Association, 83*(2), 132–134.

31. Weiss, B. (1982). Food additives and environmental chemicals as sources of childhood behavior disorders. *Journal of the American Academy of Child Psychiatry, 21*(2), 144–152.

32. Rimland, B. (1983). The Feingold diet: An assessment of the reviews by Mattes, by Kavale and Forness and others. *Journal of Learning Disabilities, 16*(6), 331–333.

33. Schwab, D. W., & Nhi-Ha, T. T. (2004). Do artificial food colors promote hyperactivity in children with hyperactive syndromes? A meta-analysis of double-blind placebo-controlled trials. *Developmental and Behavioral Pediatrics, 25,* 423–434.

34. Girardi, N. L., et al. (1995). Blunted catecholamine responses after glucose ingestion in children with attention deficit disorder. *Pediatric Research, 38,* 539–542.

35. Schoenthaler, S. J., Doraz, W. E., & Wakefield, J. A. (1986). The impact of a low food additive and sucrose diet on academic performance in 803 New York City public schools. *International Journal of Biosocial Research, 8*(2), 185–195.

36. Barkley, R. A. [Homepage]. Russell A. Barkley, Ph.D.: The Official Site. Retrieved May 28, 2008 from http://www.russellbarkley.org/

37. Armstrong, T. (1995). *The myth of the A.D.D. child: 50 ways to improve your child's behavior and attention span without drugs, labels, or coercion.* New York: Dutton.

CHAPTER 7: WHY JOHNNY CAN'T SIT STILL, PAY ATTENTION, DO WHAT HE'S TOLD, AND LEARN TO READ

1. Snyder, T. (Ed.). (1993). *120 years of American education: A statistical portrait* (excerpts from chapter 1). In *National assessment of adult literacy (NAAL).* IES (Institute of Education Sciences), National Center for Education Statistics. http://nces.ed.gov/naal/lit_history.asp

2. Sweet, R. W. (1996). Illiteracy: An incurable disease or education malpractice? National Right to Read Foundation. http://www.nrrf.org/essay_Illiteracy.html

3. Flesch, R. (1986). *Why Johnny can't read: And what you can do about it.* New York: Harper Paperbacks.

4. Sweet. Illiteracy.

5. Shaywitz, B. A., Shawitz, S. E., Blachman, B. A., Pugh, K. R., Fulbright, R. K., Skudlarski, P., et al. (2004, May 1). Development of left occipitotemporal systems for skilled reading in children after a phonologically-based intervention. *Biological Psychiatry, 55*(9), 926–933.

6. Darlin, D. (1996, June 17). Back to basics, again. *Forbes,* 46.

7. Shaywitz & Shaywitz. Development of left occipitotemporal systems.

8. Strickland, D. S. (1998). What's basic in beginning reading: Finding common ground. National Education Association. http://www.nea.org/teachexperience/rdk040225.html?mode=print

9. Shaywitz & Shaywitz. Development of left occipitotemporal systems.

10. Anderson, D., & Warshaw, M. (1996, April). For teaching kids to read, entrepreneur John Shanahan got . . . whacked! by the government, the media, and educators. *Success,* 32.

11. Gordon, N. (2005, May 26). Profiles: Organizational donors. The Center for Public Integrity. http://www.publicintegrity.org/partylines/report.aspx?aid=692

12. Olsen, D. A., & Olsen, E. (1999, April 15). Don't cry for me, head start. Cato Institute. http://www.cato.org/pub_display.php?pub_id=5483

13. Elkind, D. (1988). *Reinventing childhood: Raising and educating children in a changing world.* Cambridge, MA: Modern Learning Press.

14. Kalson, S. (2006, August 27). Back to school: From reading to algebra, everything in school is starting earlier. *Pittsburgh Post-Gazette.* http://www.post-gazette.com/pg/06239/716712-298.stm

15. National Association for the Education of Young Children. (1995). NAEYC position statement on school readiness. http://www.naeyc.org/about/positions/PSREDY98.asp. (Emphasis added by the authors.)

16. Sax, L. (2000, November 1). Ritalin: Better living through chemistry? *The World & I Online.* http://www.worldandi.com/public/2000/november/sax.html

17. Campbell, J. J. (1996). Medical professionals can't cure what ails many school children. The National Right to Read Foundation. http://www.nrrf.org/article_campbell.htm

18. LeFever, G. B., Dawson, K. V., & Morrow, A. L. (1999). The extent of drug therapy for attention deficit-hyperactivity disorder among children. *American Journal of Public Health, 89,* 1359–1364.

19. Stipek, D. (1995). Effects of different instructional approaches on young children's achievement and motivation. *Child Development, 66,* 209–223.

20. Marcon, R. A. (2002, Spring). Moving up the grades: Relationship between preschool model and later school success. *Early Childhood Research and Practice, 4*(1). http://ecrp.uiuc.edu/v4n1/marcon.html

21. Public Schools of North Carolina. North Carolina standard course of study. Retrieved May 28, 2008 from http://www.ncpublicschools.org/curriculum/computerskills/scos/06kindergarten

22. North Carolina Office of School Readiness. About us. Retrieved May 28, 2008 from http://www.osr.nc.gov/aboutUs.asp

23. Feulner, E. (2001, April 11). Grade padding at Harvard University. *Capitalism Magazine.* http://www.capmag.com/article.asp?ID=462

24. Stout, M. (2000). *The feel-good curriculum: The dumbing down of America's kids in the name of self-esteem.* New York: Perseus Books.

25. Seligman. *Learned optimism* (p. v).

26. Baumeister, R. F., Campbell, J. D., Krueger, J. I ., & Vohs, K. D. (2003,

May). Does high self-esteem cause better performance, interpersonal success, happiness, or healthier lifestyles? *Psychological Science in the Public Interest, 4*(1), 2. (Emphasis added by the authors.)

27. Twenge, J. M., & Campbell, W. K. (2001). Age and birth cohort differences in self-esteem: A cross-temporal meta-analysis. *Personality and Social Psychology Review, 5,* 326, 340–341.

CHAPTER 8: NIPPING "ADHD" IN THE BUD

1. White, B. (1978). Presentation in Raleigh, NC.
2. Ray, B. D. (2008, April 8). Facts on home-schooling. National Home Education Research Institute. http://www.nheri.org/Facts-on -Homeschooling.html
3. Galloway, R. A., & Sutton, J. P. (1995). Home schooled and conventionally schooled high school graduates: A comparison of aptitude for and achievement in college English. *Home School Researcher, 11*(1), 1–9.
4. Shyers, L. E. (1992). A comparison of social adjustment between home and traditionally schooled students. *Home School Researcher, 8*(3), 1–8.
5. Montgomery, L. R. (1989). The effect of home schooling on the leadership skills of home schooled students. *Home School Researcher, 5*(1), 1–10.
6. EduQnA.com (Education and Reference Questions and Answers Web). Can you get into college if you were homeschooled for like your entire life? Retrieved February 19, 2008, from http://www.eduqna.com/ Home-Schooling/96-home-schooling.html
7. Schneerson, M. M. (1995). *Toward a meaningful life: The wisdom of the Rebbe* (Adapted by S. Jacobson). New York: William Morrow.

CHAPTER 9: NIPPING ADHD IN FULL BLOOM

1. Trichotillomania Learning Center. Retrieved May 28, 2008 from http://www.trich.org/about_trich/
2. Strayhorn. Self-control.

INDEX

diagnosis of ADHD (*continued*)
adult ADHD, 85–86
authors' recommendation of, xv
behaviors and symptoms, 4–5, 12, 30
boundary between normal behavior
and ADHD, 18
brain scans and brain-wave activity,
xiv, 56
criteria for, 14, 16–18, 20–21, 73,
105–107, 190
disregard for criteria for, 18–19
drug development and marketing
and, 12
gender differences, 74
increase in, 20–21
objectivity of professionals and, 8
overdiagnosis of, 7–8, 105–106
by pediatrician or family physician,
68, 71–72
posthumous diagnosis of, 52–53
pseudo-ADD vs. ADHD, 56–57
by psychologists, 68–69, 72–76
at school, 68, 69–71
testing for, 36, 58, 59, 71, 72–73,
85–86
underdiagnosis of, 7
Diagnostic and Statistical Manual (DSM)
ADHD behaviors, 4, 14
diagnosis criteria in, 14–18
EOBD diagnosis, 25
mental disorders in, increase in, 12,
29–32
revision of, 23
updates to, 14
diet and nutrition, 130–134, 136, 172–
174, 205–207, 209–210
discipline. *See also* cures for ADHD, drug-
free
attitude for effective, 186–188
authoritative discipline and
parenting, 27, 120
classroom behavior and discipline
(1950–1965), 41–48, 50–52, 53
classroom behavior and discipline
(1970–present), 48–50, 70, 106,
109–110, 117–118
EOBD treatment, 27
leadership and, 163–164
outrageous discipline, 191–193

postmodern psychological vs.
traditional, 113–114, 119–120,
161–162
by teachers, 70–71
"Three strikes, you're out!" discipline
plan, 207–209
time-out, 113–114, 191
disease model of disorders, 36–37, 74–76
Down syndrome, xvi
Driven to Distraction (Hallowell and
Ratey), 53
drug abuse, 94, 95–96
Drug Safety and Risk Management
Advisory Committee (FDA), 100–101
Duke University study, 18–19
du Plessis, Susan, 144

early onset bipolar disorder (EOBD)
causes of, 27, 202
criteria for, 25–28, 30, 105–106
depression and, 98
diagnosis of, 11–12, 27–29
difference between ADHD and, 28
as fictional disease, xiii–xiv, 10
increase in diagnosis of, 28–29
misdiagnosis as ADHD, 25, 28, 98
parenting behavior, role of, 118–120
prevalence of, 12–13, 28
science behind, xi, 25
treatment of, 12, 27
validity of diagnosis, 25
Edison, Thomas, 52, 53
Einstein, Albert, 94
electronic media. *See* television and
electronic media
Eli Lilly, 85–86, 95
Elkind, David, 144
encephalitis pandemic, 13
Endangered Minds (Healy), 121–122,
135
environment
brain development and conditions
and, 65–66, 127
clutter, eliminating, 167–168
cure for ADHD, 55–56
formative environment, 121–122
triggers for gene activation, 53–56
essential fatty acids (EFAs), 130–131
ethical conduct, money-making and, xi

AVAILABLE OCTOBER 2009

THE WELL-BEHAVED CHILD
DISCIPLINE THAT REALLY WORKS

JOHN ROSEMOND

INTRODUCTION

THIS BOOK EXISTS BECAUSE CHILDREN MISBEHAVE—NOT SOME children, but *all* children. Some are blatant and loud about it, others are subtle and quiet about it, but they all misbehave. It would be one thing if their misbehavior was the result of ignorance, of not knowing that they were misbehaving, but children misbehave even when they know what they are doing is wrong. It is therefore necessary, at the outset, to explain the "why?" behind this ever-present aspect of their nature.

Most psychologists (of which I am one), if asked, "Why do all children misbehave?" would include one or more of the following words or phrases in their answers: unresolved issues or conflicts, anxiety, stress, conflicting messages, cries for help, attention-seeking, trauma, power struggles, chemical imbalances, and genes. Nope. Some of those words may help us understand why Johnny Jones of Omaha refuses to pick up his toys, but none of those words explains why *all* children misbehave, and often deliberately so.

As it turns out, the explanation is simple, so simple that most psychologists never think of it (and if they did think of it, they would immediately reject it): *children are bad*. They do not misbehave because their innocent nature has been corrupted by bad parenting or "issues" (although, and again, explanations of that sort may apply to some relatively small number) or chemical imbalances or rogue genes. Children misbehave because they are bad, and the sooner parents understand and accept this, the better for them and the better also for their children. The incontrovertible badness of children is why it takes most of two decades to fully socialize them. Their badness is the reason for this book.

I fully realize that by starting this book with the assertion that children are not good by nature will surprise if not shock many parents. That would not have shocked parents of bygone generations, however, but then those were parents who lived back when common sense had not yet been drowned in a deluge of postmodern psychobabble. When their children began to misbehave, they were not surprised; rather, they fully expected it. They understood that one could not be a good enough parent to prevent a child from behaving badly, with premeditation. Because their parenting feet were on solid ground, they were able to maintain their sense of parenting balance and respond to bad behavior authoritatively, with generally calm purpose.

> **PARENTING AXIOM ONE**
> No matter how good a parent you are, your child is still capable on any given day of doing something despicable, disgusting, and depraved.

According to a poll I take with my many parent audiences each year, today's parents are far more likely than were their parents to yell at their children. This relatively recent upsurge in parental yelling is not due to anything about children; rather, it's due to a loss of parent common sense as regards child rearing and a resultant erosion of parental confidence. Reclaiming that confidence—that sense of balance and authority— requires a restoration of common sense concerning children, and the cornerstone of parental common sense is the understanding that in any given situation, a child is inclined by nature to do the wrong thing, the self-serving thing, the bad thing. Parents who refuse to accept that are in for a rough ride.

A child's badness awakens from the slumber of infancy sometime during the second year of life. Parents put a

> **PARENTING AXIOM TWO**
> Parents who accept Parenting Axiom One will have a more relaxed, happy, and playful parenthood than those who do not. Their children will also be much easier to discipline.

sweet eighteen-month-old angel—a child who's never given them a moment's trouble—to sleep one night, and the spawn of Satan wakes up the next morning. When she's picked up, she rages to be put down. When she's put down, she rages to be picked up. When picked up again, she bites. She rages for milk, but when given milk she knocks it to the floor and rages for orange juice. Given the orange juice, she rages for milk. And so it goes.

The mentality of the awakened human being, otherwise known as a toddler, consists of five related beliefs:

1. What I want, I deserve to have.
2. Because I deserve what I want, the ends justify the means.
3. No one has a right to deny me or to stand in my way.
4. The only valid rules are those I make.
5. The rules, even ones I make, do not apply to me.

Those five beliefs are also held by criminals and dictators—and indeed, the toddler is by turns a criminal and a tyrant. It is a measure of God's grace that of all the ambulatory species on the planet, human beings do not grow to full size in one or two years. It's one thing to deal with a tantrum in a toddler who is twenty-four inches tall and weighs the same number of pounds. It would be quite another to deal with a tantrum from a two-year-old who was 5' 10" and 160 pounds. America doesn't have enough emergency rooms.

One does not need to teach badness to toddlers. They are factories of antisocial tendencies. As soon as they learn to talk, they start to lie. They assault people who don't give in to their demands. They steal other people's property and hide it. (I said this to a group of parents once, and someone rejoined that this age child does not *know* he or she is stealing. They take things because they are curious, she said, to which I asked, "Then why do they hide them?" End of discussion.)

Parents who understand that badness is the natural state of the child will not be knocked off balance when the Spawn awakens. They will simply look at each other and shrug their shoulders, realizing that the honeymoon is over. Prior to this sea change, they were mere caretakers, concerned primarily with making their child feel welcome and wanted as well as keeping her healthy, comfortable, and safe from harm. Now, however, their real job—the task of *raising* the child out of this state of narcissistic savagery into a state of civility—begins. From this point on parents are like exorcists. Their job is to exorcise the "demons" that can be exorcised and help their child learn to control those that refuse to let go. The end result is a child who willingly walks the straight and narrow path toward good citizenship.

Some children submit to this sort of discipline more easily than others. Why? The answer is anyone's best guess. These days, children who cling to their demons for all they're worth are usually called "strong willed." The fact is *all* children are strong willed. They all want their own way, all of the time. So do you. So do I. (You and I, however, have accepted that [a] we can't and [b] it's sometimes better in the long run to let someone else have *their* way.) Some children, as is the case with some adults, simply go about trying to get their own way more subtly, more cleverly than others. They charm adults into giving them their way. To charm means to cast a spell. Casting spells is wicked. These very charming kids, therefore, are just as bad as children who, lacking the talent of spell-casting, go about trying to get their way in clumsier fashion.

Raising a well-behaved child requires punishment. The operative principle is simple: when a child does something bad, something bad should happen to the child. What a wonderful world it would be if punishment wasn't necessary! What a wonderful world it would be if children could simply be talked out of misbehaving. In the 1960s, mental health professionals decided that reasoning with children was possible. Where they came up with that idea is beyond me, but they did. Lots of dumb ideas emerged during the 1960s, most of which have fallen by the wayside. This particular bad idea has proven especially stubborn, however. Nearly every issue of every popular parenting magazine contains an article suggesting that children can be reasoned with. The truth is they cannot be. When a child is old enough to be successfully reasoned with, he is no longer a child. He's ready to leave home, and he should.

Elaine Farber, the author of *How to Talk So Children Will Listen, and Listen So Children Will Talk* (Can you tell Ms. Farber and I are not on the same page?), once accused me of being "hung up" on punishing children. That's the equivalent of saying that a successful gardener is "hung up" on yanking weeds out of her garden. Punishment is every bit as necessary to raising a well-behaved child as weeding is to growing a successful garden. The analogy works at several levels:

- Gardeners do not enjoy weeding; they simply accept that it must be done. Likewise, parents should not enjoy punishing; they should simply accept that it must be done.
- A garden cannot weed itself, and children cannot discipline themselves (until they have been successfully disciplined).

- Any experienced gardener knows that the most critical time to weed is when the garden is young. The more effectively one weeds when the garden is young, the less one will have to weed later. The same is true as regards the discipline of a child: the more effectively parents punish early on, the less they will have to punish later.

This book will teach you how to be an effective dispenser of disciplinary punishment. In other words, it will help you become a more successful "gardener" of children.

It needs to be said that effective punishment can only be done out of love. A child who is not completely secure in the knowledge and feeling that his parents love him without reservation will not accept their punishment. The reader does not need to concern him- or herself with this, however, because parents who take the time to read parenting books are parents who love their children without reservation.

Another fact of living with children is that they *like* to misbehave. Here are the reasons:

- They think it's funny.
- They enjoy seeing adults get upset.
- Sometimes they get what they want when they misbehave.
- Rebelling against authority gives them a sense of power.
- They often get a lot of attention when they misbehave.
- They discover that they can control certain people and situations by misbehaving.

For all of those reasons, misbehavior is addictive, which means it is in a child's best interest that parents do all they can to make sure this particular addiction doesn't take hold, or if it does, to cure it as quickly as possible. *This book will help you more quickly recognize when your child is becoming or has become addicted to misbehavior and know what to do about it.*

Paradoxically, children also like it when adults help them to not misbehave. How is that possible? Because children don't know they like behaving properly until adults make them stop misbehaving. They like misbehaving until their misbehavior is stopped; then they realize they prefer behaving properly. They realize at that point that they *don't* like misbehaving; they *don't* like being the center of negative attention; they *don't* like entering into power struggles with adults, much less winning them; they *don't* like getting their way when they really shouldn't. They realize at that point that they are happier, more relaxed, more creative, and even smarter when they do what adults expect and tell them to do.

That is what the best research into parenting style outcomes has discovered. But common sense will tell you the same thing. Think of some very disobedient children you know. Do they seem like happy campers to you? No, they don't. They are tense, driven, uptight, petulant, explosive, loud, argumentative, complaining, irritable, disagreeable, and so on. None of those characteristics reflects happiness. Now think of some relaxed, happy children you know. Without exception, they are calmly obedient, aren't they? And just to put a potential myth to bed, they don't act like they're obeying because they're terrified of what their parents will do if they don't obey, do they? No, they don't. They just

> **PARENTING AXIOM THREE**
> The most obedient children are also the happiest children. (This is also true of adults, by the way.)

obey because they have come to realize, intuitively, that obedience is the ticket to a happy childhood. Not freedom (although obedient children tend to enjoy lots of freedom), not money, not having a lot of toys, not a brand-new bicycle or the coolest and most expensive skateboard, but obedience.

DOGS AND CHILDREN ARE HORSES OF TWO DIFFERENT COLORS

A dog trainer once told me he thought disciplining a child was really no different than training a dog. I let the remark pass, but the gentleman was wrong. Dogs aren't bad. Dogs aren't good either. They are simply dogs. If you teach a dog to walk by your side at the command to heel, it will forever walk at your side when you say "heel." There is no equivalent in the behavior of a dog to "I don't feel like it right now" or "I don't want to!" or "You can't tell me what to do!" Furthermore, teaching a six-month-old dog to heel will only take a couple of hours, at most. Teaching a three-year-old child to walk by your side in a store or parking lot will require numerous sessions over several months, yet no reasonable person would contend that a dog is smarter than a three-year-old. And just when you think you have succeeded at teaching a child to walk at your side, said child suddenly decides he doesn't want to. He wants to see what's in the next aisle. When you tell him to stop and come back, he ignores you—or worse, he laughs and keeps running away. When you finally restore control and tell him to hold your hand, he refuses. No, disciplining a child is not remotely similar to training a dog.

> **PARENTING AXIOM FOUR**
> Because it is a parent's job to maximize a child's happiness, it is also a parent's job to discipline the child properly, so that the child becomes happily obedient.

But today's parents think it is. The fellow in the above anecdote speaks for a parenting culture that was seduced in the 1960s by the notion that the simple principles of behavior modification work as well on human beings as they do on dogs. In fact, behavior modification appears to work on a human subject only when the human *consents* to it. Put another way: a dog lacks the intellectual and emotional acumen with which to mount resistance to a properly wrought behavior modification strategy, but a human being does not—and yes, I am including children as young as two in this truism. Thus, the toddler's battle cry: "You're not the boss of me!" Or, the teen's: "I don't care what you do to me!" There are no equivalents to these audacities in the behavior of a dog.

Behavior modification posits that the right consequences will produce the right behavior. Again, that's true with a dog, but it's not necessarily true with a human being. With a child, consequences that are appropriate, right, and proper may or may not produce the right behavior. Most dogs learn their lessons easily. Most children learn their lessons the hard way, and the more important the lesson, the more likely it is that a child will learn it the hard way. Furthermore, as anyone who has raised more than one child to adulthood will testify, it certainly appears that every child comes into the world destined to have incredible difficulty learning at least one particular lesson.

Yet another difference between dogs and children: reward and punishment work reliably with dogs. Reward what you want the dog to do, and the dog does it. Punish what you do not want the dog to do, and the dog stops doing it. Reward and punishment do not work reliably with children—or human beings in general for that matter. Reward what you want a child to do and the child may or may not do it, or may do it for a while and then decide he's earned enough reward and stop doing it. Punish what you want a child to stop doing and the child may keep right on doing it just to prove that there is no authority in his life that he must submit to, no authority greater than his own. Parents who

> ### PARENTING AXIOM FIVE
> When a child does the wrong thing, and his parents do the right thing, it is entirely possible that the child will keep right on doing the wrong thing no matter how consistently his parents do the right thing.

do not understand and accept that the discipline of a dog and the discipline of a child are two entirely different propositions are in for a lot of frustration.

Don't get me wrong. In saying that behavior modification doesn't work with human beings (without their consent), I am *not* saying that children should not experience consequences when they misbehave. It is vital that a child understand that bad behavior will result in consequences that are decidedly undesirable. It is equally vital that parents understand that just because a child is able to affirm that the previous sentence is true does not mean he will behave accordingly.

Proper consequences compel dogs to change their behavior. With children, as with all human beings, proper consequences only deliver information. In effect, a punitive consequence (assuming it's appropriate to the situation) conveys this message to a child: "What you are now experiencing (i.e., the consequence) is a scaled-down example of what will likely happen to you if you behave that way as an adult, in the real world." The hope is that the child will be persuaded to never behave in said fashion again—that the child will *learn the lesson*. But as I said, some children are more easily persuaded than others that the lesson is worth learning. The point, however, is that whereas a proper and properly delivered consequence will change the behavior of a dog, a proper and properly delivered consequence simply causes a child to *think*. Hopefully, the child's thinking will result in his deciding to forever abandon the misbehavior in question. But it may not. The child may only think up a more clever way of trying to get around adult authority. My point is that simply because a consequence doesn't result in better behavior doesn't mean that the consequence was improper or improperly delivered.

Do not despair, however, because even when consequences do not have any effect, it is still possible to help a child learn his lessons. Some cakes rise quickly; some, slowly. *This book will teach you what to do when every conceivable consequence has failed to move your child's misbehavior off square one.*

PERMANENT TIME-OUT FOR TIME-OUT

This is a book about strategies of discipline that employ consequences, but I dare you to find another book that employs them similarly. I endured graduate school in psychology in the early 1970s. This was psychology's romantic period, during which I was taught that children were good by nature. It followed that a child could be persuaded not to misbehave by doing something as simple as having him sit in a chair for a few minutes. Time-out, as this method has come to be called, was promoted as the be-all and end-all of discipline. During my tenure in private practice, I eventually came to the belated conclusion that the stubborn nature of a child requires discipline that is powerfully persuasive, which time-out is not. It works, I concluded, with children who are already well-behaved, in which case it is nothing more than a reminder of expectations. With a persistently disobedient, disrespectful, and/or disruptive child, however, using time-out is akin to trying to fend off a great white shark with a water pistol.

At the time, given the general infatuation with time-out (which infected me for a while), the only other disciplinary alternatives were fairly traditional ones, like spanking, that had fallen into disrepute. In fact, any discipline that smacked of how pre-1960s parents (ergo, "unenlightened") might have responded to misbehavior was eschewed, even characterized as abusive. When I suggested in a newspaper column in the early 1980s that misbehaving children be sent to their rooms and put to bed early, I received considerable complaint from counselors and therapists who claimed that children so punished stood great likelihood of developing nightmares and phobias concerning their rooms. Nonetheless, most parents who followed my advice reported positive results, and the more outrageous my recommendations were in the eyes of fellow mental health professionals, the better the results parents reported. As a child's behavior improved, so did his mood, and the emotional atmosphere of the family improved as well. Parents argued less, siblings squabbled less, and everyone communicated better. Who could argue with that?

Being the punctilious fellow that I am, I began organizing my methods into systems and later into a workshop called "The Well-Behaved Child: Discipline That Really Works!"™ Over the past several years, courtesy of parents who ask me questions through my website (www.rosemond.com), I've been able to expand and refine my approach, which is not "my" approach at all, really, but a fine-tuning of a very traditional approach to discipline.

In that regard, allow me to make one thing perfectly clear: a traditional approach to discipline was not, and is not, synonymous with spanking. Yes, traditional discipline usually included the option of spanking, but it was an option utilized rarely by most pre-1960s parents. Most people my age will tell you, as can I, that they can count on one hand the number of times they were spanked as kids. Because I believe spanking can be a reasonable response to certain outrageous misbehaviors, I have included in this book guidelines for why and when and how to spank. Oh, and by the way, the notion that spanking teaches children that it's okay to hit other people is pure, unmitigated malarkey. Research done by eminent and ethical social scientists finds that children who are occasionally (the operative word) spanked score higher on measures of social and emotional adjustment than children who are never spanked. One study found that children who have never been spanked are *more* aggressive than kids who have experienced spanking's purgative powers.

For reasons that include the fact I do not oppose spanking, I expect that this book will confirm for some that I am a draconian monster. Such is the territory that goes with being an iconoclast. I am also confident that this book will prove immensely helpful to others. In fact, I'm confident it will prove helpful to anyone who comes to the book in need and with an open mind. After more than twenty-five years of positive parent testimony and feedback, I can afford such confidence. The best of all prospects is that it might sway the minds and hearts of some. In that regard, I receive at least a dozen testimonies a year from parents who attest to once thinking I was harsh but who have since come to subscribe to "my" very traditional philosophy. One such parent recently told me that her retroconversion has been "liberating."

It is my sincere prayer that you are similarly affected by this book, and that it helps you toward raising children who are well-behaved, and therefore happy, and who therefore have the very best of starts on a successful life.

John Rosemond
Gastonia, North Carolina
May 2008

ABOUT THE AUTHORS

JOHN ROSEMOND, a family psychologist, is America's most widely read parenting expert. The author of twelve best-selling parenting books, John has appeared on numerous television and radio talk shows, including *Good Morning America, 20/20, The O'Reilly Factor, The View,* and *Focus on the Family.*

He is the busiest public speaker in the parenting field and has been for more than twenty years. In an average year he gives more than two hundred talks to parent and professional audiences across the United States. He has done both arena events and small office settings.

His weekly syndicated newspaper column appears in more than two hundred newspapers and major dailies, reaching an estimated 20 million readers every week. For more than ten years, he was the featured parenting columnist for *Better Homes and Gardens* and wrote the family counselor column for *Hemispheres,* the in-flight magazine for United Air Lines. He also writes a monthly column for *Signs of the Times* magazine.

John has been married to his wife, Willie, for forty years. They have two adult children and seven grandchildren. They live in Gastonia, North Carolina, and on a small, off-the-beaten-track island in the Bahamas.

DR. BOSE RAVENEL is a pediatrician with twenty-six years experience in private practice and eleven years teaching pediatric residents. He published a commentary in *Ethical Human Sciences and Services* titled "A New

Paradigm for ADD/ADHD and Behavioral Management Without Medication."

He is a member of several professional organizations of pediatricians, including the American Academy of Pediatrics and the Society for Developmental and Behavioral Pediatrics. He is an emeritus member of the Physicians Resource Council, a medical advisory group for Focus on the Family, and was a member of the founding board of directors of the American College of Pediatricians. He has been voted by his peers into membership of Best Doctors in America 1998–1999, 2001–2002, 2003–2004, and 2007–2008.

His experience includes publishing and speaking in the areas of child discipline and parenting. He has appeared in numerous media outlets and participated in public debates in the area of child discipline, including *CBS Evening News, NBC Dateline, ABC World News Tonight with Peter Jennings, CNN Today*, and a radio broadcast on ADHD at Focus on the Family. Speaking engagements include presentations on parenting at national meetings of Focus on the Family and the Christian Medical and Dental Association.

Dr. Bose, as he is known to his friends, has two adult children. He and his wife, Susan, live in High Point, North Carolina.